Edexcel GCSE

History B
Schools History Project
Warfare and the Impact of War

Authors:

John Child

Steve Waugh

Series Editor:

Angela Leonard

Updated for the
2013 specifications by:

John Child

ALWAYS LEARNING

PEARSON

Published by Pearson Education Limited, Edinburgh Gate, Harlow, Essex, CM20 2JE.

www.pearsonschoolsandfecolleges.co.uk

Copies of official specifications for all Edexcel qualifications may be found on the Edexcel website: www.edexcel.com

Text © Pearson Education Limited 2014

Typeset and Illustrated by HL Studios, Witney, Oxford
Original illustrations © Pearson Education Limited 2009
Cover photo © Corbis/Bettmann

First published 2014

16 15 14 13
10 9 8 7 6 5 4 3 2 1

British Library Cataloguing in Publication Data
A catalogue record for this book is available from the British Library

ISBN 978 1 446906 84 2

Printed by Neografia

A note from the publisher
In order to ensure that this resource offers high-quality support for the associated Edexcel qualification, it has been through a review process by the awarding organisation to confirm that it fully covers the teaching and learning content of the specification or part of a specification at which it is aimed, and demonstrates an appropriate balance between the development of subject skills, knowledge and understanding, in addition to preparation for assessment.

While the publishers have made every attempt to ensure that advice on the qualification and its assessment is accurate, the official specification and associated assessment guidance materials are the only authoritative source of information and should always be referred to for definitive guidance.

Edexcel examiners have not contributed to any sections in this resource relevant to examination papers for which they have responsibility.

No material from an endorsed resource will be used verbatim in any assessment set by Edexcel.

Endorsement of a resource does not mean that the resource is required to achieve this Edexcel qualification, nor does it mean that it is the only suitable material available to support the qualification, and any resource lists produced by the awarding organisation shall include this and other appropriate resources.

2014/12

Acknowledgements

The author and publisher would like to thank the following individuals and organisations for permission to reproduce photographs:
(Key: b-bottom; c-centre; l-left; r-right; t-top)

akg-images Ltd: 22, 41, 43, 64, 69, 142, Bibliothèque Nationale 32, 33, British Library 23, British Museum / Erich Lessing 13, Dmitriy Nikolaevich Kardovsky 62b, North Wind Picture Archives 17, 36; **Alamy Images:** akg-images 70, Image Asset Management Ltd. 82, Lordprice Collection 98b, 124r, Mary Evans Picture Library 15, North Wind Pictures 31; **Bridgeman Art Library Ltd:** Atkinson, John Augustus (1775-1831) / Private Collection 53, Bibliotheque de L'Arsenal, Paris, France / Archives Charmet 28, Bibliotheque des Arts Decoratifs, Paris, France / Archives Charmet 8bl, 12, 30, British Library, London, UK / © British Library Board. All Rights Reserved 49tr, © Central Saint Martins College of Art and Design, London 57, Musee de la Tapisserie, Bayeux, France / With special authorisation of the city of Bayeux / Giraudon 19, 20, 21tl, 21br, National Army Museum, London 52, 62cl, Private Collection 77, Private Collection / © Look and Learn 135, Private Collection / Photo © Barbara Singer 99, Private Collection / The Stapleton Collection 55, 65, 91l, Universal History Archive / UIG 134; **British Library Images Online:** 25, 34, 35; **Corbis:** 88, Bettmann 10, 40, 63, 104, Christel Gerstenberg 29, David Pollack 159, David Spurdens 79, Gianni Dagli Orti 58, Historical Picture Archive 49br, 51, 68, Hulton-Deutsch Collection 73, 167, Jonathan Blair 44, Nagasaki Atomic Bomb Museum / epa 81, Peter Turnley 89, Reuters 83, Stapleton Collection 11, 39, Stefano Bianchetti 8cr; **DK Images:** Stephen Biesty 26; **Daily Express:** 105; **Fotolia.com:** jelwolf 86; **Getty Images:** Hulton Archive 8tr, 72, 80, 98t, 102, 114, 116, 126, 136t, 146, 161tl, Hulton Royals Collection 115, Moviepix / Silver Screen Collection 148, Popperfoto 103, 156, Time & Life Pictures 74; **Image courtesy of The Advertising Archives:** 152; **Imperial War Museum:** 113, 119, 161tr; **iStockphoto:** Alex Slobodkin 170br, Chris Schmidt 170cr, Efendi Kocakafa 170cl, Stockphoto4u 172, ZoneCreative 170bl; **Vinmag Archive Ltd:** 163; **Mary Evans Picture Library:** 144, Illustrated London News Ltd 124l, Paul Brown 27; **Mirrorpix:** 8br, 91r; **National Archives:** 130; **Political Cartoon Society:** 140; **Rex Features:** ITV 85; **The Art Archive:** Eileen Tweedy 112, 122; **The National Library of Wales:** / Solo Syndication / Associated Newspapers Ltd 132; **TopFoto:** 100, 101, 120, 150, Ann Ronan Picture Library / HIP 9, AP 118, HIP / LordPrice Collection 106, HIP / The Print Collector 47, Public Record Office / HIP 127, The Granger Collection 60, Topham Picturepoint 107, 108, 109, 121, 128, 131, 139, 154, 158, ullsteinbild 24, 111, World History Archive 67, 136b

All other images © Pearson Education

We are grateful to the following for permission to reproduce copyright material:

Source B page 26 from *The Medieval Castle: Life in a Fortress in Peace and War* (Penguin Classic History) ISBN-13: 978-0141390703 Penguin (Philip Warner) December 1, 2001; Source G page 36, Source B page 65, Source F page 66, Source B page 89 from *The Cambridge History of Warfare* ISBN 978-0521618953 Cambridge University Press (Geoffrey Parker) 22 Aug 2005; Source A on page 51, Source C page 65 from *Cassell's World History of Warfare* ISBN 978-0304363520 Weidenfeld & Nicolson (Holger Herwig) 13 Feb 2003, Orion Publishing Group Ltd with permission and University of Nebraska Press with permission; Source C page 52 from *War in European History*, ISBN-13: 978-0199546190 Michael Howard, OUP Oxford (Michael Howard.) 15 April 2009, with permission; Source B page 61 from *Making Saints: Religion and the Public Image of the British Army* ISBN-13: 978-0838637296, Fairleigh Dickinson University Press, U.S (Kenneth E Hendrickson) p. 44, 31 Mar 1998, with permission Associated University Presses; Source C page 61 from *Events That Formed The Modern World* ISBN 978-1-59884-901-1, ABC-CLIO, LLC, California.(W. Thackery and John E Findling 2012) p22, republished with permission of ABC-CLIO; permission conveyed through Copyright Clearance Center, Inc.; Source B page 85 from Commanders Blamed For Marine's Death, *The Guardian*, 27/11/2006, http://www.guardian.co.uk/uk/2006/nov/27/military.iraq, © Guardian News and Media Ltd 2006; Source A page 102 from *The Memoirs of Field-Marshal Kesselring* ISBN 978-1853677281 Greenhill Books; reprint edition (Kesselring) 15 Feb 2007, Frontline Books with permission; Source C page 103 from *Mrs. Milburn's Diaries: An Englishwoman's Day to Day Reflections*, 1939-45 ISBN 978-0349106236 Abacus (Clara Emily Milburn) 4 May 1995, with kind permission of the copyright holder for Clare Milburn; Source C page 110 from *Accrington Observer*, 19th September 1914, with kind permission of Trinity Mirror Syndication; Source B page 110 from Lloyd George 1917, with kind permission from the Estate of David Lloyd George; Source B page 120 from *Echoes of the Great War* (OUP (Reverend A Clark 1985) p190, by permission of Oxford University Press; Source D page 129 from *No Time To Wave Goodbye* ISBN-13: 978-0747500834, Bloomsbury Publishing PLC; 6th. Reprint edition (Ben Wicks and Michael Caine) 25 Aug 1989, © Ben Wicks,25 Aug 1989, Bloomsbury Publishing Plc; Source E page 133 from http://www.labour-party.org.uk/manifestos/1950/1950-labour-manifesto.shtml, reproduced by permission of the Labour Party; Source A page 138 from *A History of the Second World War: Surgery*, Editor, Sir Zacharay Cope, 1953. *Introduction to A History of the Second World War:* Surgery, Ed. Cope, HMSO, 1953. Contains public sector information licensed under the Open Government Licence (OGL) v2.0.http://www.nationalarchives.gov.uk/doc/open-government-licence; Source G page 145 from Early suffragist campaigning, http://www.parliament.uk/about/living-heritage/transformingsociety/electionsvoting/womenvote/overview/earlysuffragist/ Contains Parliamentary information licensed under the Open Parliament Licence v1.0.; Source H page 145 from *Twentieth Century Britain*, ISBN 0 631 91320 3, Blackwell (Jon Nichol) p20; Source B page 147 from the *Daily Mail*, April 1916; Source C page 147 from *English History 1914-1945* ISBN-13: 978-0198217152 OUP Oxford (A. J. P. Taylor) 21 Oct 1965, by permission of Oxford University Press; Source C page 148 from *Women's Suffrage in Britain, 1867-1928* ISBN-13: 978-0852782255 The Historical Association (Martin Pugh) Feb 1980; Source B page 150 from *Bombers and Mash* ISBN-13: 978-1844088737, Virago (Minns R 1999), Virago, an imprint of Little, Brown Book Group as publishers and Johnson and Alcock Ltd; Source F page 151 from Modern World History for Edexcel Coursework Book: Britain in the Age of Total War 1939-45 Heinemann, (Malcolm Chandler) 24 Jan 2002, Modern World History for Edexcel Coursework Book: *Britain in the Age of Total War 1939-45*, Malcolm Chandler, Pearson Education Limited; Source B page 152 from http://www.history.ac.uk/reviews/review/689, Review of Gender, Work and Education in Britain in the 1950s (review no. 689), with kind permission from Professor Ruth Watts; Source D on page 153 from *The Second World War* ISBN-13: 978-0340814215 p54 (Neil DeMarco) 1997, Hodder Education Group; Source A page 156 from *Twentieth Century Trend in Social Mobility in Britain*, Anthony Heath and Clive Payne 1999, http://www.crest.ox.ac.uk/papers/p70.pdf, p.14 Working Paper Number 70 June 1999, with kind permission from Anthony Heath, Emeritus Professor of Sociology, Emeritus Fellow of Nuffield College; Source B page 157 from Paul Addison, http://www.ibiblio.org/hyperwar/UN/Canada/Natl_Exp/NatlExp-4.html, p 39, Britain and the Politics of Social Patriotism p39, with kind permission from Professor Paul Addison; Source C page 159 from Winston Churchill speaking to the Commons June 1940, Curtis Brown with permission; Source C page 161 from Siegfried Sassoon: Declaration against the War Estate of George Sassoon/The Siegfried Sassoon Literary Estate, 1917; Source D page 161 from The estate of J B Priestley 5th June 1940, with permission of United Agents; Source F page 161 from World War II today, http://ww2today.com/21st-august-1940-british-morale-reported-to-be-excellent-2, with kind permission from Martin Cherrett; Source B page 162 from East Grinstead Observer, 1944, http://www.spartacus.schoolnet.co.uk/2WWtaxation.htm,courtesy of egcourier.co.uk.

Every effort has been made to contact copyright holders of material reproduced in this book. Any omissions will be rectified in subsequent printings if notice is given to the publishers.

Contents

■ Option 1C: The changing nature of warfare

■ The changing nature of warfare c50AD–c1350

■ The changing nature of warfare c1350–c1700

■ The changing nature of warfare c1700–c1900

■ The changing nature of warfare c1900 to the present day

Option 3C:
The impact of war on Britain c1903–c1954

Welcome to this Edexcel GCSE History B: Schools History Project Resource

Option 1C: The changing nature of warfare and 3C: The impact of war on Britain c1903–c1954

These resources are appropriate for GCSE History students on the linear GCSE course certificated from 2015. This specification has a focus on change and development through studies of societies in depth and of key themes over time. Packed with tips and activities, the book includes lots of engaging features to enthuse students and provide the range of support needed to make teaching and learning a success for all ability levels.

Your Development Study

This first part of the book helps you to understand how warfare has changed over the years. By the end of this part of the book you will be able to explain:

- what warfare was like in c50AD and how it has changed over the years to the present day
- the effects of these changes
- patterns of change
- causes of the changes
- how changes in warfare fit into changes in wider society.

Your Source Enquiry

This second part of the book helps you to understand the effects war had upon Britain from c1903 to c1954. By the end of this part of the book you will be able to understand:

- the impact of war on British society, for example social mobility and the role of women
- the impact of war on civilian life and public opinion about warfare
- how war enabled the government to have more influence over the lives of ordinary people.

How to use this book

Edexcel GCSE History B: Schools History Project Warfare and its impact is divided into the two units that match the specification. Unit 1 is divided into four sections:

- c50AD-c1350
- c1350–c1700
- c1700–c1900
- c1900 to the present day.

Unit 3 contains guidance, instruction and practice questions on the source requirements for the exam. This book does not cover the content for your Unit 2 depth study.

Features of this book

Learning outcomes structure learning at the start of each topic.

A topic **Summary** captures the main learning points.

Activities provide stimulating tasks for the classroom and homework.

 A dedicated suite of revision resources. We've broken down the six stages of revision to help you ensure that you are prepared every step of the way.

 How to get into the perfect 'zone' for your revision.

 Tips and advice on how to plan your revision effectively.

 A checklist of things you should know, revision activities and practice exam questions at the end of each section plus additional exam practice at the end of the book.

 Last-minute advice for just before the exam.

 An overview of what you will have to do in the exam, plus a chance to see what a real exam paper will look like.

 What do you do after your exam? This section contains information on how to get your results and answers to frequently asked questions on what to do next.

These features help you to understand how to improve with guidance on answering exam-style questions, tips on how to remember important concepts and how to avoid common pitfalls.

There are two different types of ExamZone features throughout this book:

Build better answers

Why did it take so long for gunpowder weapons to change how warfare was fought? (12 marks)

You may use the following in your answer.
- Inaccuracy of early cannon
- Shortcomings of the matchlock

You must also include information of your own.

■ **Basic, Level 1**
Answer gives a simple description of gunpowder weapons with a little detail.

● **Good, Level 2**
Answer gives a more developed description of gunpowder weapons with more detail and some support from relevant material and/or own knowledge.

▲ **Excellent, Level 3**
Answer shows understanding of the focus of the question, makes relevant points and gives good supporting detail from the stimulus, but explores other aspects from own knowledge as well. For example: explaining that early cannon were inaccurate, difficult to transport, often exploded and expensive.

Build Better Answers give you an opportunity to answer exam-style questions. They contain tips for what a basic, good and excellent answer will contain.

Build better answers

Why was there stalemate for so long on the Western Front in the First World War? (12 marks)
You may use the following in your answer: • Defensive weapons • The tactics used by generals
You must also include information of your own.

Build Better Answers: The Know Zone Build Better Answers pages at the end of each section include an exam-style question with a student answer, examiner comments and an improved answer so that you can see how to improve your own writing.

Student answer	Comments	Improvements
The German attack on France in 1914 was stopped short of Paris. Neither side could defeat the other so they dug trenches.	The answer mainly describes what happened rather than explains why it happened.	Extract from improved answer: The German attack was stopped because their infantry could not advance; defence was stronger than attack. Attacking infantry were mown down by machine gun and rifle fire.
When one side attacked, the other side fought off the attack with powerful defensive weapons.	To improve, the answer needs to: • give reasons why there was stalemate and why it lasted so long	Armies could dig in and defend; but neither side had weapons to attack and capture enemy positions, so it was stalemate.
So the two sides just fired artillery shells at each other and launched new attacks with even more men, e.g. when the British attacked at the Somme.	• give relevant information from the source to support those reasons • use own knowledge to add to the information from the source.	The stalemate went on so long because generals kept attacking enemy defences with artillery and gas. But they did not work because defenders used dug-outs and gas masks. Generals attacked with more men and tanks, but the tanks were not reliable. New tactics didn't work so the stalemate went on until 1918.
They tried new weapons, such as tanks and gas, but the stalemate went on until 1918.		

The changing nature of warfare

Introduction

This part of your course looks at developments in warfare from c50AD to the present day.

You will be asked to think about:

- what changed in warfare; turning points, patterns of change
- what caused those changes and what the effects of the changes were
- how these changes in warfare were related to society and wider historical change.

In this section of your study, you will learn about:

- warfare from c50AD to c1350, the time of Boudicca's Revolt and the Battle of Hastings
- warfare from c1350 to c1700, the time of British archers at Agincourt and the Battle of Naseby in the English Civil War
- warfare from c1700 to c1900, the time of the British victories at the Battle of Waterloo and in the Crimean War
- warfare from c1900 to the present day, including case studies on the First World War and the First Gulf War of 1991.

c1350–c1700

c1700–c1900

c50AD–c1350

c1900 to the present day

c60AD	1066	1415	1645	1815	1854	1914	1991
Boudicca's Revolt	The Battle of Hastings	The Battle of Agincourt	The Battle of Naseby	The Battle of Waterloo	The Crimean War	The First World War	The First Gulf War

1.1 The Roman army in Britain

Learning outcomes

By the end of this topic you should be able to:

- describe the key features of the Roman army in Britain
- explain how Roman society affected the key features of the Roman army.

In 43AD, Britain was invaded by the Roman army. The Roman Empire already circled the Mediterranean Sea and stretched into northern Europe. Now the Roman Emperor, Claudius, ordered the conquest of Britain.

Within one hundred years, the Roman army had conquered all the area we would now call England, Wales and southern Scotland. What was that army like?

Roman society and the Roman army

All armies are shaped by the societies which create them. The Roman army is an example of this.

The Roman Empire was large, wealthy and highly organised. So it created a large, well-funded and highly organised army. For example, at this time, the Roman army:

- was a permanent **standing army** of about 300,000 men; it was not just formed during periods of war
- recruited men for 20 years of service, so that they could be trained to a high standard
- recruited only men who passed medicals and met standards for age, intelligence, eyesight and height – 5 foot 10 inches.

Source A: A Roman carving.

This is a Roman carving showing a legionary. Like most Roman soldiers he is an infantryman or foot soldier.

His main weapons were daggers and swords. You can see his dagger in the picture. Soldiers used two-foot long, double-edged swords; they were mainly used for stabbing, but could also sever limbs when swung.

Most soldiers also carried two seven-foot throwing spears with an effective throwing range of 30 metres.

Roman soldiers wore coarse tunics. As you can see, they were bare-legged. They wore leather marching sandals.

To protect themselves, Roman soldiers wore light armour. Notice how it is made up of interlocking metal plates and metal helmets, with metal flaps to protect the neck and cheeks.

Also note the soldier's shield. These were usually cylindrical in shape, over a metre long and almost a metre wide. They were strong, made of wood and edged with metal. A group of soldiers could make a solid wall of shields to protect themselves from arrows or spears.

Roman society had well established metal and textile industries. So equipment in the Roman army was well developed.

As well as his weapons and armour, a legionary had to carry tools for building and a spade for digging. A Roman army never struck camp without pitching tents and digging latrines.

Organisation of the Roman army

Legionaries, like the one on page 9, were the most important weapon of the Roman army. They were organised into **legions** of about 6,000 men.

- Each legion was led by several **centurions** (senior soldiers) and an officer.
- Each legion would also have specialist archers and 120 horsemen to act as **scouts**, and it would have its own medical staff, carpenters, vets, armourers, surveyors and priests.

Legions were the key units of the Roman army. They were self-contained, flexible fighting units. There were 28 legions; this meant 150,000 regular soldiers. The Roman army also had about 150,000 auxiliary troops, from conquered armies and allies.

Roman army tactics

A society as organised as the Romans produced an army with organised tactics. It used discipline, training and fitness more than weight of numbers. The Roman writer, Flavius Vegetius, said, 'Victory comes not by numbers and courage, but by skill and training. To this, Rome owes the conquest of the world.' Officers had manuals for tactics, such as using high ground when defending, and having the wind behind them to help arrows. Roman generals would normally position infantry in the centre of their army, with cavalry at the sides and archers and spear throwers behind the infantry.

- First, a hail of arrows and spears would be sent over the infantry to disrupt the enemy.
- Then the infantry would drive forward into the enemy, forming a wedge shape or a series of wedges, protected by their shields.
- This would force the enemy back and crush them together, allowing the Roman soldiers to stab at their enemy between their shields.
- **Cavalry** then cut down retreating enemy troops.

Sometimes the army had to attack towns instead.

- Legions had specialist engineers to build artillery: catapults to hurl rocks or large spears at the enemy.
- They also built towers, sheds and ladders to attack fortified walls.

Life in the Roman army

Life in the army was as organised as Roman society. For example, for army training:

- soldiers used standardised weapons made in army weapons factories
- training took place in special camps with artillery ranges
- officers and troops practised their skills by fighting **gladiators** – slaves trained as fighters.

Source B: A modern picture showing a Roman army besieging a town. Note the ladders, sheds, tower and catapult, as well as the use of shields to protect soldiers under the walls.

The Roman historian, Josephus, wrote that the Roman army's 'manoeuvres are like bloodless battles and their battles like bloody **manoeuvres**.'

Roman society was wealthy enough to care for soldiers well:

- soldiers travelled with leather tents and generous rations – 3lb of bread, 2lb of meat and two pints of wine per day
- Roman forts had fresh water and safe ways to dispose of sewage
- larger forts had hospitals; army doctors had herbal medicine for routine ailments and opium for dealing with pain.

As a result, on average, Roman soldiers lived five years longer than other citizens.

But discipline was also taken very seriously:
- the penalty for breaking regulations during a campaign was death
- troops who misbehaved were 'decimated' – one tenth were chosen by lot and flogged to death as a warning to others.

The army leaves its mark

Technology was also a feature of Roman society. Ancient Rome is famous for engineering feats like **aqueducts** and roads. The Roman army was used to build many of these.

As a result, one effect of the Roman army was to change the appearance of Britain by:
- building fortresses and walls (such as Hadrian's Wall) which were used for centuries afterwards
- building roads, such as Watling Street (a paved road about 270 miles long, from the Welsh borders to Kent), which still shape modern routes
- boosting the growth of cities in Britain; London, for example, thrived under the Romans; other cities, like Chester, grew up around army camps
- building Britain's first drainage and sewage systems in towns.

The Roman army leaves

When the Roman Empire gradually weakened and lost its control of western Europe, the Roman army abandoned Britain, in about 410AD. The Britons who remained had no such armies. There were to be no armies in Britain as large and organised as the Roman army for well over a thousand years.

Source C: A modern drawing based on Roman carvings. It shows Roman soldiers involved in a building project.

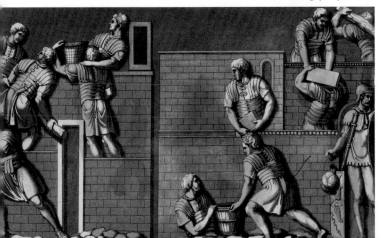

Activities

1 Describe:
   a) how the Roman army was organized
   b) the weapons and tactics of the Roman army
   c) the life and routine of a Roman soldier.
2 Describe three ways in which Roman society shaped the key features of the Roman army.

 examzone **Build better answers**

The bullets below show two aspects of the Roman army in Britain. Choose **one** and describe its key features. (6 marks)

- The organisation of the Roman army
- Life in the Roman army

 Basic, Level 1
Answer gives simple statements about the Roman army with no detail. For example: *The Roman army was well organised* or *Soldiers were treated well.*

Good, Level 2
Answer gives a range of features of the Roman army with good, detailed support for each feature. For example: *One feature of life in the Roman army was that soldiers were well fed. They had generous rations of 3lb of bread, 2lb of meat and two pints of wine per day.*

Summary

- The origins, culture and organisation of Roman society shaped Roman warfare and the Roman army.
- The Roman army was large, well funded and highly organised.
- Roman officers used carefully thought-out tactics.
- Roman troops were paid, trained soldiers who were well looked after, but discipline was harsh.

1.2 Warfare in the Celtic World

> **Learning outcomes**
>
> By the end of this topic you should be able to:
> - describe the key features of warfare
> - explain how Celtic society affected warfare in the Celtic world.

When the Roman army invaded Britain in 43AD, it was occupied by people called the Celts. In fact, Celts occupied most of northern Europe. Unlike the Romans, the Celts never tried to unify all the land they occupied to make one country. In Britain, for example, there were many small, independent Celtic tribes living in scattered villages, growing corn and raising cattle and pigs. These Celtic tribes included the Iceni, the Trinovantes and the Catuvellauni, who had settled in southern and eastern England, and the Brigantes, who lived further north.

Celtic society created very different armies and fought very different wars from those of the Roman Empire.

How Celtic society affected warfare

Celtic armies did not have any of the Roman systems for recruiting, training or organising troops. Celtic society was mainly too poor to recruit large, permanent, paid armies like the Romans had. Anyway, the Celts did not want to rule large areas of land, so they had little need for large armies. Celtic warfare was mostly raids on nearby villages. They just wanted cattle, valuables or slaves – or to weaken their enemies by killing families and burning villages and crops. So Celtic society expected untrained volunteers to turn up with their own weapons to defend their village or raid others.

Sometimes, the Celts did all they could to avoid battle. Celtic society relied upon their men to work the land. They could not afford to lose men in battle. So, sometimes, instead of all-out-war, a small number of men were chosen to fight each other in a staged battle, which decided the outcome of the war.

Celtic weapons and fighting

The Celts were skilled in metalwork. This enabled the spear to become a key Celtic weapon. They had long spears for stabbing and smaller throwing spears. Most Celtic warriors also had swords up to a metre long, used for slashing the enemy, and large, decorated wooden shields, often covered in leather, with a metal **boss** in the centre.

Few Celtic warriors had armour. Most wore normal clothes for fighting – coarse trousers, shirt and cloak, often dyed in bright colours.

Celtic warrior leaders

With no standing army, there were no officers in Celtic fighting. But Celtic society did have leaders, who had better equipment.

- These noble warriors had leather smocks and helmets; some had bronze or iron helmets, decorated with coral or even gold.
- A few nobles fought on horseback. Their four-cornered saddles gave them stability, enabling them to use their swords and spears better.

In some Celtic tribes, noble warriors used battle-chariots. These were two-wheeled vehicles, about four metres long. A charioteer drove while the warrior threw his spears, before dismounting and fighting on foot.

Source A: From a modern drawing of Celtic warriors. The artist based this on Roman accounts written by Romans such as Julius Caesar, a Roman general who fought the Celts.

Celtic warrior bands

The Celts had no standing armies, but some Celtic tribes became wealthy enough to pay a few full-time warriors. These formed small war bands. They had warrior training schools to practise their skills. They claimed special powers from Celtic gods and held religious initiation rituals for recruits.

Celtic battle strategy and tactics

The Celts rarely fought large-scale wars, but sometimes they had no choice.

As the Roman Army fought its way across Europe and Britain, the Celts were at constant war with the Romans. Sometimes the tribes joined forces to fight the Romans. For example, in 60AD, the Iceni gathered an army of over 200,000 men, under their leader Boudicca, by combining forces with several other Celtic tribes (see page 14).

But Celtic warriors were not suited to large battles. There were several reasons for this.

- Celtic society produced very few permanent, trained soldiers, and none of them were drilled in fighting in large groups.
- Celtic society valued heroic individual warriors; so they had no interest in fighting as units.
- Celtic society had no written language, so it had no war manuals to spread information about battlefield manoeuvres or tactics.
- There were no clear leaders in Celtic society. Celtic armies formed up in tribal groups, warriors fighting alongside those they knew. These groups did not all have the same weapons or equipment.

So, as befitting a simple society, Celtic tactics were simple – mainly mass attacks. One simple tactic they used was to try to frighten the enemy.

- Before battles, warriors beat their weapons against their shields, shouting, blowing horns and beating drums.
- They destroyed the enemy's sacred sites to show that they were not afraid of their gods.
- Some warriors fought naked, with their bodies painted in dye, their long hair dyed blond with lime, and with beards and droopy moustaches.
- They displayed the bodies of their victims to intimidate their enemies.

Diodorus Siculus, a Roman historian from the 1st century AD, wrote: 'They cut off the heads of enemies slain in battle and parade them on the necks of their horses.'

When they attacked, the Celts often centred their attack on one point, but this cramped them for space: and Celtic warriors needed space to swing their swords.

In contrast, the Romans trained for combat in compact spaces, using short swords and daggers to stab, particularly into the armpits.

Roman victories over the Celts show that a trained, disciplined and motivated army will often defeat a much larger army that lacks training and discipline.

Source B: A Celtic helmet from the 1st century BC found in the River Thames near Waterloo Bridge. Celtic helmets, finely decorated shields and chariots show us that not all Celtic warriors would have been equipped as simply as those in the picture opposite.

Activities

1   Describe details of the following features of Celtic warfare:
    a) **recruitment**
    b) training
    c) tactics and strategy.
2   Explain four ways in which Celtic society shaped fighting and tactics in Celtic warfare.

Summary

Celtic society shaped the fighting and tactics involved in Celtic warfare.

1.3 Boudicca's Revolt – Celts v. Romans

Learning outcomes

By the end of this topic you should be able to:

- describe the events of Boudicca's Revolt and her importance as an individual
- highlight key features of Roman and Celtic warfare in the events of Boudicca's Revolt.

Historical sources

The Celts left no written accounts of Boudicca's Revolt. Our two main written sources are histories written by Romans.

- Tacitus was the most important Roman historian of this period. He wrote about 40 years after the Revolt and was not an eyewitness. However, his father-in-law, Agricola, was probably an eyewitness to the revolt.
- Cassius Dio wrote after Tacitus. We only have a summary of his account and we don't know on what sources he based his account.

The background

Boudicca was the wife of Prasutagus, king of the Iceni, a Celtic tribe who lived in Britain, where Norfolk is today. Cassius Dio tells us she was tall, had long red hair, a piercing stare and a harsh voice. When Prasutagus died, in 60AD, he left half his wealth to the emperor Nero and half to his wife, hoping the Romans would allow her to rule as queen. In the words of Tacitus, the Roman historian:

Source A:

The event was otherwise. The king's land was ravaged by the centurions; they pillaged his house. His wife, Boudicca, was whipped; her daughters were ravished. The relations of the king were reduced to slavery.

Boudicca called a rebellion amongst the Iceni. She was joined by other Celtic tribes. The Trinovantes joined because they had been mistreated by Roman soldiers who settled in Colchester, their capital. They also resented being told to worship the ex-Roman emperor Claudius and to pay for a temple in Colchester dedicated to him.

The Revolt

Boudicca decided to rebel. Tacitus describes her as a forceful woman and she was able to inspire other tribes to join her.

At the head of a large army of Celts, her first target was the city of Colchester. Raiding neighbours was a common feature of Celtic warfare; it was what they were good at.

The Roman inhabitants of Colchester appealed for help, but they were sent only 200 troops. Boudicca's army were triumphant. In the words of Tacitus:

Source B:

Unguarded, they were surprised and overpowered by the Barbarians in one assault. The colony was laid waste with fire and sword.

Petilius Cerealis marched to relieve the city with 200 men, but the British horde [attacked him]... the Roman infantry [was] cut to pieces.

Soon afterwards, Boudicca's army attacked London. At that time, it was a new commercial centre, founded after the Roman conquest of Britain in 43AD. The rebels torched so many buildings there, that archaeologists can still find a thick layer of burnt debris under the current city. Finally, Boudicca and her army attacked the city of St Albans. In the words of Tacitus:

Source C:

The inhabitants of Verulamium [St Albans] were put to the sword. The ways of a savage people lead them always to plunder… The number massacred in the [three] places which have been mentioned, amounted to no less than seventy thousand. To make prisoners was not in the idea of a people who despised all the laws of war... [They made] sure to glut themselves with the blood of their enemies.

Dio's account gives more detail: he says that the noblest women were displayed, impaled on spikes with their breasts cut off and sewn to their mouths, 'to the accompaniment of sacrifices, banquets, and wanton behaviour' in sacred places.

The Battle of Watling Street

Suetonius, the Roman governor of Britain, decided to end the revolt. He led an army of 10,000 to meet the rebels. Near Watling Street, London, he confronted Boudicca's army of 230,000 Celtic warriors. He drew up his troops carefully in a narrow gorge which protected his flanks; a forest behind made an attack from the rear impossible. The Britons just spread out on the open plain. Tacitus says:

Source D:

> They formed no regular line of battle. Detached groups arrived… so sure of victory, that they placed their wives in wagons at the edge of the plain, so they could see the British valour.

In the typical style of Celtic leaders, Boudicca inspired her army. She drove along the front of her warriors, insulting the Romans and rousing her troops, with words like, "I am fighting as an ordinary person for my lost freedom. That is what I, a woman will do – let other men die in slavery if they will!"

Boudicca led her attack bravely – but not wisely. She charged the Roman legions. As she attacked, her troops were channelled by the sides of the gorge into a tightly packed mass.

Suetonius' soldiers replied with great discipline. They waited until the Celtic army had advanced to about 36 metres away and then hit them with a volley of Roman spears. The spears took a heavy toll on the Britons, very few of whom had armour. Those who had shields and intercepted the spears either had to discard their shields or fight with their shields weighed down by a heavy iron spear embedded within. A second volley followed, as each Roman legionary carried two throwing spears. The Celtic attack fell into disarray.

Suetonius then ordered his legionaries and auxiliaries to move forward in formation. Protected by shields, and with their superior discipline, the Romans were able to stab the Britons though gaps in their shield wall. The Celts, in contrast, were crowded together and had too little space to use their long stabbing spears or slashing swords.

The Roman cavalry, spears extended, then entered the fray and attacked the Britons from the flanks.

They also rode to the rear and attacked Boudicca's supply wagons, which she had left unprotected.

As their losses mounted, the Britons lost heart and tried to retreat. But their path was blocked by their wagons. As they retreated, they were massacred by Roman cavalry.

The Romans killed the warriors – and also the women and children. Tacitus reports that 'Boudicca, by poison, ended her life' and, altogether, '80,000 Britons fell' whilst 'the Romans lost only 400'. The revolt was over.

Activities

1   From the events of Boudicca's Revolt, what can you find that was typical of:

    a) Roman warfare   b) Celtic warfare?

2   During the revolt, how far do you think Boudicca was responsible for:

    a) its successes   b) its failure?

3   'In warfare, a smaller, disciplined, trained army will often defeat a larger, untrained and ill-disciplined force.' Use the events in the Battle of Watling Street to explain why this happens.

Summary

- Boudicca's Revolt illustrates several key features of Roman and Celtic warfare.
- The Roman army, weapons and tactics were superior to the Britons.

Source E: A modern picture of Boudicca. There are no mosaics or sculptures from the time that show us the events or what Boudicca looked like.

1.4 Saxon warfare

> **Learning outcomes**
>
> By the end of this topic you should be able to:
> - describe the key features of Saxon warfare
> - explain how Saxon society affected warfare.

The Saxons come to Britain

During the 1,000 years after Boudicca's revolt, Britain was transformed. The character of society in Britain changed dramatically and, as the social context changed, warfare in Britain changed too.

- Between 200 and 400AD, the Roman Empire went into decline. Eventually, the Roman army withdrew from Britain in 410AD.
- From about 400 to 600AD, waves of Germanic people from northern Europe travelled across the seas to settle in Britain. These were the Angles, Saxons, Jutes and Frisians – often called Anglo-Saxons or just Saxons.
- The Celtic Britons remained in control of the areas we now call Wales and Scotland. But, by about 600AD, the Anglo-Saxons had set up their own kingdoms, like Wessex, Essex, Sussex, East Anglia, Mercia and Northumberland, in what we now call England.
- Finally, by about 900AD, all these separate kingdoms were unified into one Saxon kingdom, which became known as England.

By 1066 – a key year in British history – the Saxon King of England was King Harold. What kind of Saxon society did he rule? And what kind of army did he have?

Saxon society

Saxon society was mainly rural. There were a few towns, but land was the main source of wealth. In theory, the king owned all the land: but, to protect his kingdom, the king needed soldiers. He could employ a few, but not enough for a large army. So the Saxons developed a system in which the king gave land to loyal followers in exchange for their military support.

It was influenced by a similar system in Europe, but it was not as well developed.

Saxon society, land and armies

The King
Saxon England was ruled by a king. The king had palaces around his kingdom, which he visited regularly to maintain control of his lands. The king was expected to protect his kingdom from invasion, so he had his own small army and even a navy, which was paid for by taxes.

Earls
To control his kingdom, the king gave land to loyal followers. These were called earls; they were given large areas of the kingdom – in theory, only for their lifetime. In return, the earls had to support the king. They recruited full-time soldiers, called **housecarls**, to guard them and support them in battle.

Thegns
These earls parcelled out control of their land to thegns. Thegns would be wealthy enough to support large households. In return, they were expected to support their earl. Many of them employed some full-time housecarls.

Freemen
The freemen of England – ceorls - were mainly small tenant farmers. For most of the time they worked on their lord's land. But they were expected to join the **fyrd** – the emergency army which was raised or released according to need.

Slaves
Slaves were mainly prisoners captured in battle, but some were bought at markets and used to work on the land or as servants.

Saxon armies

The Saxon king had two main kinds of soldiers, housecarls and the fyrd.

- Housecarls were professional soldiers paid by the king, earls and thegns. They were recruited when young from the strongest boys and trained to use weapons. They were clothed, armed and fed by their lord. When fighting, they were either fed by their lord's supply wagons or lived off the land – stealing their food.
- The fyrd was an army made up by freemen, who were expected to volunteer in times of danger. In early Saxon times, the fyrd was very disorganised and made up of farmers with only scythes and axes for weapons. But, over the centuries, there were so many wars – first between the various Anglo-Saxon kingdoms and then against invading Vikings – that, by 1066, the fyrd had become a hardened force. Because it was based on local men, the king could raise the fyrd in any part of the country he needed.
- The Saxons did not use mounted soldiers.

Source A: Saxon housecarls. Note the spear, sword, shield, chainmail and helmet.

Saxon weapons and armour

Soldiers in the fyrd brought their own weapons. They usually had swords, a spear and a shield, and some kind of protective clothing, like a helmet and leather jerkin. However, some fyrdmen arrived only with farm tools, like scythes, for weapons.

Housecarls were much better armed. For attack, they had swords, spears and, sometimes a battleaxe. These had metal axe-heads, with cutting edges about 30cm long, mounted on a long pole. In the hands of a strong man, these could easily behead an enemy. Some housecarls were also trained as bowmen.

For defence, housecarls had a coat of chainmail, called a byrnie, a pointed helmet to deflect blows and a wooden shield, usually a long one, to protect the legs as well as the body.

Saxon warfare

Saxon armies were mainly used for defence against invading forces, such as the Vikings, or rebellions. Their tactics involved:

- forming a defensive front line of housecarls behind a wall of shields
- strengthening this defensive line with fyrdmen behind the housecarls
- rebuffing attacks with this shield wall
- using spears and arrows, from behind the shield wall, to weaken the enemy
- moving forward in formation, using swords and axes to attack enemy lines.

Activities

1 Describe Saxon:
   a) recruitment of soldiers
   b) provision of soldiers' equipment
   c) weapons and tactics.
2 In what ways was Saxon warfare shaped by Saxon society?

Summary

Saxon society shaped the armies, weapons and tactics of Saxon warfare.

1.5 Norman warfare

> **Learning outcomes**
>
> By the end of this topic you should be able to:
> - describe the key features of Norman warfare
> - explain how Norman warfare reflected Norman society.

The Normans lived in northern France (Normandy), just the other side of the English Channel from Saxon England. They had originally come from Scandinavia and northern Germany. The name 'Norman' actually means 'norsemen' or 'northmen'.

Like the Vikings, from about 800AD they began to move into warmer areas of Europe. In 911AD, they were allowed to settle in northern France, under the rule of the Frank (French) king.

Norman society

Norman society was partly shaped by its Viking origins. The Normans who settled in northern France were warlike marauders; experienced soldiers, hungry for land (see Source A).

Warfare was a constant feature of Norman society. The young William (later William the Conqueror), who became Duke of Normandy in 1035, had to fight off two serious rebellions and two attacks by the King of France before his famous invasion of Britain in 1066.

Source A: Written in about 1090, by Geoffrey Malaterra, a monk and historian, probably of Norman origin. He lived in areas occupied by Normans and knew at least one Norman ruler.

> [The Normans are] …cunning, discontented with what they have, always hopeful of gaining more and desperate for wealth and power.
>
> They are able to endure of toil, hunger, and cold whenever fate brings this on them.
>
> They love hunting and hawking and delight in the pleasure of horses and of all the weapons and the trappings of war.

The constant fighting in Norman society meant that young men in wealthy families were normally trained to fight on horseback, using swords, shields, bows and lances.

Norman society was also shaped by the Franks who lived around them. Since about 700AD, the Franks had developed the feudal system. This changed how society was organised and it also changed how armies were formed. Under the feudal system:

- A ruler granted land to his leading supporters. They became his **tenants-in-chief**, often called barons. In return, they supported him with military service. In the Frankish tradition, they served as heavily armed knights on horseback; they also employed other soldiers.
- These barons usually divided their land among their own sub-tenants. These tenants did not pay rent as we do today; instead, they promised to give support and military service to their lord. Again, in the Frankish tradition, they too served as mounted knights and employed other soldiers.

As the Normans settled in Normandy, they adopted this system. As a result, their style of warfare became a mixture of their aggressive Viking heritage and the mixed army of mounted knights and foot soldiers of the Franks.

The Feudal System

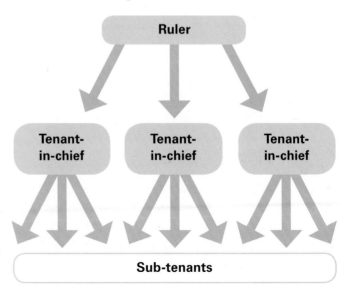

The Norman army

The main difference between the Norman and Saxon armies were the Norman mounted knights. These were usually the men of wealthier families and they considered themselves the cream of the fighting forces. The Saxons did not fight on horseback, whereas up to half of the Norman army might consist of mounted knights.

The Normans also had foot soldiers – infantry. There was no tradition of calling up the fyrd in Norman society, so the infantry were normally professional soldiers, employed by the leaders of the army.

The Normans also had large numbers of archers in their armies.

Norman weapons and armour

For attacking, Norman knights mainly used spears, but also swords, small axes and lances.

To defend themselves, they wore knee-length chainmail shirts, called hauberks. Sometimes they had chainmail hoods and a pointed helmet, typically with a 'nasal' to protect the face. They also used shields – usually kite-shaped.

Norman foot soldiers also used spears, swords and axes. The bows they used were quite short and they only drew the strings back to their bodies, not fully to the ear. The Normans also used crossbows.

Norman infantry were less likely to be wealthy than the knights. As a result, though they had helmets and shields, they were less protected. Few wore chainmail; it was too heavy and expensive.

Norman warfare

Norman armies were more aggressive than the Saxons. Spears, arrows and cavalry charges were often used to soften up an enemy before the infantry moved forward. The cavalry were often deadly when chasing fleeing enemy foot soldiers.

Another difference between Norman and Saxon warfare was the development of castles. These stone fortresses were common homes and military bases for wealthy knights in Europe, long before they were introduced to Britain.

Activities

1 Describe the troops, weapons and tactics of the Norman army.

2 Describe how Norman society shaped the key features of the Norman army.

 examzone **Build better answers**

Read the description of the Normans in Source A. How useful is this to a historian who is investigating Norman warfare? Use Source A and your own knowledge to explain your answer. (8 marks)

■ **Basic, Level 1**
Answer uses valid, but simple, assertions, e.g. *It must be useful because it is Norman.*

● **Good, Level 2**
Answer uses reasoned arguments based on how useful the content or the author is.

▲ **Excellent, Level 3**
Answer evaluates how much the source can be trusted by evaluating how reliable the content or the author is, for example by looking at the nature, origin or purpose, and also uses own wider knowledge.

NB: The best answers use information from the source and their own knowledge.

Summary

Norman society shaped the armies, weapons, and tactics of Norman warfare.

Source B: An extract from the Bayeux Tapestry which shows Norman knights and archers.

1.6 The Battle of Hastings 1066

Learning outcomes

By the end of this topic you should be able to:

- understand the key features of the Battle of Hastings and William I's leadership there
- recognise key features of Saxon and Norman warfare at the Battle of Hastings.

In early August 1066, Duke William of Normandy gathered an invasion fleet. He intended to attack England and claim the throne, but northerly winds kept him in port. It was 28 September before he could set sail.

During those weeks the English king, Harold, suffered set-backs.

- Firstly, many of his soldiers became impatient and returned home to harvest their crops.
- Then a gale weakened his fleet.
- Finally, a Viking army of 10,000 men invaded the north of England. Harold had marched his army for six days to defeat the invaders at the Battle of Stamford Bridge.

All this left the south coast unguarded; William landed unopposed. He ravaged local villages, taking supplies and goading Harold to fight him.

Harold's war council urged him not to rush to battle. Harold ignored their advice. He tried to surprise William by the speed of his response and set out on the 190 mile march south. But William had sent out scouts, who spotted his approach.

Source A: An extract from the Bayeux Tapestry, a Norman record of William's invasion. This part shows the Norman knights foraging for food.

The armies

Norman army	Saxon army
Army size: 8,000 in total • 2,000 knights • 4,000 infantry • 2,000 archers	Army size: 7,500 in total • 2,000 elite **housecarls** • 5,500 **fyrd** militia with no cavalry
Arms: • Knights were well-armed with lances, spears and swords. • They also had mail shirts and metal helmets. • Archers had short bows with a killing range of 100 yards. • Other archers were armed with crossbows.	Arms: • Housecarls used swords and 5 foot long battle axes. • They were also armoured in mail shirts and metal helmets. • The fyrd were partly farmers who had little military training. Most would have a spear and shield and little else.

The Battle

So on the morning of 14 October, Harold drew up his forces near the road from Hastings to London, on Senlac Hill, about 10 miles inland.

It was a fine defensive position, his right flank protected by a marsh and the centre and left flank by a steep slope. The battle began at about 9.30a.m.

William's strategy was:

- to weaken the enemy with arrows,
- followed by an infantry attack,
- then a cavalry charge.

But Harold's men had formed a strong **shield wall** on the hill, with his housecarls at the centre.

- Norman arrows hit shields and had little effect.
- The English fought off the infantry charge, hurling down stones and javelins.
- When the Norman cavalry charged, the Saxon shield wall was intact and bristling with spears.

Source B: This extract from the Bayeux Tapestry shows the Norman cavalry failing to breach the Saxon shield wall.

The Norman cavalry charge stalled. Many horses were killed or shied away. The Normans retreated and the Saxon infantry chased them down the hill. In the melee, William's horse fell.

Norman sources – like the Bayeux Tapestry - say that William raised his helmet, showed his face, declared that he was alive and rallied his knights. The Normans turned and set upon the English infantry. Many, including Harold's two brothers, were killed before they could scramble back to the safety of the shield wall.

The battle then resumed, as before. The Norman knights even tried to use the tactic of feigned retreats to lure the Saxons off the hill again. The battle became a matter of **attrition**, with heavy face-to-face, hand-to-hand combat at the edge of the shield wall.

For hours, the Norman assaults failed.

- But gradually, as housecarls fell, their places were taken by less powerful fyrdmen.
- Then Harold was killed, possibly shot in the eye by an arrow and ridden down by knights.
- This deflated Saxon morale and the fyrdmen fled, pursued by Norman knights.

About 5,000 English and 3,000 Normans had died.

Summary

The Battle of Hastings shows:
- several features typical of Saxon and Norman warfare
- the importance of individuals in warfare.

The verdict

William's victory was a triumph for the feudal army of mounted knights, archers and infantry.

It was also a victory for leadership.

- Harold chose his ground well.
- But he would have been better to wait for reinforcements.
- William marshalled his troops well and inspired them when needed.
- William also benefited from good luck.

Activities

1 What can you learn from the Bayeux Tapestry about the armies that fought at the Battle of Hastings?
2 How did each of these contribute to victory at the Battle of Hastings?
   a) Strength of the Norman army.
   b) The leadership of William.
   c) Luck.
3 Overall, how far should William get the credit for winning the Battle of Hastings?

Source C: The death of Harold.

1.7 Warfare 1066-1350

Learning outcomes

By the end of this topic you should be able to:

- know how feudalism developed after 1066
- know that feudalism shaped the key features of warfare in this early medieval period.

The feudal system

After the Battle of Hastings, William became King of England. To protect and control his kingdom, he needed a strong army. So he, and later Norman kings, used the feudal system (see page 18).

Source A: An illustration from the 14th century showing mounted knights, archers and, in the top left, pike men.

The Norman kings gave huge areas of land to loyal barons. In return, the barons gave military support to the king. Then, to control their lands, the barons gave parts of their land to sub-tenants, who promised military support to the barons.

This is how Norman kings and their supporters imposed their rule on the Saxon population and raised armies for wars against foreign enemies.

The Assize of Arms

The feudal system provided large numbers of mounted knights and also some infantry, but infantry was the biggest part of a medieval army. In 1181, King Henry II extended the feudal system by passing the Assize of Arms. This law said that all freemen who owned a small amount of property had to provide their own arms and fight for the king. This re-shaped early medieval armies.

The early medieval army

Between 1066 and 1350, the early medieval army was composed of knights and infantry.

Infantry made up most of the army. Some were the permanent men-at-arms employed by knights. But most were poorer men doing their feudal duty.

Some were pike men. Pikes were three-to-six-metre spears. Pike men gathered around knights or archers and pointed their pikes towards enemy cavalry or infantry charges. An axe-head fixed near the top of pikes made **halberds** to thrust and cut.

Mounted knights were the elite of the army. Made up of wealthy landowners, knights could provide their own horses, swords, shields and lances.

At first, they had **hauberks** – chainmail tunics; then, armour developed. By 1300, metal breastplates and back plates were common. After about 1400, knights wore full suits of armour, though these were soon seen to be impractical.

Archers made up about half the infantry.

Some shot crossbows; these were very accurate and so powerful their bolts could pierce armour. But crossbows were slow to re-load, so most archers used short bows, about 50cm long, with a 100 metre range.

Training

A knight's fighting skills were part of the culture of noble families, so training came in the form of mock fights and tournaments for young noblemen.

Most soldiers were commoners, not nobles. So, laws were made requiring common men to practise archery. There was little other training. Feudal armies were not permanent. They only formed for wars, so there were no barracks or training camps.

Provisioning

The feudal system provided men for an army; but food and supplies had to be provided in other ways.

- **Baggage trains** of carts, mules and horses carried supplies. Each man in the army needed about 3lbs of food per day and each horse 20lbs of fodder – grass or hay. River water caused illness amongst soldiers, so armies carried mead, beer or wine instead.
- **Supply by sea or river** made it easier to carry heavy goods. On the Third Crusade in the 12th century, Richard I of England supplied his army by sea. An army supplied by ships could move at about 20 miles per day.
- **Plunder** was common. Soldiers were sent to forage in the countryside or steal from villages. An army that needed to **forage** as it marched slowed to about five miles per day. Foraging left a wasteland that could cause more civilian deaths from starvation than deaths in battle.

Movement

Feudal armies moved at the speed of a walking man. Knights travelled on horseback; horses pulled an army's carts. But infantry had to march to battle and living off the land slowed a march down. To march 15 miles in a day was good going. In 1346, it took Edward III over 30 days to march his army of about 10,000 men 300 miles to the Battle of Crécy.

Care of combatants

No medieval commanders had the means to care properly for their soldiers. More died from a lack of general or medical care than were killed outright on the battlefield.

General care was provided by the knights' servants or the women – usually wives and family – who travelled with the army in their hundreds. They would cook, wash and mend clothes. They searched men and clothes for lice and fleas, which could cause the deadly diseases which spread through armies.

Medieval armies had few, if any, medical staff. Any wound which pierced the intestines or the chest normally caused fatal infection. Wounded men were often left, unattended, on the battlefield overnight after a battle. Many died from blood loss, infection or exposure. It was an act of mercy for the victorious side to return to the battlefield the next day and kill the wounded.

The weaknesses of feudal armies

As we have seen, feudal armies were:

- small – they relied on feudal ties: William had only 8,000 men at Hastings
- temporary – a knight or soldier's feudal duty was normally limited to 45 days
- poorly trained and drilled – tactics had to be simple
- ill-disciplined – knights were very independent and often more concerned with ransoms and glory than orders.

Gradually, kings became frustrated by this. They began to accept money in exchange for feudal service and hired professional soldiers. But this only happened gradually before 1350.

Source B: A contemporary picture of men-at-arms fighting at the Battle of Bannockburn, in 1314.

For weapons, the infantry used swords, axes and bows, and sometimes a small dagger or a mace. For defence, they used shields and helmets. Some had chainmail or plate armour; most could only afford leather jackets, called **gambesons**.

Generally, the infantry were badly equipped. Most bought their own weapons. In around 1300, a pike, mace, axe and mail shirt cost about half a year's average wages.

Limited warfare

The feudal system produced small armies. William the Conqueror's army of 8,000 at the Battle of Hastings in 1066 was considered large. King Henry II of England could only call upon 6,000 knights in the 12th century.

The **campaigning season** was limited too. Fighting was only possible from the late spring – after crops had been sown – until the autumn, after which the weather could make it impractical to move troops and fight battles.

These factors meant that this was an age of limited warfare.

The aims of most wars were limited too. Rulers often used their armies like private possessions – to force a rival to give him land or money, or to settle a dispute between royal families. Unlike in later wars, rulers rarely destroyed their enemy's army or conquered their country.

Fighting was also limited. In feudal society, rulers had good reasons to avoid battles:

- at a time when rulers led armies, losing could mean they were killed, like King Harold at the Battle of Hastings in 1066;
- or they could be captured, like King Richard I of England in 1192.

Being captured meant paying a huge **ransom** in exchange for freedom.

So, instead of fighting, commanders might spend most of their time manoeuvring their armies to avoid a battle or to trap their enemy in a hopeless position. This manoeuvring might involve **skirmishes** or raids. Occasionally an army would just **plunder** an area, either to destroy an enemy's food supplies or capture a town to seize **booty**.

Even if you wanted a battle, it was not easy:

- it was difficult to know where your enemy was; commanders relied on **intelligence** from scouts using imperfect means like smoke signals, church bells or pigeons;
- if the commander of a feudal army wanted to fight, he would have to hold a council of war with his leading noblemen to get their agreement.

Battlefield tactics

So, in feudal society, battles were not the most common means of waging war. But when battles were fought, these were the tactics employed:

Preparing for battle

Generals would try to draw up their armies in positions which were difficult to attack – on the top of slopes or protected at the back and sides, perhaps by woodland, marshes or rivers.

They would then try to weaken the enemy, perhaps using arrows or, commonly using cavalry.

Cavalry attack

Knights considered themselves the elite of feudal society, and they liked to take the leading role in battles. They were the tanks of medieval warfare. They would form into a tightly packed group and charge, hoping to burst through the enemy defences. A mounted knight (150lb), his armour (60lb) and weapons (40lb) required a sturdy horse. At a top speed of about 15 miles per hour – probably as fast as you could run – the combined weight of the knight and horse made a colossal impact.

Source C: A 14th-century picture of knights leading a charge at the Battle of Muldorf, 1322.

Defence

The defending infantry would try to weaken the cavalry attack. They would:

- fire arrows into the attacking cavalry;
- position troops behind spiked posts;
- put troops in tight squares, protected by pikes;
- lay **caltrops** on the ground to injure the attacking horses.

The infantry charge

Befitting their place in society, the attacking infantry followed the mounted knights, to exploit gaps in the enemy defences. If necessary, knights dismounted and also fought on foot.

Once hand-to-hand combat began, fighting was like frenzied butchery. Face-to-face, men tried to smash an opponent's skull or arms with a mace or axe, or to pierce his armour joints, or slash his belly or cut the tendons in arms or legs with an axe or a sword.

Retreat

Sometimes mounted knights charged and then pretended to retreat; this sometimes tricked infantry into chasing them. Once they were away from their protective spears or pikes, the knights then turned upon the disorganised infantry.

The same was true at the end of a battle. In hand-to-hand fighting, once one side turned and fled in disorder, it usually led to slaughter. It was common for more soldiers to be killed in the final retreat than in the battle itself.

Leadership

There was usually little difference in the size of medieval armies or their weapons. Often the outcome of a battle was therefore determined by the quality of leadership or the discipline of the troops.

Source D: Infantry at the Battle of Courtrai in 1302, using halberds, swords and axes, while stumbling on the bodies of the dead.

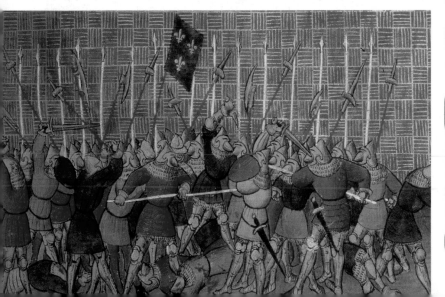

The age of mounted knights?

The noble, mounted knights were the most powerful force on the battlefield. They are often described as the decisive force.

This is partly because records of battles come mainly from histories, songs, poems and novels written by the noble classes themselves, boosted by romantic images of jousting tournaments. So, even in early medieval times, the importance of the mounted knight may have been exaggerated. Infantry were always the largest part of feudal armies.

The decline of mounted knights?

By 1350, towards the end of medieval times, the power of the mounted knight was in decline – because of tactics and technology. From about 1300, commanders changed their tactics to use longbow archers to weaken cavalry. They also used pike men with halberds to hook knights off their horses and hack them to death with their axe-heads.

By 1350, gunpowder brought muskets and cannon; horsemen were very vulnerable to these. Although cavalry remained a feature of armies for some time, they were never the powerful force they once were.

Activities

1. What were the key features of an early medieval army?

2. How did the feudal system shape the key features of early medieval armies?

3. How much did early medieval armies change between 1066 and 1350?

Summary

- The feudal system shaped the composition and tactics of medieval armies.

- Medieval armies were small and temporary; they had limited training and care for soldiers; provisioning and movement were difficult.

- Medieval armies fought limited warfare.

1.8 Siege warfare 1066-1350

Learning outcomes

By the end of this topic you should be able to:

- describe the key features of castle design and how this changed over time
- describe the key features of siege technology
- explain how castles fit into the overall picture of early medieval warfare.

Castles

The Romans had built forts in Britain, but these had decayed and disappeared by the Middle Ages. When the Normans began to build castles in Britain, after 1066, it marked a distinct change.

A castle had several functions. It was:

- a safe place for the Norman barons to live amongst the hostile Saxon population
- a stronghold which could be defended against attack by another baron or a foreign army
- a military base from which to launch attacks.

The nobles could only build these castles with the king's permission.

At first, the key consideration was speed; the Normans needed to be safe. So, cheap, plentiful materials – wood and earth – were used for the first castles. They were 'motte and bailey' castles.

Motte and bailey castles

The motte was a mound, made of layers of earth. It usually had a circular wooden palisade (barrier) at the top, with wooden huts leant against the inside walls. It was the last place of refuge in an attack.

The bailey was the courtyard below the motte. It provided the housing and storage for normal life – but it was also surrounded by a wooden palisade on an earth bank, as the first line of defence.

Ideally, a castle was sited high up, with views all around and wells to provide water in the bailey and motte. Sometimes, water in the ditch around the bailey strengthened the defences of the castle.

Source A: A motte and bailey castle.

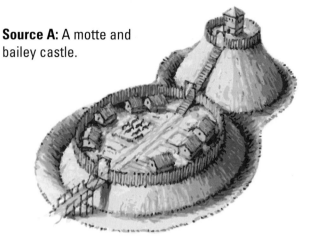

William the Conqueror built one near Hastings, in just 15 days. The Bayeux Tapestry shows that he had with him sections of castle wall built in advance to speed up this process. By 1100, the Normans had built motte and bailey castles all over England.

Source B: From *Life of John Commines,* by Walter the Archdeacon, 1130.

It was customary for rich men and the nobles [to build castles], because of their carrying on of feuds; and so they may be safe from enemies, and may have greater power for either conquering their equals or keeping down their inferiors.

Changes in castle design

Wooden castles had problems. They were easily attacked by fire and the wooden palisades rotted. Improvements were soon developed.

Stone keeps

One solution was a circular stone tower, or keep, on the motte. A circular keep was built at Carisbrooke Castle in about 1100. But circular keeps were too small for lavish living space for barons. So the next solution was tall, square keeps. These were too heavy to sit on the motte, so they were usually built inside the bailey. Henry II built several square keeps after becoming king, in 1154, such as Orford Castle in Suffolk.

Stone curtain walls

From about 1100 onwards, the wooden palisades around castles were also replaced by high stone walls – called curtain walls.

Later changes to castle design

Over time, castle designers found ways of changing the features of castles to make them easier to defend. There were many changes.

Crenellations and shutters

It was not long before the curtain walls were topped with crenellations [A]. These had gaps, called embrasures [B], for defenders to fire through, separated by merlons [C] for them to shelter behind. Over time, wooden shutters were placed over embrasures for extra protection.

Bratticing and machicolations

Later, castle designers found ways to build overhangs on the outside of the top of the walls, so defenders could fire arrows or drop rocks on attackers at the base of the wall. At first, these structures were wooden and called bratticing. Eventually, they were made of stone and called machicolations [D].

The glacis and towers

Tall, thin walls could easily be breached. The first solution to this was to make the base of the walls thicker, and sloped, to make attack harder. This slope was called the glacis [E].

Towers [F] were another improvement to defence. From a tower, a defender could shoot along a wall at any attackers trying to breach it. At first, the towers were square. Soon, designers realised that rounded towers were less easy to attack. The towers at Conisborough Castle, for example, built in about 1200, were circular. One square tower, at

Activities

1 For extra information, try an internet search for images of castles and the technical terms named on pages 26-29.
2 What does Source B tell you about the reasons castles were built?
3 Describe four key features of castle design.

Rochester Castle, which was breached in an attack in 1215, was replaced by a round tower.

Gatehouses

Castle designers also realised that the weakest point of the curtain walls was the large hole designed into every one – the entrance. To counter this, they began to develop gatehouses around the entrances. Gatehouses [G] included lots of defensive features, like towers, drawbridges, portcullises and something called 'killing ground'. This was the heavily fortified space that attackers would have to cross to get to the entrance.

Ditches and concentric castles

To stop attackers easily getting to the castle walls, designers began to put a series of concentric ditches around the walls. Eventually, this idea turned into concentric walls [H]. These replaced single curtain walls with double rings of walls – low external ones and higher internal walls for extra security. Edward I build such a castle at Conway in Wales in about 1283-1289 – part of his 'iron ring' of castles to keep the Welsh at bay.

Source C: Conway Castle. Note the concentric walls, towers, crenellations, machicolations, glacis and gatehouse.

Siege technology

When attacking armies came across castles or towns protected by stone walls, they had to tackle them. If ignored, opposing forces could sally forth from inside the walls, harass the attackers and then return behind the walls to safety.

A full frontal attack on the castle or town walls was never the first option. Attackers usually decided upon encirclement, then battery, then negotiation, then attack.

Encirclement

Encirclement by the attacking army cut the town or castle off from reinforcements, supplies and, possibly, the water supply. Sometimes this alone was enough to starve the castle or city into surrender, unless a relief force drove the attackers away.

Battery

Battery involved weakening or breaching the walls. This was done in a variety of ways, for example, using siege engines, **battering rams**, fire and mines (see page 29 for details).

Source D: A 15th century manuscript showing a siege of a fortified city in 1099 by British and other troops. How many defensive features can you see? How many techniques for attacking fortified walls can you see?

Negotiation

Attackers always preferred to negotiate if they could. They knew that, if the defenders thought their plight was hopeless, they would sometimes agree to surrender. This would usually involve paying the attacking army large amounts of money either to go away or, at least, not to kill the inhabitants when they took over.

Attack!

If negotiating failed, after weakening the walls, attackers could then mount an assault. They used ladders and **siege towers**. It took great bravery and discipline. Attacking armies were often bigger than defending garrisons so, once inside, the result could be slaughter.

Attacking the walls

There were several ways of attacking the walls of castles or fortified towns.

Siege engines

Siege engines were devices created to break down the walls of fortified towns or castles.

- A **mangonel** was a catapult which worked by winding rope to create tension – like stretching an elastic band. It had a long, flat trajectory.
- A **trebuchet** was like a large sling. It had a long beam on a pivot; the beam had a sling on one end and a heavy weight on the other. When the weight dropped, the sling on the other end catapulted a rock, on a high trajectory, over the walls.

Source E: A medieval mangonel.

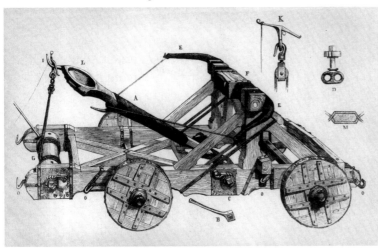

Mangonels hurled rocks at walls. Trebuchets hurled rocks, spears and rotting carcasses over walls to cause death and disease.

Rams, sows and penthouses

Attackers also used battering rams to break down walls or castle doors. To get close, they advanced under a long hut on wheels, called a penthouse or sow. A metal-tipped battering ram was slung from the roof of the sow. While defenders tried to kill them with arrows, rocks and fire bombs, attackers under the shelter swung the ram against the walls.

Mining

Sometimes attackers dug a mine under the castle walls. They propped up the roof of their tunnel with timber props as they dug. Once under the walls, they would start a large fire. This destroyed the props, causing the tunnel to collapse. The attackers hoped this would also make the walls above collapse, creating a weak point to attack.

Storming the walls

Once the walls were weakened, attackers had to storm the walls in a frontal assault. This was a very dangerous task, since defenders used arrows, spears, rocks and swords to fight them off from above.

The simplest way for attackers to get to the top of the walls was to use ladders. But it was hazardous, since only one attacker at a time could ascend the ladder. Defenders frequently tipped the ladders, and attackers, back down onto the ground.

Attackers also used wheeled siege towers, called belfries, to make a more concerted attack. These were made of wood and covered with wet animal hides to prevent fire being used against them. Attackers could shelter in the towers and then, many at a time, emerge from a platform at the top of the tower and leap onto the walls.

Who won?

Most sieges failed. Attackers often ran out of food, money or patience, or they fell ill from exposure or infected water. Defenders suffered dreadfully from hunger in long sieges or were slaughtered if the walls fell, so many decided to negotiate a solution.

Activities

4 In what ways did castle design improve between 1066-1350?

5 How did attackers try to overcome these improvements?

6 Study the picture of a Roman attack on fortified walls on page 10. What similarities and differences can you see compared to the medieval attack shown on page 28?

Summary

Norman warfare included castles. Sieges revived earlier Roman methods of warfare.

1.9 Summary: Warfare c50AD–c1350

In the preceding pages, we have looked at:
- Roman and Celtic societies in c50AD
- Saxon and Norman societies before 1066
- Early medieval feudal society 1066-1350.

These different societies cover almost 1,500 years.

Today, we are used to things improving as time goes by. When this happens, we can picture progress in a simple diagram, like this.

Source A: Graph showing continuous, steady improvement.

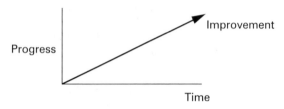

However, the story of warfare from Roman times to 1350, is not a simple story of steady progress.

- Things certainly improved at the start of the Roman Empire; the Roman army which conquered Britain was improving in weapons, organisation, leadership and training.
- During exactly the same years, there was no improvement at all in Celtic armies or wafare.
- When the Romans left Britain, in 410AD, all their improvements were lost.
- After 1066, the Normans brought feudalism to Britain; armies began to improve again. But, in some ways, they were still less advanced in 1350 than the Romans a thousand years before.

What we learn from this is that change is much more complicated than we might have thought.

Activities

1   To illustrate how complex change is, try drawing a graph for 50AD to 1350 to accommodate the four bullet points above. It is possible; but it's not simple!

Another thing about modern life is that many things seem to be constantly changing, very fast. Take fashion, computers and holiday travel, for example. They are all totally different now from how they were 50 years ago.

This constant change sometimes hides how common **continuity** is. Throughout the long period we have been studying, some key features of warfare stayed the same. For example:

- Most armies remained small – usually no more than 10,000 men.
- Infantry remained the biggest part of armies.
- Infantry decided the outcome of most battles.
- Swords and spears, of various kinds, remained the most important weapons.
- The feigned cavalry retreat remained a useful tactic and, for infantry, they were never more vulnerable than when in retreat.

Activities

2   Look back at Boudicca's Revolt and the Battle of Hastings. They were a thousand years apart. List the similarities between them.

Source B: A modern picture of Celtic warriors. The picture is based on written descriptions of Celtic warriors from about 50AD.

We have also discovered something else about:
- Roman and Celtic societies in 50AD
- Saxon and Norman societies before 1066
- Early medieval feudal society after 1066.

Each one had a very different kind of society. This meant that each society's warfare was different from that in the other societies. Differences in society caused differences in weapons, tactics, the organisation and recruitment of armies and army life.

For example:
- The Roman Empire was centralised; power and wealth were concentrated in the hands of the emperor. He could therefore afford a permanent, paid and well-equipped army. This meant that ordinary citizens did not normally fight in battles.
- Celtic society was decentralised; power and wealth were divided among thousands of Celtic villages. There was no central army; each village or tribe arranged their own forces. The quality of weapons varied. Every man was expected to fight.
- Feudal society was also decentralised. A king gave his supporters power over much of his land and, in exchange, received military service. Most men might expect to fight. Soldiers had to provide what weapons they could. Leadership was often disputed.

So at any given time changes in the organisation of society will often explain changes in the key features of warfare at that time.

Source C: A 19th-century picture showing an army of soldiers gathering in about 1250AD.

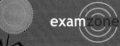

Activities

3 Take the issue of training for armies. How did the different societies in:
- the Roman Empire
- Celtic society
- medieval feudal society

affect the degree of training in each of their armies?

---

exam zone **Build better answers**

How much did the organisation of armies change between Celtic Britain in 50AD and Saxon Britain in 1066? Explain your answer. (16 marks)

You may use the following in your answer.
- Boudicca's tactics at the Battle of Watling Street
- Harold's tactics at the Battle of Hastings

You must also include information of your own.

 Basic, Level 1
Answer makes simple comments about the armies supported by a little knowledge.

 Good, Level 2
Answer gives slightly more developed information with more supporting detail.

Better, Level 3
Answer concentrates on the issue of change, with accurate information to support ideas and use of own knowledge.

Excellent, Level 4
A well-developed, sustained argument is made on the issue of change, with accurate examples and use of own knowledge for support. Analyses both continuity and change to come to a judgment on the nature of change.

Make sure you write accurately – there are three extra marks available for spelling, grammar and punctuation in these questions.

2.1 Warfare 1350-1450

Learning outcomes

By the end of this topic you should be able to:

● identify areas of change and continuity in warfare 1350-1450

● describe changes in recruitment

● describe the rise and impact of the archer.

The period 1350-1450 was, overall, a time of gradual change. In many ways, warfare during this time continued to have the same key features as the period 1066–1350.

The two main changes were:
- increased recruitment of **mercenaries**
- the impact of archers using long bows.

Source A: This is a battle scene from about 1450. In many ways it is similar to battles 150 years earlier.

Continuity

Methods of fighting changed little

1350 to 1450 was a period of almost constant warfare across Europe.

The biggest conflict was the Hundred Years' War. This was a series of wars, from 1337 to 1453, between the English and the French. The major battles were fought at Crécy, Poitiers and Agincourt.

Although the amount of fighting increased, in many ways the methods of fighting during this period changed very little from earlier years. See Source A for details.

Armies remained small

As we shall see, new methods of recruiting armies were found, but armies still remained small.

● When Prince Edward invaded France in 1356, he had an English army of only 6,000 men.
● In the last conflict of the 100 Years' War, the Battle of Castillon in 1453, the English army consisted, again, of 6,000 men.

Pictures of medieval warfare can mislead. Some paintings give a romantic view of mounted knights, all in full suits of armour. This is wrong. Most mounted soldiers wore far less armour than the paintings show.

Compare the fighting with the battles shown on pages 24 and 25. Nothing much has changed.

The infantry make up most of the combatants. They fight with pikes, swords and shields. They have helmets, but are otherwise poorly protected.

Mounted knights attack using lances swords and shields Often medieval artists exaggerated the number, but not here.

Edward III of England led several armies during this period. He won the battles of Crécy and Poitiers. But even his small armies were a huge expense.

- When he transported 4,000 troops by sea, he had to send with them 1,300 sides of bacon, 200 tons of grain, 56 tons of cheese and 30 tons of peas and beans.
- In 1360, to equip his armies with spare weapons, he was storing 11,000 bows and 24,000 arrows at the Tower of London.

The limited wealth of kings in medieval times just did not allow the employment of very large armies.

Limited warfare remained the norm

As before, wars were rarely waged to conquer other countries. Instead, kings fought wars to:

- pillage riches from foreign lands. In 1346, for example, King Edward III spent months pillaging France before the Battle of Crécy
- cause economic damage to enemies by destroying crops and property in raids called **chevauchées**
- capture enemies for ransom. In 1356, at the Battle of Poitiers, the English captured the French king and demanded a sum twice the annual tax revenue of France for his return.

So warfare often consisted of raids, sorties and skirmishes, rather than battles. The aim was often to force the enemy into concessions in a treaty.

Since kings often led their armies, battles meant personal danger for them; capture could bring their country financial ruin. At the Battle of Poitiers, in 1356, the English captured King Jean II of France. He was held for ransom until 1360. France had to agree to give England 3 million gold coins and a large area of south-west France for his release.

Kings avoided battle if possible. In 1415, Henry V gave battle at Agincourt only because he had to.

Sieges remained common

Europe had many castles and fortified towns at this time. When threatened, people and armies sought safety there. So wars continued to involve many sieges of towns and castles. As before, attackers had either to starve people out – a slow process – or attack the walls – a dangerous one.

Source B: 15th century illustration of peasants attacking a knight. They might kill and rob him, else hand him over for ransom.

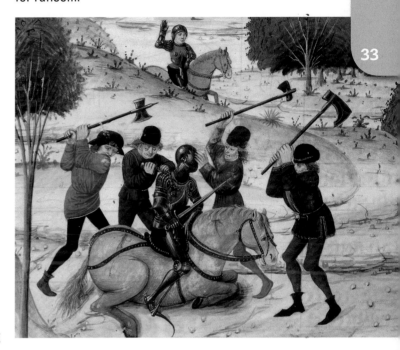

Tactics changed little

Since the weapons, size and composition of armies changed little there was also little change in tactics.

- Mounted knights and, increasingly, archers were used to mount attacks.
- Pikemen and archers were used to defend against attacks.
- The feigned retreat, a tactic used to fool the enemy in the Battle of Hastings 300 years before, was still used.
- What usually ended battles was brutal hand-to-hand combat. So infantry remained essential to an army's success. The English at the Battle of Crécy, in 1346, had 16,000 men, of whom 12,000 were infantry.

Change 1: Recruitment

Despite the large areas of continuity we have seen, some things were changing in warfare between 1350 and 1450. One was recruitment.

Problems with feudal armies

During the Hundred Years' War, the kings of England needed armies to fight abroad. They also needed them throughout the campaigning season – spring and summer – when the weather suited fighting. Feudal armies didn't meet their needs.

- Feudal duty was limited to about 45 days' service in one year – enough to fight off an invasion, but not to fight overseas or in a prolonged siege.
- Feudal troops were limited in number. In theory, English kings could call upon a total of 6,000 feudal knights. In practice, they could call on far fewer. Many knights said their feudal duty was to defend England and refused to go overseas.
- Feudal armies were badly trained. Young noblemen took part in jousting tournaments, but there was no proper training as a group, so battle tactics had to be very simple.
- Moreover, feudal knights were difficult to control. They were independent, wealthy men who resented military discipline. Some, especially in France, saw war as an exercise in the code of **chivalry**, where doing what was honourable was more important than doing what would win.
- Feudal armies provided their own weapons. So the quality of arms and protection, especially in the infantry, was very varied.

Source C: Knights jousting in about 1400. This is as close as feudal knights came to formal training.

Paying for professional soldiers

Because of these problems, kings hired troops to supplement their feudal armies. But this cost money. Where was it to come from?

- Kings had some income from the rents they charged on royal land; but this was limited and could not easily be increased.
- From about 1150, kings found a second source of income. They began to accept payment of money instead of military service. This payment was called **scutage**. By 1350, it was common for kings to use this money to hire soldiers to supplement their feudal forces.

Source D: Richard Fitzneal, in 1180, describing the beginnings of scutage.

> When the realm is threatened or attacked by enemies, the king orders that a certain sum, usually one pound, shall be paid by each knight. From this source are derived wages for soldiers. King Henry prefers to expose foreign mercenaries rather than his native knights to the fortunes of war.

The Hundred Years' War created an even more pressing need to hire troops; kings needed armies year after year to serve on long campaigns abroad. So they looked to a third source of income - taxes. Edward III, King of England in 1350, charged his subjects a new levy on property – in effect, a tax on wealth. He raised taxes on the export of wool as well and also borrowed money.

Gradually, the kings of England increased their income. As a result, they were able to employ mercenaries – professional soldiers for hire. This was not new in itself; mercenaries had been used before. What was new was the *number* of mercenaries. During the Hundred Years' War, English armies were made up mainly of mercenaries.

Activities

1   What were the advantages and disadvantages to a medieval king of:

   a) a feudal army

   b) professional soldiers?

34

Mercenaries

Mercenaries are men willing to do military service for a fixed period of time in exchange for pay.

If the king (or his nobles) wanted to hire soldiers, they would pay a sum of money to a mercenary leader, often called a 'captain'. In exchange, the captain would provide a number of soldiers, whom he paid a daily wage. The contract between the soldiers and the employer was called an **indenture**.

Mercenaries – typical daily wage
- Mounted knight   1 shilling (12 pence)
- Mounted archer   6 pence
- Archer on foot   3 pence
- Foot soldier   2 pence

A typical labourer's wage at this time was 4 pence per day. However, soldiers also shared the booty or ransom money from successful campaigns.

There was a wide variety of mercenaries.

- Some mercenaries were bands of soldiers from smaller states in Europe, such as Hesse in modern Germany. They were often willing to fight in European wars for any ruler who would employ them.
- Some mercenaries were Englishmen. Young men looking for adventure might be employed as foot soldiers. Archers were employed from English farming communities. Knights were employed from noble families.

An indenture

In 1371, the earl of Salisbury hired an army to fight in France. He contracted Roger Maltravers to serve for one year.

In his indenture, Maltravers agreed to provide his own horse, to bring two archers and to give one third of any booty or ransoms to the earl. The earl agreed to pay wages and the cost of transport to France.

For his Agincourt campaign, in 1415, Henry V raised an army of about 8,000 men, most of whom were mercenaries.

The impact of mercenary armies

In some ways, hired armies were similar to feudal armies.

- Mercenaries did not make *bigger* armies – they were too expensive.
- Neither did they form a *permanent* army, like the Romans had. Mercenaries were dismissed at the end of their contracts.
- They did not make much difference to the *provisioning* of armies either. Mercenaries made their own arrangements for food and lodgings.

However, mercenary armies did cause some changes.

- Training improved. Some captains trained their troops. Archers often practised firing a hail of arrows towards a common target (see page 37 for details).
- Before 1350, there was no specialist medical support for armies; wounded treated themselves or relied on friends. When mercenary armies were formed, some men and women claiming medical expertise joined the baggage trains of the armies and charged for giving help.

Source E: A medieval painting showing soldiers pillaging the baggage train of their defeated enemy. They would also steal booty – money or weapons – from battlefield bodies.

Change 2: The age of the archer

The other major change in warfare between 1350 and 1450 was the development of the longbow.

Archers in armies were not new. Of the 8,000 men in the Norman army at Hastings, 2,000 had been archers. But, from about 1350, two things changed.

- Firstly, the *size* of the bow changed. In early medieval times, archers had used a small bow, about 50cm long and effective only up to 100 metres. Now, longbows of about two metres in length appeared in English armies.
- Secondly, the *number* of archers changed. Of the 12,000 English infantry who defeated the French at the Battle of Crécy in 1346, 8,000 were longbow archers. They had grown from a quarter to two-thirds of the army.

What made the longbow so special?

For the period 1350 to 1450, the longbow was the most feared weapon on the battlefield. It terrified the enemy for several reasons.

- It could fire arrows a distance of 400 metres.
- The archer could fire 15 arrows per minute. The French crossbow could fire three.
- Its 2-foot long arrows could penetrate plate armour. Knights could be pinned to their mounts by arrows that went through armour, **chain mail**, flesh and bone, and pierced the saddle!

The impact of longbows

Fighting: decline of the mounted knight

The longbow changed the battlefield.

- In an attack, archers softened up enemy forces before the infantry launched an assault.
- In defence, archers brought down charging mounted knights or oncoming enemy infantry. Pikes had already weakened mounted knights as a force on the battlefield. The longbow now made them even less effective.

Archers wore metal or leather skull-caps and padded jackets, sometimes reinforced by chainmail. In addition to bows, archers were armed with small swords and shields. When needed, they put down their bows and fought like normal infantry.

The longbow was the decisive factor in battles like Agincourt in 1415. They remained the most deadly weapons on the battlefield until the later development of gunpowder weapons.

Source F: A modern picture of a 15th-century archer. Some archers had quivers to carry arrows. Others just lodged them in their belts.

Activities

2 Write a one minute speech advising the king whether to rely upon a feudal army or to raise taxes and pay for professional troops. Give reasons.

Source G: From *The Cambridge History of Warfare*, edited by Geoffrey Parker.

> The days of the feudal horseman were numbered, for the longbow (and later the handgun), combined with the pike, gave the advantage to the footsoldier.

Recruitment: rise of mercenaries

Longbows speeded up the replacement of feudal troops with mercenaries.

This was because longbows were so difficult to use. They were very powerful weapons; only those who practised from an early age could develop the muscles to pull the bowstring fully back. The infantry recruited to feudal armies would not do; expert archers had to be selected and employed.

Often these came from the yeoman class of small, rural landowners, especially those from the Welsh borders, where the longbow had been developed.

Training: need for expert archers

The age of the longbow changed training in English armies.

Firstly, English kings passed a series of laws to encourage individual young men to practise with longbows.

- In 1252, the Assize of Arms required all Englishmen aged 15–60 to own a bow.
- In 1363, Edward III ordered all Englishmen to practise archery on Sundays and holidays.
- But the real change was training in groups. Units of archers were **drilled** to improve their accuracy.
- The archers were organised into units of 20 or 100. They practised forming up ten ranks deep.
- An experienced knight skilled in the longbow (unlike most knights) was in overall command. This was the Master of Archers.
- On his command, **centenaurs** (leaders of units of 100) ordered the archers to 'loose arrows'.
- Archers learned to angle arrows to land on a white sheet (to represent a group of enemy troops) at various ranges – a practice called 'clout shooting' (i.e. cloth shooting).

This was a distinct change. Very little regular, organised drilling of groups of soldiers had taken place in the feudal armies before the longbow.

Society: rise of the yeomanry

We have seen how society can shape warfare. The feudal system, for example, produced small armies led by noble knights. But sometimes warfare can shape society. The long bow is an example of this.

- Firstly, the long bow reduced the need for feudal mounted knights. This boosted the power of the king. Kings no longer relied upon their nobles for military strength. They could employ their own armies, using taxes; this made kings much more powerful.
- Secondly, the longbow boosted the wealth of the English yeomanry. Yeomen were farmers who owned small farms. They provided many of the archers for English armies. After battles like Crécy, Poitiers, or Agincourt, many yeomen came home with 100,000 **ducats** from pay, booty and ransom. Yeomen became very wealthy farmers and a much more important feature of medieval society.

Activities

3 Compared to the period 1066–1350:
   a) what stayed the same in warfare 1350–1450
   b) what changed?

4 What were the key features of recruitment 1350–1450?

5 What impact did the longbow have on warfare 1350–1450?

exam zone
Build better answers

Choose **one** period of time and describe the key features of warfare in that period. (6 marks)

- 1066–1350
- 1350–1450

■ **Basic, Level 1**
Answer makes limited, general comments, with little supporting detail.

● **Good, Level 2**
Answer makes precise statements about key features with accurate and relevant supporting detail.

Summary

- 1350–1450 was a period of gradual change in medieval warfare.
- Two key changes were the increased use of mercenaries and longbows.

Boom!

The period 1350 to 1450 was one of gradual development. This changed after 1450. **Gunpowder** was the reason.

Very slowly, since about 1350, cannon had developed. By 1450, they were decisive. In 1453, the Battle of Castillon ended the 100 Years' War; it was won by cannon.

Warfare would never be the same again.

2.2 The Agincourt campaign 1415

Learning outcomes

By the end of this topic you should be able to:

- describe the Agincourt campaign and the role of Henry V
- recognise features of warfare that were typical from 1350 to 1450.

The Agincourt campaign of 1415 was part of the Hundred Years' War. These were several wars between England and France stretching from 1337 to 1453. When Henry V became King of England in 1413, he thought he could conquer land in northern France for England.

The siege of Harfleur

Henry invaded France in August 1415, with an army of about 6,000–8,000. He needed a base, so he besieged the port of Harfleur in Normandy. The town was defended by fortified stone walls and about 400 soldiers. After five weeks, the town surrendered. Any townspeople who swore allegiance to Henry were allowed to remain; the rest were ordered to depart.

How typical was the siege of Harfleur?

In some ways, this was a typical medieval siege – it followed the typical pattern of encirclement, battery, attack, negotiation and ransom.

- First, Henry surrounded the town, cutting off supplies. A French convoy carrying food and ammunition for the town was captured.
- Then Henry pounded the walls with catapults and prepared his men to attack.
- Seeing their position was hopeless, the town's commanders asked for a deal. They gave up the town in exchange for ransom.

But, in another way, the siege was not typical. As well as medieval catapults, Henry also pounded the walls with twelve cannon. This was one of the earliest uses of cannon by the English army.

Henry's strategy was to avoid a full-scale battle. So, after the siege, he left a small garrison in the town and took the rest of his army to winter in the town of Calais, at that time an English stronghold.

He could have safely sailed to Calais, but Henry thought this cowardly. Instead, he chose to march; this was an error. The French had gathered a much larger army, led by Charles d'Albret, who shadowed Henry's movements in order to try and force him into a battle.

Source A: Henry's reputed speech, 1415.

"Let them assemble their great armies, there is hope in God they will hurt neither my army nor me. I will not suffer them, puffed up with pride... They would say through fear I had fled away, acknowledging the injustice of my cause."

The French eventually trapped the English in a narrow stretch of ploughed land between two woods. The French army was between Henry and Calais. Henry had been outmanoeuvred.

- Henry V's army had only 6,000 men and 5,000 were archers.
- The French had 20–30,000 men, many of whom were powerful mounted knights.

On 25 October, Henry was forced to fight but would have preferred not to. His small army had just marched 250 miles in bad weather, whilst suffering from dysentery. Defeat would also mean the end of the campaign, with the risk of Henry being captured or even killed.

The Battle of Agincourt

The French intended to soften up the English defences with cavalry attacks and then send in the infantry to finish them off.

Henry's tactics were defensive. He placed his army where the gap in the woods was most narrow, about 750 metres. This was important;

it meant he could not be outflanked or swamped by overwhelming numbers. He also had angled stakes dug into the ground to slow the French cavalry.

He then sent archers to hide in the trees and fire into the French lines. This was called **'galling'**; the French regarded it as unchivalrous.

It provoked an angry response. A small group of 450 French cavalry made a charge at the English lines. The infantry moved up behind them.

The longbows now showed their value:
- when the cavalry was about 200 metres away, English archers fired in volleys;
- wounded French horses fell or panicked, careering into others;
- the charge failed and cavalry retreating in the narrow space slowed down the infantry;
- arrows rained down on the French infantry, slogging through mud, some in heavy armour;
- the bodies of fallen men slowed their advance still more.

When hand-to-hand fighting began, the narrow battlefront made the extra French troops useless.

Source B: A 19th-century painting of Agincourt. Look at the soldiers, their weapons and clothes. Also look at the battlefield. How accurate do you think it is?

The French monk of St. Denis wrote: *'The first wave of about 5,000 men was so tightly packed that the third rank could not use their swords.'*

Henry then attacked. His archers put aside their bows and attacked from the flanks with swords. His foot soldiers pressed forward too. The French, crowded together and stumbling on bodies, retreated.

Heralds were sent to ask the French if they were conceding. The answer came back that they were. The battle had lasted only about 3 hours.

What was the outcome of the battle?
The English suffered no more than 500 deaths.

The French deaths numbered between 2,000 and 11,000, according to sources at the time, and 1500 nobles were captured for ransom.

The decisive factors seem to have been:
- the leadership of Henry V
- the indiscipline of French knights
- the impact of English archers
- the heavy ground.

The Battle of Agincourt was important because it saved the English army and earned them ransoms. It also showed the strength of the English longbow.

But successful sieges, at Harfleur and other towns, were important too. These gave Henry V military and political control of the surrounding countryside.

Activities
1. Use the text and Source B to make a list of the types of soldiers and weapons used at Agincourt.
2. Pages 32-37 describe warfare 1350-1450. In what ways were the siege of Harfleur and Battle of Agincourt typical of warfare at that time?
3. The bullet points in the column above list four factors in the English victory at Agincourt. Explain the importance of each one.

Summary
The Agincourt campaign illustrates a number of typical features of warfare from 1350 to 1450.

2.3 The age of gunpowder 1450–1700

Learning outcomes

By the end of this topic you should be able to:

- describe the gunpowder weapons that dominated warfare 1450–1700
- explain the impact that gunpowder weapons had on warfare.

Cannon

The formula for gunpowder arrived in Europe from China during the 13th century. Soon after, it was being used in warfare. The first known use of a gunpowder cannon in Europe is recorded in Metz (now in northern France) in 1324.

The Bad News…

Early cannon were not very effective:

- the first cannon were wooden and shot stone balls; it took time to develop metal cannon
- they had a range of only 100 metres and were so inaccurate they could only be used against large targets, like town walls
- they often went wrong – in 1460, King James II of Scotland was killed by a cannon, which blew up when firing.

Improving cannon was a slow business. For a hundred years, rather than replacing traditional medieval **artillery**, cannon were used alongside it.

Source A: A contemporary drawing of the siege of Dublin in 1577. Attackers and defenders are using gunpowder weapons alongside traditional weapons like lances and pikes.

The Good News…

Weapon manufacturers used improved technology to make cannon more effective. By about 1450:

- **trunnions** made it easier to change cannons' range of fire
- **quadrants** were used to improve aim
- then specialist cannon were developed – like **mortars** or **howitzers**, which lobbed cannonballs on a high trajectory over walls
- there were massive long-distance cannon, like 'Mad Margaret', which had a barrel five metres long and half a metre wide
- from about 1500, field guns were developed. These were smaller cannon, called light artillery, which were pulled around battlefields by horses. This meant cannon were not just used against stationary targets, like walls. They were now used against enemy infantry.

Expense was another thing which slowed down the use of gunpowder weapons. The impact on transportation was huge – to transport just 50 cannon took hundreds of wagons and oxen. But cannon were essential. In 1415, it had taken Henry V five weeks to take Harfleur; in another siege in 1449, 16 cannon reduced its walls to rubble in two weeks. By 1450, cannon were a normal part of all armies.

FASCINATING FACT

One huge cannon, used in 1453, was nearly 10 metres long and fired stone balls weighing half a ton. To transport it by road, 50 carpenters were used to strengthen bridges; it was then put on 30 wagons and pulled by 60 oxen.

Firearms – the matchlock

In about 1450, the first effective firearms also appeared. These were the matchlock musket and the smaller matchlock **arquebus**.

The Good News…

Matchlock muskets could:

- kill at 400 metres
- pierce armour at 200 metres
- and, unlike archers, musketeers did not tire during battle.

The Bad News…

Matchlock muskets:

- were very inaccurate
- frequently misfired – they were useless in rain
- were heavy – over 10 kilos – as heavy as 10 bags of sugar. The gunner had to balance it on a stick
- caused smoke, which made aiming difficult
- took two minutes to reload. Reloading under fire took courage – it was easy to lower the musket and lose the shot out of the barrel before firing, or to overcharge the weapon and knock yourself out with the recoil.

Source B: A musketeer pictured in the Drill Book for the Dutch army, issued in 1607.

FASCINATING FACT

The matchlock had a slow-burning match-cord, held in a lever, or cock. When the trigger was pulled, the cord set off gunpowder in a flash pan which then fired the gun.

Some modern phrases come from musketeers. A misfire was ' just a flash in the pan', whilst firing before you were ready was 'going off at half cock'.

Firearms – the flintlock

For 200 years, these problems with matchlocks meant that they were used alongside other weapons, like bows. Then technology came to the rescue. By 1610, a new firing mechanism had been found. Flintlock muskets were invented. These used flints to make a spark, which set off the gunpowder. They were widespread in armies by 1650.

More Good News…

Flintlock muskets:

- could be pre-loaded, so a soldier could carry several loaded muskets into battle and fire them rapidly, without having to re-load
- could be used by cavalry. Horsemen could not re-load matchlocks, but **dragoons** (mounted soldiers) could tuck several loaded flintlocks in their belts and ride, firing, into battle.

So, despite their limitations, from about 1450 onwards cannon and firearms were used more and more. By about 1600, they dominated battlefields. Warfare would never be the same again.

As Robert Barret reported in 1598, *'Then was then, and now is now. Wars are much altered since the fiery weapons.'*

Activities

1. On a timeline, plot the development of gunpowder weapons from 1200 to 1600.
2. What were the limitations of early gunpowder weapons?
3. What were their advantages?

The military impact of gunpowder weapons

Musketeers

Musketeers became a major new group of combatants in the infantry.

- They completely replaced archers by 1650.
- They gradually replaced pike men. They attached long knives, or **bayonets**, to the end of their muskets. This turned muskets into thrusting weapons, so pike men were not needed.

Cannoneers

Cannoneers also became a major new group of combatants. They worked in teams to transport, maintain and fire the cannon.

Cannon were so feared by the enemy that it was known for captured cannoneers to be tied up and blasted out of their own cannon!

Cavalry

Gunpowder weapons finally brought an end to mounted knights.

- Muskets and field cannon easily cut them down.
- After 1450, mounted knights were replaced by cavalry with specialist roles.
- The New Model Army (1645) had lightly armoured, fast-moving dragoons armed with flintlock muskets and pistols.

Transport and logistics

Cannon were very difficult to transport.

- In 1550, an army advisor calculated that, during a campaign, just to move one siege cannon required 60 horses. Moving the powder and shot it used in one week required another 160 horses!
- In 1660, moving a train of just ten siege guns and ten mortar cannon needed 750 carts and almost 2,000 oxen.

All these horses and oxen needed feeding. Just 200 draught animals needed a ton of fodder every day, which had to be transported too!

Armies had always had wagons, horses and wagon drivers for their baggage trains. But gunpowder weapons meant that transport and the logistics of armies – organising its resources – became even more important than before.

Military impact of gunpowder weapons

Infantry lines

Throughout medieval times, infantry had attacked and defended by forming solid blocks of men, or 'squares'. But, from about 1600, generals realised that lines of muskets were better:

- they used up to 10 ranks of men
  - each line would fire, then retreat and re-load, whilst the next rank came forward to fire
    - this way they achieved a constant **volley of fire**.

Training

Gunpowder weapons demanded regular training.

- Musketeers needed to load under pressure and quickly fire, retreat and re-load.
- Cannoneers needed to be able to practise in order to improve their aim and speed up their rate of fire.

Armies therefore had to spend more time training their troops.

Standardised weapons

Before this, soldiers could replace their weapons by stealing from bodies on the battlefield. Mixing swords or spears caused no problems.

With gunpowder weapons, the whole army needed standard issue. Ammunition which did not fit the barrels of guns was ineffective and dangerous.

The impact on siege warfare

Gunpowder weapons also had an effect on the way castles and towns were defended and attacked.

New town defences

At first, castles and towns used cannon along their walls as a form of defence, but medieval walls were tall and thin. They were easy for attackers' cannon to hit. Worse, the vibration of the defensive cannon made the walls crack and fall.

So, castle and town walls had to be re-designed. At first, defenders just strengthened their walls by piling earth banks against the inside. In the longer-term, the walls were re-designed.

The new design for fortifications involved short, thick walls with arrow-shaped **bastions** (towers). These were harder to hit and allowed defending cannon to fire out at many angles. After about 1500, they became the norm for town and castle fortifications. So attackers needed new tactics.

Attacking fortified towns

Attacking cannon could no longer easily knock down these new town and castle walls. So the first change was that sieges became longer.

Secondly, attackers had to defend themselves against the defenders' cannon. Therefore, attackers dug trenches around the towns and castles they besieged.

Attacking troops sheltered in these trenches. They also set up cannon in there and bombarded the enemy for months on end. After weakening the town defences, they sent in infantry attacks.

Source C: Arrow-shaped bastions on a 16th century fort.

Activities

4   Make a list of the military changes caused by the rise of gunpowder weapons. Say which one you think is the most significant and explain your choice.

 **Build better answers**

Why did it take so long for gunpowder weapons to change how warfare was fought? (12 marks)

You may use the following in your answer.
*   Inaccuracy of early cannon
*   Shortcomings of the matchlock
You must also include information of your own.

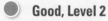

■   **Basic, Level 1**
Answer gives a simple description of gunpowder weapons with a little detail.

●   **Good, Level 2**
Answer gives a more developed description of gunpowder weapons with more detail and some support from relevant material and/or own knowledge.

▲   **Excellent, Level 3**
Answer shows understanding of the focus of the question, makes relevant points and gives good supporting detail from the stimulus, but explores other aspects from own knowledge as well. For example: explaining that early cannon were inaccurate, difficult to transport, often exploded and expensive.

Summary

Using gunpowder created new weapons. These weapons were so powerful that they changed:
• battlefield and siege warfare
• the composition and training of armies, creating, for example, musketeers and cannoneers.

2.4 Army life 1350–1700

Learning outcome

By the end of this topic you should be able to:

● describe the key features of the gunpowder armies which emerged after 1350

● describe the key features of daily life in them.

Larger, professional armies

Life in the army for the typical soldier changed in many ways between 1350 and 1700. One change was that troops served in bigger and bigger armies.

- In 1415, for his Agincourt campaign, Henry V had at most 8,000 men.
- In 1645, the New Model Army (see page 45) had 22,000 men.
- Another change was that the typical soldier of 1700 was much more likely to be paid.
- In 1350, many soldiers in the king's army were doing their feudal duty. They would often serve for only a few weeks before returning home.
- By 1450, some were feudal troops, but many more were mercenaries, who contracted to serve, for pay, for a fixed term, maybe a year.

The decline of the feudal system

The Norman kings relied upon their most loyal barons for troops to defend and keep control of their kingdoms. For about 300 years, the country depended upon feudal armies.

But feudal armies had weaknesses (see page 34). Once expensive gunpowder weapons became an essential part of armies, feudal volunteers were even more unsuitable.

So, after about 1350, kings increasingly used scutage, taxes and loans to raise money to employ and equip mercenary troops instead.

Once they had their own income and their own armies, kings were no longer so dependent upon powerful barons for support. The government of England became more centralised and the feudal system gradually came to an end.

- By 1700, most troops were permanently employed in a better trained, standing army – rather like the New Model Army in the 1640s. The old feudal armies were no more.

Uniforms

Feudal armies and mercenaries usually supplied their own protective clothing and weapons. This remained the case in the first permanent armies. Soldiers sometimes wore ribbons or sashes to indicate which side they were fighting for. But this was not foolproof.

At the Battle of Marston Moor, in 1644, Sir Thomas Fairfax became stranded amongst the enemy and, in his own words, 'Removing the signal [a white scarf] from my hat, I passed off as one of their commanders.'

However, the New Model Army adopted coats of red and white and, by 1700, most permanent armies had standard uniforms such as the now infamous English 'redcoat'.

Source A: A modern representation of musketeers in typical mixed 1640s uniforms with coloured ribbons.

The New Model Army

The New Model Army was created by the English Parliament in 1645 to fight against King Charles I in the English Civil War. Its commander was General Fairfax; its cavalry was led by Oliver Cromwell.

Size

The New Model Army had 22,000 troops.

- 14,000 were infantry – two-thirds musketeers and one-third pike men.
- 7,000 were cavalry, of whom 1,000 were dragoons, mounted musketeers.

It had 50 cannon, mainly light field artillery.

Recruits

- were paid a standard 8 pence per day rather than doing their feudal duty
- were a full-time standing army, not part-time **militia** raised in a crisis
- were a permanent army, not mercenaries on short-term contracts.

Training and discipline

Recruits were put through proper military training. There was a Drill Book with set activities, so the troops learned to march and manoeuvre better, and musketeers and cannoneers learned to fire quicker.

By the time they went into battle, they were trained and disciplined.

- Drinking or gambling in camp and pillage or rape on campaign were banned.
- Desertion was punished by death.

Logistics

The administration of the New Model Army was centralised, in London.

- The management of food, clothing and equipment was better than before.
- For one campaign, in Scotland, quartermasters organised standardised seven-day rations.
- Infantry were issued with standardised red uniforms, the first of the British 'redcoats'.

Care of troops

Food

Food supplies for troops improved little between 1350 and 1700. Large armies were very expensive to feed. An army of 30,000 men needed 20 tons of bread and the meat equivalent of 1,500 sheep every day!

There were also severe logistical problems. Armies did carry food, but you needed 250 carts just to carry the flour needed to bake bread for 30,000 troops. So, like medieval armies, troops still had to rely on foraging or stealing food on the march.

Living conditions

Most armies continued to sleep in the open. Even the New Model Army was not issued with tents until 1650. Water supplies were often contaminated; diseases like dysentery were rife in camps. Up to 1700, more men died of disease on campaign than from battlefield injuries.

Medical care

Medical treatment hardly improved either. Troops could pay camp hangers-on for medical care, but it rarely worked. No-one understood the causes of infection at this time, so operations on wounds were often more likely to kill than the original wound.

So, the general care of troops improved little:

- partly due to the expense
- partly because of logistical problems
- partly because of a lack of knowledge.

Activities

1. In what ways was the New Model Army typical of changes taking place in armies between 1350 and 1700? Was it in any way not typical?
2. Life in the army was harsh. Why were governments so slow to improve the conditions of troops during the years 1350–1700?

Summary

- Gunpowder weapons made armies larger and more professional by 1700.
- These armies were hard to clothe, feed and care for.

2.5 The Battle of Naseby 1645

> **Learning outcomes**
>
> By the end of this topic you should be able to:
> - use events of the Battle of Naseby to show typical features of 17th-century warfare
> - use events to the Battle of Naseby to show the importance of military leadership.

The English Civil War (1642–1646) was fought between the Royalist army of King Charles I and forces supporting Parliament, led by Sir Thomas Fairfax and Oliver Cromwell.

In April 1645, campaigning resumed after a winter break. Fighting typically only took place during the spring and summer months at this time.

King Charles was more interested in picking off enemy towns than a pitched battle. He sent 5,000 of his troops to besiege Taunton, a key town in the south-west of England.

Fairfax wanted to engage the King in battle instead. For weeks, he pursued the Royalist army. There were occasional skirmishes.

Eventually, the King decided to fight. He did not wait for his troops to return from Taunton.

On 14 June:
- Fairfax positioned his army on top of a steep slope leading to Mill Hill. Its flanks were protected by thick hedging on one side and rough ground on the other.
- The King's general, Prince Rupert, set out his army opposite.

The battle begins

- First, Fairfax ordered his cannon to fire shots to soften up the Royalist infantry.
- But their initial **salvos** went high.
- After this, the infantry of the two sides were too close for cannon to be used.

So cannon were not a decisive factor.

Next, the King ordered his infantry to leave its high ground and march up the slope to attack the main Parliamentary army.

The distance between the armies was small; there was time for only one volley of musket fire before hand-to-hand fighting began.

So muskets were not decisive either.

The first key action was taken by Cromwell, in charge of the cavalry. He sent Colonel Okey and his dragoons behind the western hedging, to harass the Royalist troops with musket fire.

Stung into action, Rupert's lightly armoured cavalry charged the Parliamentary army, using pistols. They broke Fairfax's lines; two of the Parliamentary cavalry **regiments** fled.

Source A: A map of the Battle of Naseby.

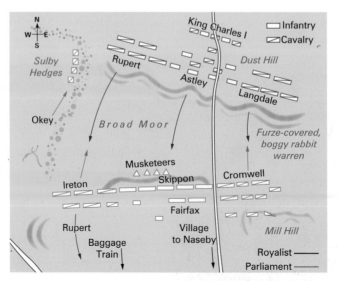

Parliamentary Army
Commanded by:
- Sir Thomas Fairfax
- Oliver Cromwell

13,000 men, including:
- about 7,000 infantry, armed with muskets and swords and protected by pike and artillery
- about 6,000 cavalry, armed with swords and muskets

The King's Army
Commanded by:
- King Charles I
- Prince Rupert

8,000 men, including:
- about 4,000 infantry, armed with muskets and swords and protected by pike and artillery
- about 4,000 cavalry, armed with swords and muskets

Then Rupert made a mistake. He failed to control his cavalry, who chased the fleeing Parliamentary troops and attacked their baggage train. Vital Royalist cavalry thus missed the next stages of fighting.

Cromwell made no such mistake.

Cromwell wins the cavalry contest

The infantry were now engaged in hand-to-hand combat using swords and musket buts. Neither side was winning, so the next stage was decisive.

The remaining Royalist cavalry tried to break the deadlock.

As they charged up the slope to attack Cromwell's cavalry, they lost momentum. By this time, they were outnumbered two to one, due to the earlier cavalry attack on the baggage train. They also attacked in a narrow channel, with boggy land on their left. This reduced the impact of the attack.

Cromwell's cavalry took heavy casualties, but kept their formation and held firm. The Royalist charge faltered, stalled and fell back.

Unlike Rupert, Cromwell had good control of his cavalry and sound tactics.

- He sent part of his cavalry to pursue the retreating Royalist horsemen.
- He wheeled the rest of his force to his left and attacked the Royalist infantry from the flank.

Source B: A 19th-century picture of the Battle of Naseby. It shows Royalist (left) and Parliamentary cavalry. Note the differences from earlier, heavily armoured, medieval knights.

The Royalist infantry were trapped between Okey's dragoons to the west and Cromwell. Assaulted from all sides, their advance stalled and they fled.

The bloody retreat

The Royalists were now in chaotic retreat. The Parliamentary army chased them for about 12 miles and slaughtered all the men they caught. One group of Royalist horsemen rode down a cul-de-sac: they were trapped and killed to a man.

100 Welsh women in the Royalist baggage train were mistaken for Irish **Catholics** and the staunchly **Protestant** Parliamentary army killed them all.

About 1,000 Royalists were killed and 5,000 captured. The battle raised the profile of Oliver Cromwell and ended the King's chances of winning the war.

Activities

1 Make a table with these headings:

Typical features of C17th warfare	Naseby was typical because...	Naseby was not typical because...

Here are some typical features:

Limited warfare; Improved discipline; Weakening enemy with cannon; Decisive cannon fire; Dragoons harassing enemy; Cavalry charges; Decisive musket fire; Hand-to-hand infantry combat; Weakness in retreat; Decisive leadership.

Now read the story of the battle. Every time one of these features appears, write beside the feature an explanation of why Naseby is – or is not – typical of 17th-century warfare.

2 How far do you think Naseby was typical of 17th-century warfare?

3 How far do you think leadership decisions made by King Charles, Prince Rupert and Cromwell determined the outcome of the battle?

Summary

- The Battle of Naseby shows several typical features of warfare at that time.
- It shows the importance of military leadership.

2.6 Summary: Warfare c1350–c1700

Simple change

To help us get an overview of a long period of time, such as 1350–1700, it is sometimes useful to think about change as a simple process.

For example, if we were to think about:
• a period of no change or
• a period of rapid change
we could put them on simple graphs such as these:

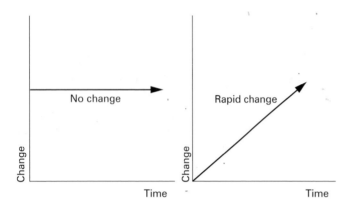

This kind of simple picture of change can help us see 'the big picture' – the overall view.

For the period 1350–1700, an overall view of change in warfare could be seen as the following:
• a period from 1350 to about 1450, when there was slow change – there were changes, but they took place gradually and had limited impact
• a period from about 1450 to 1700 when bigger changes occurred, more rapidly and with more significant effects; the biggest cause of all this change was the use of gunpowder weapons.

The year 1450 could be called a watershed because it was a time between two very different periods of change.

Complex change

But change is more complex than simple graphs can show. They give a useful overall impression, but they hide the complexity of change.

During the period 1350-1700, several key features remained much the same. For example:
• infantry remained the biggest part of armies
• hand-to-hand weapons – swords, daggers, clubs etc. – remained much the same
• the feigned retreat remained a useful tactic
• sieges remained a common form of war
• provisioning the army remained a hard task
• medical care for the wounded remained poor.

These are examples of *continuity*.

However, there were some gradual changes. For example:
• feudalism declined as a way of raising armies; rulers increasingly used taxes to pay for troops
• mercenaries became a bigger part of armies
• standing armies, though small, emerged
• standardised weapons began to be issued
• uniforms appeared, then slowly became the norm
• training of groups, like cannoneers, increased
• cannon increased army transport difficulties.

This type of change is often called development.

Some changes had a much bigger impact. They made things completely different afterwards. For example:
• muskets transformed the battlefield

This type of change is a *turning point*.

Activities

1 Using the graphs on this page as examples, draw your own graph showing an overall picture of change for the period 1350–1700.

Activities

2 Would you consider the following features of warfare 1350-1700 to be examples of continuity, development or a turning point?

  a) the decline of the mounted knight

  b) the use of cannon after 1450

  c) disease in army camps.

Key features of battles

Because history is a combination of continuity and change, over the history of warfare, battles show some features that are the same and some that are different.

For any battle, we can look at key features such as:
- the size of the armies
- the composition of the armies – infantry, archers, cavalry, etc.
- the weapons used
- the tactics used
- the influence of the site of the battle
- the influence of training and discipline
- the influence of leadership decisions.

Activities

3 Look at the events of
- the Battle of Agincourt
- the Battle of Naseby.

Using the features of these battles as a guide:

a) list the similarities you can find

b) list any key differences.

examzone   Build better answers

What do Sources A and B show about changes in warfare 1350-1700?

Explain your answer, using Sources A and B and your own knowledge. (8 marks)

■ Basic, Level 1
Answer gives simple statements but does not address 'change'; just describes things from the source or from own knowledge.

OR

Answer makes very simple statements about change with little supporting detail from the sources or from own knowledge.

● Good, Level 2
Answer describes change and supports this with references to specific details in each of the sources and/or from own knowledge.

▲ Excellent, Level 3
Answer makes valid **inferences** about the nature or extent of change in warfare, which can be worked out from specific details in the source and uses own knowledge to put these changes in their historical context.

Source A: An illustration in a prayer book called *Luttrell's Psalter*, made in about 1340. It shows young men doing archery practice.

Source B: An engraving made in about 1650. It shows men casting cannon and cannon balls in a forge. There is a battle scene in the background, shown in the top right-hand corner of the engraving.

3.1 Warfare in the 18th century

Learning outcomes

By the end of this topic you should be able to:

- describe the key features of 18th century warfare
- explain how these key features affected the organisation of armies and the experience of combatants.

Warfare in the 18th century was a mixture of continuity and gradual change. Look out for these features as you read these pages.

18th-century armies

One change was standing armies. We have already seen how permanent standing armies developed in the 17th century. During the 18th century, a standing army with paid troops became the norm for countries like Britain.

Another change was the size of standing armies. Even in peacetime, England had an army of about 50,000 troops. In wartime, extra troops were recruited, often foreign mercenaries.

- In 1709, in the War of Spanish Succession, the British Army rose to 150,000 troops.
- 80,000 of these were mercenaries.

There was also continuity. For example, the composition of standing armies barely changed.

- Infantry continued to make up about 75 per cent of troops.
- Infantry were mainly foot soldiers, with muskets and bayonets, but also included artillery units.
- Cavalry, now lightly armoured and restricted to specialist roles, made up the remainder.

Weapons in the 18th century

Weapons changed only very slowly during the 18th century. For example, an improved flintlock musket, called by troops the 'Brown Bess', came into service in 1715. It stayed in service for 130 years and 7.8 million were manufactured.

However, we should note two changes to do with 18th-century weapons.

Improved use of muskets

The Brown Bess changed little during the 18th century, but it was better used.

Socket bayonets were introduced. Before the 18th century, 'plug' bayonets were fitted down the barrel of a musket – preventing the musket from firing.

By the end of the 1690s, socket bayonets were being used. These fitted around the barrel of a musket and made it possible to fire with the bayonet fitted.

Firing drills improved. The effective range of the Brown Bess was quite short, only about 100 metres. Loading was so slow that opposition infantry could cross the killing ground during only two **volleys** of fire.

During the 18th century, musketeers became better drilled and therefore more deadly. In the Battle of Dettingen in 1743, British musket fire defeated the French army in 30 minutes.

Improved use of light artillery

By 1700, cannon were devastating against fortified walls. They had an effective range of 500 metres. But they were very heavy.

A modest 12-pounder gun weighed well over a ton. Combined with its carriage, this could rise to four tons – as much as a fully grown elephant! This made them hard to move around a battlefield and use against infantry.

After 1700, there were two main changes:

- Lighter, bronze cannon were made.
- Gun carriages were also made lighter.

This meant that light field guns, mounted on carriages and pulled by horses, became a key part of 18th-century armies. They fired:

- 'grape shot' (clusters of small metal balls)
- 'canisters' (tin or wooden canisters filled with metal fragments).

In 1709, British light field guns blew ranks of French troops off their feet using exploding canisters, at the Battle of Malplaquet.

Strategy

Limited warfare remained the norm. It continued to dominate the overall strategy of 18th century warfare.

This was the last century when armies were often led by rulers not generals. These rulers feared decisive defeats, with heavy loss of expensive troops. So they fought wars for limited gains, happy with an agreed peace rather than total defeat for one side.

As a result, skirmishes and sieges remained more common than full-scale pitched battles.

This strategy of limited warfare reduced the impact on civilians. Even in besieged towns, once a siege was fully laid, a surrender was normally negotiated with few casualties, as in medieval times.

Source A: From *Cassell's World History of Warfare*.

> British soldiers who fought in the War of the Spanish Succession (1701–1713) used weapons similar to those used 100 years later in the armies at the Battle of Waterloo in 1815.

Source B: 19th-century painting of late-18th century light artillery. Cannon and musket smoke made battlefields in 1750 look very different from battlefields in 1350.

Activities

1 List the key features of 18th century armies, weapons and strategies. Give one piece of supporting detail to illustrate each feature.

2 Make two lists to show 'Continuity' and 'Change' in 18th century warfare.

Logistics

Problems of logistics – the management of army resources – also limited change in 18th century warfare. There were three problems.

Firstly, large armies had to be supplied with large quantities of weapons, ammunition, uniforms, equipment and food. When on campaign, all this had to be carried with the army in slow-moving baggage trains (the wagons, stores and people that followed armies around).

Secondly, campaigns were only possible from April to October. Outside these times:
- supply wagons and cannon carriages became stuck in mud
- it was impossible to graze the cavalry horses and draught horses
- deaths from diseases rose.

Third, manoeuvring armies in a coordinated way was difficult.

- Roads and maps were poor. It seems odd, but some armies wanting to fight just couldn't find each other.
- Clocks were rare and there were no agreed European time zones. Generals timed attacks with phrases like 'the crack of dawn'.
- Communication between an army and its HQ was very slow. It took at least six weeks to send orders to British troops in America. News of the victory at Waterloo reached London by private homing pigeon before the War Office found out!

Recruitment

Recruitment to the larger professional standing armies of the 18th century took a variety of forms.

Officers

Officers were recruited from noble families. They bought **commissions** for their younger sons.

- The higher the rank, the higher the price, so only the wealthiest families could afford the most senior ranks.
- Seniority within a rank depended on the date of the commission, so families often bought the commission when the boys were very young.

Lower ranks

Bigger armies in the 18th century meant that recruitment of enough men was hard. Employing foreign mercenaries was one solution, but armies were keen to recruit from home.

Recruits could sign up for a term of 8–12 years. If they signed up for life, they were paid a bounty – an attractive lump sum of up to £20. They volunteered for the ranks for a variety of reasons.

- Some wanted to swap their hard lives for the **camaraderie** and adventure of the army.
- Some wanted a career, advancement to non-commissioned officer rank as sergeants.
- Some wanted the regular pay – or the cash bounty sometimes paid on signing up.
- Some were offered early release from prison if they joined the army.
- Some were signed up by local recruiting officers– see Source D.

But the life of a foot soldier was hard. Many men soon found that they regretted their decision to sign up.

Source C: *From War in European History,* by Michael Howard.

> …it became more difficult to recruit into the ranks of the armies anyone except social drop-outs, criminals, dupes and half-wits who could only be kept under control by ferocious discipline.

Local militia

Keeping large armies fully recruited became an ongoing challenge.

During the Seven Years War, in which Britain fought from 1756 to 1763, the warring armies typically lost 20 per cent of their troops each year from disease, **desertion** and death in combat.

Sometimes the army fell back upon using local militia. These were part-time soldiers who signed for local military groups which were originally intended to help out in times of crisis in their local area.

In the Seven Years' War, there were fears that Britain might be invaded by France. So, in 1757, a Militia Act was passed in Britain to improve the size and quality of the militia. Parishes in England and Wales had to produce lists of men aged 18-50 from which men were chosen by ballot to train as militia.

At first, this caused resentment – and even riots in places, because of fears that militia men might be forced into the regular army. But, despite this, the quality of militia did improve and, during the Wars against France in 1798, its size grew to 118,000.

Source D: A British painting from about 1800 showing soldiers drinking with locals. Some young men were signed up by recruiting sergeants who plied them with alcohol.

Organisation of 18th-century armies

Because of the growing size of these standing armies, a level of organisation was required far beyond that needed by any earlier British armies.

The War Office

In 1722, a new War Office was created to run the British Army from grand new buildings on Horse Guards Parade in London. From here, it ran army administration, finance and supplies.

To make it easier to administer, smaller units were formed called regiments. These had their own administrative bases, staff and emblems. For example, the Grenadier Guards trace their history back to this time.

The War Office organised standardised weapons, and set standards for equipment and uniforms.

Standardised uniforms

Purchasing standardised uniforms for 50,000 troops was beyond the powers of 18th century government. Officers bought their own uniforms. Regimental colonels usually organised the purchase of uniforms for the other ranks, including:

- brightly coloured frock coats
- waistcoats and shirts
- knee breeches and **gaiters**
- stockings and buckled shoes
- cross belts and cartridge pouches
- scabbards for bayonets
- knapsacks for equipment, spare clothes, tent pegs and food preparation kit.

It was part of the daily routine of soldiers to look after their kit – for example, using white pipe clay to whiten belts and gaiters.

Despite this, uniforms were constantly grubby. They had to be routinely replaced every three to six years.

Training 18th-century armies

Having permanent armies meant that more time could be spent, during peacetime, in barracks, training for battle.

Source E: Drill for 18th-century soldiers. Note the bayonets and standardised uniforms, which were typical by the 18th century.

Training for the rank and file

Soldiers constantly practised marching, manoeuvring, reloading and firing. The whole army used the same, rigid drills. They learned to march onto a battlefield in columns at 75 steps per minute and then, without pausing, wheel into firing lines.

Firing in ranks from the firing lines was vital to the success of the infantry. So they practised this over and over again. On a constant basis, the front ranks fired a volley and then retreated to the back of the line, to be replaced by the ranks behind. This gave them repeated volleys every 15 seconds.

Better trained armies meant that generals could use more complex tactics on the battlefield. For example, at the Battle of Waterloo in 1815, the Duke of Wellington manoeuvred into an excellent defensive position and organised his troops into defensive squares as well as traditional defensive lines.

Training for officers

Training also improved, a little, for officers. For example, the Woolwich Engineering and Military Academy opened in 1741.

However, the impact of training schools for officers was limited, since not all officers attended. Most went straight into their regiments as cadets and learned their skills as apprentice-officers.

Looking after 18th-century armies

Creating a large standing army in the 18th century created the huge problem of how to look after it.

Accommodation

When armies were small, soldiers were **billeted** in houses and inns during peacetime. This was not practical for bigger armies, so barracks were built. Ravensdowne Barracks, constructed in 1717, was among the first to be built in England. But the cost meant that barracks were basic:

- Men slept two or more to a bed.
- There were no kitchens, so they cooked in the sleeping quarters.

Provisions on campaign

Provisions, like food, were another challenge, especially when an army was on campaign.

The large armies of the 18th century were too big to live off the land. So, the army had to supply its men with bread, biscuits, meat or fish, and drink.

On the march, soldiers were given four days' rations. Typically, this was 1lb of bread and 1lb of beef per day, sometimes with cheese.

When food ran out, troops could forage for food and pillage local houses, but this was not enough. So, every four days, armies had to stop, set up kitchens, bake bread and re-ration.

At times during the century, beer money or rum rations were added. But alcoholism caused problems amongst troops, so it was not regularly issued.

Feeding livestock

Armies on the move also had problems feeding their animals – horses for the cavalry and for pulling wagons, for example.

- An army of 50,000 men needed 40,000 horses.
- Unless fed from the fields, all 40,000 required 20lb hay and 9lb oats every day.

Meeting all these needs meant that, as well as troops, an army needed a second 'army' of bakers, cooks, blacksmiths and barrel-makers! If this baggage train was damaged or captured, the army would be fatally weakened.

Medical care

As in earlier centuries, the 18th century saw only slow progress in the medical care of troops.

However, once there was a standing army, medical officers were appointed to every army regiment. This improved medical practice.

Date	Event
1743	Sir John Pringle was physician general to the British Army in Flanders. He began the practice of agreeing with the enemy that field hospitals should be neutral safe havens for the sick.
1752	Pringle published his *Observations on the Diseases of the Army*. This set out good practice for the medical treatment of soldiers. However, the bloodletting, **emetics** and **purging** recommended were of little use.
1760	Dr John Hunter was with the British Army in Portugal and he could see the problems of bleeding patients as a treatment. His public criticism reduced the extent of this unhelpful practice.
1761	After extensive experience treating soldiers, Hunter introduced new methods to probe gunshot wounds.

All this was of little real help. The basic problem was that, in the wider world, medical science was still at an early stage in its history. No doctors at this time yet understood how infection was caused.

So a healthy soldier was at risk from his normal living conditions, such as:

- sleeping in the open, under improvised tents made from blankets, rifles, branches – anything they could find
- polluted water, which caused cholera and dysentery – known as the 'bloody flux' from blood in the diarrhoea
- and, since there were no proper latrines, the faeces of the sick soldiers all around him.

A wounded soldier was even more at risk.

- Amputation was the normal treatment for limbs with bullet wounds.
- Surgeons did no more than wipe their hands on filthy aprons between operations.
- They therefore killed more soldiers than they saved with their surgery, mostly through spreading infection.

It wasn't that the government didn't care about its soldiers. But the logistics of such a large army were new. No one had experience of organising and looking after so many people.

Discipline

Discipline was very harsh, for several reasons.

- The Duke of Wellington described his men as 'the scum of the earth, enlisted for drink'. Poor quality recruits needed a strong hand.
- Poor living conditions made troops rebellious unless they were strongly controlled.
- Officers maintained strict discipline in battle. They felt troops 'must fear officers more than danger'.

Minor punishments included reduction of rank or patrol duty; worse offences were punished by corporal punishment, such as whipping; the most serious offenders had their contracts lengthened, were sent to serve overseas, or were hanged or shot.

Source F: A British soldier being flogged at Chatham barracks near London.

examzone

Build better answers

How much did the British Army change between 1700 and 1800? Explain your answer. (16 marks)

You may use the following in your answer.
- The use of light artillery
- The creation of the War Office

You must also use information of your own.

■ **Basic, Level 1**
Simple comment with a little knowledge.

● **Good, Level 2**
More developed descriptions of the army, with some support from relevant knowledge.

▲ **Better, Level 3**
A consistent focus on change, with accurate and relevant material to support points made.

▲ **Excellent, Level 4**
A sustained argument, focusing on change throughout, with precisely selected supporting knowledge.

An extra three marks are available for spelling, punctuation and grammar.

Activities

3 Add the key features of these aspects of the 18th century army to your list of features (Q1): administration; recruitment; training; barracks, provisioning, medical care.

Then add one piece of detailed information to support each key feature on your list.

4 Organise these key features onto your lists showing 'Continuity' and 'Change' (Q2).

Summary

- The 18th century saw larger standing armies.
- Weapons and strategy changed very little.
- Organising and caring for the army was an increasing challenge.

3.2 1793-1815 French Wars and the Battle of Waterloo

> **Learning outcomes**
>
> By the end of this topic you should be able to:
> - identify key features of the Battle of Waterloo
> - understand Wellington's part in the battle
> - describe how the wars against France 1793-1815 changed British warfare.

1793–1815 Wars against France

In 1789, in the French Revolution, the people of France overthrew – and later beheaded – their king. The revolutionaries, later led by Napoleon, declared that they would spread 'Liberty, Equality and Fraternity' throughout Europe.

This struck fear in the hearts of monarchies all over Europe. They were determined to restore monarchy to France. This led to a series of wars between France and the rest of Europe. In Britain, they are known as:
- the French Revolutionary Wars 1793-1802
- the Napoleonic Wars 1803-1815.

The melting pot of war

Over 20 years of intermittent fighting forced Britain to search for ways to improve its:
- army, weapons and methods of fighting
- organisation of the army.

> **A watershed**
>
> These wars were part of a watershed – a dividing line – between 18th-century and modern warfare.
>
> France poured all its manpower and wealth into war in a battle for the survival of the Revolution. This forced other nations to do the same.
>
> The limited warfare of the 18th century was moving towards the total warfare of the 20th century.

Effects on warfare in Britain

The wars against France 1793-1815 had a number of effects upon the British Army and the way it was organised.

The size of the British Army

In 1793, the British Army had 40,000 men under arms. At the height of the wars, in 1813, it had 250,000 men under arms:
- about 190,000 infantry
- about 40,000 cavalry
- about 20,000 artillery and engineers.

The relative size of the different parts of the army was no great change, but its scale was a clear change and sign of the future.

Recruitment

Recruiting regular troops was a challenge; but so was officer recruitment: The army needed 10,000 high quality officers by 1813. This led to two changes.

- Promotion from the ranks was encouraged. Over the course of the wars, only 20 per cent of new commissions were purchased.
- Promotion amongst officers was improved. Purchase or promotion to captain required at least two years' service, to major at least six years'.

The cost of war

Another clear change and sign of the future was the cost of warfare. The cost of funding the army during the Napoleonic Wars doubled from £20 million to £40 million, 1803-15.

Britain also lent her allies in Europe a total of £100 million in war loans during that time.

Weapons

There may have been a Revolution in France, but there was no revolution in weaponry.

- As noted on page 50, light field artillery continued to grow in use during this time. In 1793, the Royal Horse Artillery was formed to provide mobile light artillery on the battlefield.
- In 1800, the British Army's first Rifle Brigade was formed as sharpshooters and scouts. Rifles were more accurate than muskets, but rifles were at an early stage of development and had no real impact for another 50 years.
- In 1806, the British Army fired its first ever rockets at French ships near Boulogne. They were metal rockets, powered by gunpowder, and they carried an explosive head which spread shrapnel and fire. Again, they had very limited effects at this stage.

Generally, weapons remained the same as the previous 100 years: so did battlefield tactics.

Typical battlefield tactics

- Skirmishing, feints and positioning your forces was vital, to use any advantages in the terrain.
- Artillery was the main shock force, weakening the enemy for infantry attacks.
- Cavalry were used at times to soften up the enemy, notably by Napoleon, but they were mainly for specialist roles, like raids, protecting infantry flanks and pursuing defeated troops.
- Infantry was the main weapon of attrition.
- Musket fire was saved until the enemy advance was 50-80 metres away. Advancing at walking pace into fire, and the hand-to-hand combat which followed, took immense bravery. But it eventually decided the day.
- Both sides at Waterloo had about 50,000 infantry.

The Battle of Waterloo

In June 1815, the French Emperor, Napoleon, decided upon a pitched battle at Waterloo. He had 105,000 troops divided into three divisions.

Napoleon faced two armies.

- 68,000 mainly English and Dutch troops led by the Duke of Wellington.
- 45,000 Prussian troops led by Field Marshal Blücher.

The first skirmish was on 16th June at Quatre Bras. Wellington stood firm, but Blücher's army was repelled. Napoleon sent Marshal Grouchy's division of 33,000 troops to pursue him.

So, when the two sides settled into their positions on 18th June at Waterloo, it was Wellington's 68,000 troops facing Napoleon's remaining 72,000.

Wellington chose his defensive position well.

- He drew up his troops on the reverse side of a ridge, to reduce the impact of enemy artillery.
- The battle area was narrow, with villages on each side – good for defence.
- He also set up two positions in front of the ridge to break up the French assault, manned by elite units.
  - One was at a chateau held by the Coldstream Guards.
  - The other was a farmhouse held by the King's German Legion.

Source A: A 19th-century engraving. French infantry on the left fire in ranks as the British infantry advance.

Fighting begins

Wellington had prepared his ground well. In contrast, Napoleon had not.

Napoleon was not well. He was suffering with piles, making him snappy and unable to ride his horse to survey the battle. He also made three early errors.

- Firstly, he did not recall Grouchy's 33,000 French troops. They took no part at Waterloo.
- Secondly, he delayed his attack. He judged the battlefield too muddy for cavalry until 11.30am.
- Thirdly, he tried a diversion. He attacked the chateau protecting Wellington's line, hoping to make him use his reserves. But Wellington's outpost stood firm and Napoleon's troops were weakened by serious casualties as a quarter of his troops became caught up in the 'diversion'.

The French artillery attack

At 11.30am, Napoleon began his offensive with artillery – normal tactics to weaken the enemy.

- But soft ground swallowed the cannonballs and canisters, preventing ricochets and shrapnel.
- The British position behind the slope meant many shots just sailed over their heads.

So Napoleon delayed his main assault again. By this time, 30,000 Prussians, sent by Blücher, arrived to help Wellington's defence, whilst Napoleon was still without Grouchy's division.

Source B: A 19th-century painting of Waterloo, showing heavy artillery and cavalry. Napoleon had 246 cannon.

The French infantry attack

So, it was 1.00pm – six hours after dawn – when Napoleon finally launched his infantry attack.

Contrary to normal practice, Napoleon arranged his infantry advance, not in a line, but in a column formation, 200 men across.

An infantry column has less firepower than an infantry line, and is more easily hit by the enemy's artillery, but it has much more impact when it hits the thin enemy lines and can rapidly punch through them.

Wellington responded with an untypical formation of his own. He did not set his men up in a line to face the enemy. Instead he used hollow squares, four ranks deep.

Because it is narrower, a square is not as powerful as an infantry line. But, with corners reinforced by cannon, and the first three rows of infantry firing volleys in rotation, it was hard to break down.

The British defences stood firm. Wellington had two more cards to play.

- He had hidden mobile field artillery behind a heavy hedge on the French right flank. They blasted the French column from the side.
- Then he sent in cavalry and 3,000 British redcoats, firing muskets.

Napoleon's first assault failed; 3,000 French troops were captured.

59

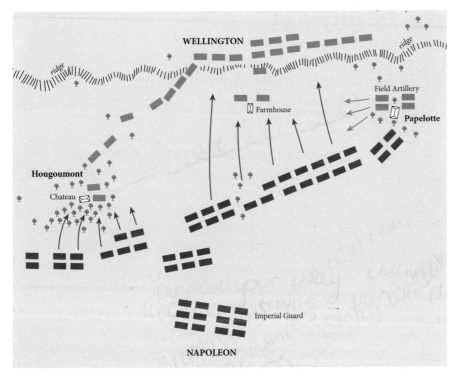

Source C: The battlefield at Waterloo.

The final French errors

Napoleon now made another error. It was 3.00pm. Napoleon's troops were more or less intact. He could have withdrawn, met up with Grouchy's 33,000 troops and fought another day. Instead, he decided to launch another attack on the centre of Wellington's defences.

At about 4.00pm, the French made a breakthrough. Marshal Ney's division captured the farmhouse defences protecting the centre of Wellington's line.

Ney could now bring in his field artillery and use them there to pound the tiring British forces. So Ney called for reserves for an all-out assault. He asked Napoleon to send in the elite Imperial Guard.

Possibly annoyed by Ney's slow progress, possibly unwilling to use his reserves, Napoleon refused.

Wellington, on the other hand, acted decisively. He personally led troops to the heart of his line, where Ney's assault was most fierce. The line held.

Then came the turning point. Grouchy's 30,000 French troops had failed to manoeuvre Blücher's Prussian troops away from the battlefield. As a result, the full Prussian force arrived to reinforce Wellington's tiring troops.

It was only now that Napoleon finally sent in the Imperial Guard. It was too late. Napoleon's tired troops were now out-numbered.

Wellington finally switched from defence to attack. His infantry advanced. The French were overrun.

About 60 per cent of the French troops were killed, wounded or taken prisoner. Their battle was lost.

Wellington at Waterloo

Wellington's key successes were:

- the initial manoeuvring and skirmishing, and the placement of his main troops at Waterloo
- setting up buffer outposts at the chateau and the farmhouse
- his defensive infantry squares
- his use of mobile field artillery
- adopting a patient, defensive strategy – to give time for Blücher's Prussian troops to arrive.

Activities

1 How far were the wars against France a period of change in British warfare? Explain your answer.

2 How typical was the Battle of Waterloo of warfare at this time?

3 Why did Wellington win the Battle of Waterloo? Consider his leadership and other factors.

Summary

- The Battle of Waterloo has features typical of this time.
- Wellington was a key figure in what was a fairly typical battle at Waterloo.

3.3 1815-50: Return to normal

> **Learning outcomes**
>
> By the end of this topic you should be able to:
> - analyse the extent of change in the years 1815-50
> - explain the reasons for lack of change, including the influence of Wellington.

When the wars against France came to an end in 1815, some of the changes which had taken place since 1793 were reversed.

The size of the army went back to something approaching 18th-century levels. It had:
- 230,000 men in 1815
- 98,000 men by 1838.

Spending on the army also fell. The budget was:
- £70 million in 1815
- £17 million by 1820.

Even the growth of artillery, a long-standing trend, began to slow down during these years.

Ignoring improvements

Worse still, the army ignored improvements which it could have been making.

- New technology, like the **telegraph**, became available from the 1830s. But it was ignored by the army. Senior staff said telegraph wires were difficult to lay and move with troops – and easy for the enemy to intercept. Instead, communication was by lights, flags and despatch riders.
- Tactics went out of date; there were no large-scale army manoeuvres between 1815 and 1850 in which to practise new tactics.

As a result of all this, the British Army looked much the same in 1850 as it had done in the 18th century.

The core of the army remained well-drilled infantry in highly coloured uniforms. Artillery – and even cavalry – continued to be their main support.

When Britain needed an army in the Crimea in 1854, it had so many soldiers who were old, untrained or stationed abroad defending the Empire, that it barely scraped together 25,000 able men.

Source A: Cavalry controlling a political meeting at St Peter's Field, in Manchester, in 1819. This was a time of political unrest in Britain, when many people were demanding the vote. The army was used to control political protests. Old-fashioned military methods, like cavalry charges, worked for controlling unarmed crowds.

What was slowing down change?

It is interesting to analyse what was causing the lack of change. Several factors seem to have been at work.

Strategic reasons

After 1815, Napoleon had gone. The threat from France was over and almost 40 years of peace in Europe followed. Free of any serious threat from abroad, the British Army settled into lesser roles, guarding the empire and putting down domestic unrest (see Source A). Complacency set in.

Economic reasons

The national debt had risen sharply as a result of the cost of the wars against France. It was:

- £250 million in 1790
- £800 million in 1816.

Taxes had gone up to pay for the wars against France. Once the wars finished, the government and the taxpayers wanted a smaller army so that taxes could be cut. They did not want to spend money on improvements in the army.

Social reasons

Warfare is always a product of its time. For various reasons, these were times when society – or, at least, the most powerful parts of it – were against change.

The main reason was that the French Revolution had frightened the upper classes in Britain. In their view, it showed how change caused disruption. The ruling classes therefore became suspicious of all new ideas – even in warfare.

Social reasons were also a reason for the survival of the cavalry in this period. Cavalry was now weak in battle, but it was still admired by the upper classes. One reason was that there was no police force and cavalry were very good at controlling public protests.

In 1819, a large crowd demonstrated for political reform in St Peter's Field in Manchester. The 15th Hussars were called in to control the crowds. Eleven people died and several hundred were injured. With Waterloo in mind, people dubbed it the Peterloo Massacre.

Conservatism in the army

There were also strong forces in the British Army itself which wanted to prevent change.

Most army officers were from the aristocracy; they were naturally conservative, preferring to keep things the same rather than change them. Those in charge of the army – politicians and old soldiers – were men of the past. Wellington, for example, was in the Cabinet as Master of the Ordinance (i.e. army weapons and equipment) from 1818 to 1827. He was made Army Commander-in-Chief in 1842, a post he held for ten years until the age of 83.

Wellington's influence

According to two historians, Wellington was an obstacle to change (see Sources B and C). He opposed reform of the army.

Source B: Kenneth E Hendrickson (1998).

> [Wellington] opposed experimentation with weaponry, change in uniform and the conditions for other ranks. To his mind, reforms implied destabilisation.

Source C: Thackery and Findling (ed) (2012).

> Conservative in military as well as most other matters, he (Wellington) held up reform of the British army for a decade.

Activities

1 Try to find examples of the following in the years 1815-50:
   - continuity (things staying the same)
   - regression (turning back the clock)
   - progress (things improving)
   What do your findings tell you?
2 How far was Wellington the reason for the lack of change, 1815-50?

Summary

- 1815-50 saw a lack of change. What change there was turned back the clock.
- There were several reasons for the lack of change; one was Wellington's role.

3.4 The Crimean War 1854–1856

> **Learning outcomes**
>
> By the end of this topic you should be able to:
> - recognise features in the Crimean War typical of an earlier age of warfare
> - recognise features of the Crimean War typical of a later age of warfare.

Source A: A cavalry charge at the Battle of Alma in 1854, looking much like Waterloo.

The Crimean War was fought between Russia and an alliance of Britain, France and Turkey. It was fought mainly on the Crimean Peninsula in the Black Sea, 4,000 miles by sea from London.

It had features of earlier warfare because:
- it featured small armies far from civilians;
- using troops clad in brightly coloured uniforms;
- deployed in infantry lines or cavalry charges.

But it also showed that armies were starting to use weapons and tactics typical of later wars.

- Britain's French allies used new iron-clad warships against Russia's wooden ships.
- British and French troops were starting to experiment with new percussion rifles and rifled cannon (see page 64).
- Around Sebastopol, shelling was so severe that the troops dug into trenches, rather like the First World War 60 years later.

Leadership

Generals sometimes disastrously used 'old' methods against 'new' weapons. Massed frontal assaults against superior firepower was very costly.

- In 1854, Russian infantry at Inkerman charged troops whose rifles had a longer range. The Russians lost 12,000 men in one attack.

These were not the only examples of poor leadership. The British commander, Lord Raglan:
- failed to look for a suitable landing site;
- took months to establish an efficient supply line for his troops from the port of Balaclava;
- delayed his attack on Sebastopol, allowing the defenders to complete their defences.

These errors caused many people to question the way that Britain selected its army officers.

> - Using newer weapons, the British and French combined lost about 150,000 men.
> - The Turks used older weapons and, though on the winning side, lost 400,000 men, killed or wounded.
> - Also using older weapons, the Russians lost 500,000.

Source B: Russian troops dug defences like First World War trenches 60 years later.

Improvements in medical care

The war sits on the watershed between 'old' and 'new' medical practices at war. For example, at first, diseases such as cholera and typhus and exposure caused 80 per cent of deaths in the Crimea. But then there was a change.

The Times publicised the filthy conditions in the military hospital at Scutari, causing public outrage. As a result, the sewers under the hospital were cleaned and Florence Nightingale was sent to the Crimea with a team of nurses to improve the hospital's organisation and cleanliness. The hospital death rate eventually fell from 40 per cent to two per cent, though the exact cause is unclear. What is clear is the effect of Nightingale's campaigning on her return. It prompted improved nursing standards in military hospitals, improvements in medical care, better designed hospitals and the founding of the Army Medical College.

Source C: This is an engraving from the time of a military hospital, sent back to Britain from the Crimea. Such information outraged public opinion and ensured changes in the ways wars were fought afterwards.

War reporting and public opinion

The Crimean War also changed war reporting.

At the start of the war, *The Times*, in London, used an officer in the British Army for war reports. Sent by horse and ship, his letters took a week to arrive.

Later, they sent a reporter, William Russell, who sent reports to London by telegraph on a daily basis. This new method of communication had a huge impact on public opinion. Russell's reports of the conditions at Scutari and the Charge of the Light Brigade shocked the public.

Transportation and supply

The war also illustrates new methods of wartime transportation.

Using steamships and railways, the British and French could transport men, weapons and supplies to the Crimea in under three weeks – despite the great distance.

They also built the first ever military railway – a 25-mile track from the Crimean coast to British trenches at Sebastopol. It could deliver 240 tons of food and supplies per day.

FASCINATING FACT

Technology allowed the French assault on the Malakoff fort at Sebastopol to be precisely timed. As soon as their shelling stopped, their infantry attacked. It was the first use of the order 'Gentlemen, synchronise your watches'.

Activities

1 List the features of the Crimean War which could be called typical of 'old' warfare.

2 List the features of the Crimean War which could be called typical of 'new' or later warfare.

3 In what ways does the Crimean War show the influence of public opinion upon warfare?

Summary

The Crimean War illustrates old features typical of 18th-century wars and new features typical of late-19th-century warfare.

3.5 1850-1900: Rapid change

Learning outcomes

By the end of this topic you should be able to:

● know the key features of change 1850–1900

● understand the causes and impact of change.

Industrialisation and warfare

1850-1900 was a period of rapid change in warfare. One reason was industrialisation.

In the second half of the 19th century, Britain was the leading industrial nation in the world. Other countries, such as France, Germany and the USA, were not far behind. Production of goods like iron and steel – vital for making weapons - were growing and prices were falling. For example, in 1855, Henry Bessemer patented a process for mass-producing cheap steel. Before 1850, the price of steel was £60 per tonne; the Bessemer process reduced the cost to £7.

Other industrialists found ways to make cheap iron and steel into standardised weapon parts using conveyor belt production. For example, the Royal Small Arms Factory, at Enfield in London, made rifles. In 1856, they built a new machine shop, with 1,000 workers, who could make 1,750 rifles per week. They were soon mass-producing the famous Lee-Enfield rifle.

This kind of industrial progress changed weaponry.

Source A: The mitrailleuse, an early French machine gun in use from the 1860s.

Weapon type	Improvement
Rifles	Rifles replaced muskets. The spiral groove (or rifling) inside the barrel made the shot spin so it flew further and straighter. By the 1860s they could kill from almost a mile away.
Bullets	Percussion cartridges were developed, with explosive caps at the back of the bullet. They did not need flints or sparks to fire, meaning soldiers could fire reliably in damp weather. Conical bullets were made; they could be loaded into the breech of a rifle and fired from revolving magazines containing several bullets. Soldiers could now load quickly, lie down and fire several shots in succession.
Machine guns	Gatling guns were introduced from the USA. They were like small cannon, with several thin revolving barrels. They could fire 150 bullets per minute. By the 1880s, there were smaller and lighter machine guns. Some, like the Maxim, could be moved around by individual soldiers.
Cannon	Cannon could now be reliably made from steel, improving their strength. Cannon were also given breech-loading actions which could fire 10 rounds per minute, and rifled barrels which made them more accurate.
Shells	By the Boer War (1899–1902), cannon had percussion shells, which would explode on impact.

FASCINATING FACT

In 1898, at Omdurman, North Africa, British troops with machine guns and rifles killed 11,000 Sudanese for only 28 casualties.

Effects on the battlefield

These new weapons transformed battlefield tactics.

Defence beats attack

Crude frontal attacks by infantry or cavalry became useless. Defenders, using rifles, machine guns and cannon, could just mow them down or blast them to pieces. Defence now dominated battlefields.

Source B: From *The Cambridge History of Warfare,* edited by Geoffrey Parker.

> [The British] encountered a Russian attack by the Alma river… Well aimed fire from rifles slaughtered the Russians well before the British lines came within reach of the enemy muskets.

Cavalry

Cavalry was finally dealt its death knell by rifles, machine guns and cannon. Horses remained a feature of battlefields for a while, but mainly as transport to battle and as draught animals.

Source C: Cassell's *World History of Warfare.*

> Cavalry [had been] the premier branch of the service. But the Franco-Prussian War showed that its only real choice was idleness or suicide.

British industry in the Crimean War (1854-56)

New weapons changed warfare in the Crimea. But British entrepreneurs also directly affected the war.

- The army's railway from the port at Balaclava to the front line was built – at cost price – by the **entrepreneurs** Peto and Brassey.
- The mining industry in Leeds paid for two locomotives for this railway.
- Joseph Paxton, architect of the Crystal Palace, set up an Army Works Corps to erect a township of wooden huts to house troops in the bitter winter.
- I.K. Brunel, the railway engineer, designed and built a hospital from prefabricated components, made in Britain and constructed on site.

- William Fairbairn, the ironmaster and shipbuilder, sent a pair of floating workshops to be stationed in the Black Sea to do repair and maintenance tasks for the army in the Crimea.

Transport and warfare

Industrialisation was one cause of change in warfare after 1850. Transport was another. Steamships and trains could transport troops and heavy supplies quicker than earlier forms of transport – and in any weather.

Railways

The world's first regular passenger railway opened in Britain in 1830. Britain used a railway to fight the Crimean War in 1854-56.

- The British Army built a railway from the port of Balaclava to take troops and supplies to its trenches 25 miles away.
- Transporting troops by rail was 15 times faster than marching.

Steamships

In normal, variable weather, sail ships averaged 5 knots. From the 1840s, screw propellers meant that steamships could average 10 knots.

The Royal Navy requisitioned 11 steamships from the Cunard Line to carry men and supplies to the Crimea.

Source D: Unloading supplies from steam-ships to rail at Balaclava, painted in 1856.

Communication and warfare

As well as industrialisation and transport, new methods of communication also changed warfare.

The electric telegraph

The telegraph was a way of sending messages along electric wires. The British Army first used it in the Crimean War, when a Telegraph Detachment was created as part of the Royal Engineers.

The telegraph had a big impact on the government of war and general staff communicated with commanding officers on campaign.

Source E: Diary of Staff Officer Calthorpe (1855).

> Lines have been laid down from Headquarters to Balaklava, [and to the front line]. Lord Raglan [the commander-in-chief] can therefore now communicate in a few minutes with any of his generals at any time, day or night. It is also a great advantage in the trenches, as if there is a sortie by the enemy, reinforcements can be sent.

The press

The telegraph also had another effect on warfare. It speeded up the reporting of wars by the press and this changed public opinion about warfare. Particularly influential were the reports of William Russell and the photographs of Roger Fenton.

Source F: From *The Cambridge History of Warfare,* edited by Geoffrey Parker.

> Then winter settled over the region… conditions in the front lines and in hospitals were appalling; some commanders wintered in their yachts. Correspondents reported the dreadful conditions under which the army was suffering, and the public outcry resulted in substantial reforms.

William Russell's reports for the *Times* arrived daily. He revealed the poor conditions of soldiers in the Crimea, claiming that, because of cholera, only 9,000 out of 30,000 troops were fit for duty. He also publicised the blunders of British officers – he wrote "Lord Raglan is utterly incompetent to lead an army".

Roger Fenton was one of the first war photographers. In four months in the Crimea, he took 360 photos, which sold widely in England. They were not deliberately critical of the war like Russell's reports. But his photos – and those of others later – greatly increased public knowledge and interest in warfare.

Public opinion and warfare

By 1870, public and political opinion combined to change how Britain waged war.

- In 1868, a new Liberal government was elected, led by William Gladstone. He wanted to modernise society, including schools, the Church – and the army.
- The public had been outraged by what they had read in the press about the Crimean War. They wanted a fairer and more efficient army.
- Success abroad (against China, in Africa) created a taste for war. The public demanded a modern army which could expand British territories abroad. This new enthusiasm for war was called **jingoism**.

This combination of public and political opinion brought about reform of the army.

Army reforms

In 1872, the Secretary for War, Edward Cardwell, improved recruitment by:

- reducing the period of enlistment to 12 years (six years active service and six years in reserve)
- creating a regional organisation for regiments, e.g. the Warwickshires, the Yorks and Lancs
- developing 'linked battalions', in which one battalion stationed overseas whilst its linked battalion was at home, training and recruiting
- abolishing the purchase of commissions and, instead, promoting on merit; this improved the quality and professionalism of Army officers.
- abolishing the flogging of soldiers.

He also improved the quality of equipment by introducing the new Martini-Henry rifle as the main infantry rifle. It was more accurate than its predecessor and had a longer range. It was also breech-loading. This meant it was faster to load and, even more importantly, soldiers could now load, fire and re-load from a prone position, which made them safer from enemy fire.

Medical improvements

Medical services in the army also improved.

- From 1855, medical orderlies were organised into the Medical Staff Corps.
- From 1863, medical officers were trained at an Army Medical School at Netley, in Hampshire. This was based at a new military hospital, inspired by Florence Nightingale, called the Royal Victoria Hospital.
- From 1873, the regimental medical officers were united into the Army Medical Department.

Florence Nightingale

Nursing also improved. During the Crimean War, Florence Nightingale saw there was a connection between hospital cleanliness and death rates – though she didn't understand what the connection was. Eventually, as a result of her work, nursing improved and hospitals became cleaner. Survival rates improved (see page 63).

Wartime surgery

Surgery on wounded soldiers improved after 1850.

- Ether (1846) and chloroform (1847) were more widely used as **anaesthetics**.
- Steam sterilising (1878) made surgical supplies cleaner.
- X-rays were used to detect broken limbs (1895).

Source G: Contemporary image of wounded soldiers under the Red Cross flag, 1877.

The Red Cross

Troops also benefited from two other changes.

- In 1863, the Red Cross was created to provide impartial help to those wounded in wars.
- Then, in 1864, the Geneva Convention was agreed. It set out how the wounded should be treated in wars. Britain signed in 1865.

Activities

1 (a) List the main improvements in weapons 1850-1900.

(b) What were their effects on the battlefield?

2 What effect on warfare 1850-1900 did the following have?
- industrialisation
- public opinion

Build better answers

The bullets below show two causes of change in warfare 1850-1900. Choose one and describe the key features of the way it changed warfare. (6 marks)

- Transport
- The telegraph

Basic, Level 1
Generalised answer with little detail.

Good, Level 2
Key features identified, with relevant details to illustrate these. For example, the use of railways and steamships identified as the key features of transport improvements with details to show how these affected warfare.

Summary

- The period 1850-1900 was a period of rapid change in warfare.
- The main causes of this rapid change were industrialisation, improved transport and communications and public opinion.
- Weapons changed, armies were modernised and medical care on the battlefield improved.

3.6 Summary: Warfare c1700–c1900

Simple change

The period between 1700 and 1900 was not a time of consistent change in the history of warfare.

On a simple level:
- 1700–1790 was a time of continuity.
- 1790–1815 was a time of rapid and significant change, for example the size and cost of armies increased greatly.
- 1815–1850 was a time of stagnation – even regression.
- 1850–1900 was a time of rapid change.

Activities

1 Look back at the sections on the period 1790–1900.

a) Write a sentence or two to justify each of the four statements bullet-pointed above.
For example:

'1700–1790 was a period of continuity because limited warfare remained the norm, cavalry continued to decline in importance, and infantry, using the same weapons, remained the biggest part of all armies.'

b) Using the guide graphs on page 48, draw a graph showing a simple view of the course of change 1700–1900.

Complex change

Change is normally more complex than it is possible to show on a simple graph. For example, the period 1700–1790 was, in general terms, a time of continuity. Most things stayed the same and any changes were slow. But looking more closely, we can find examples of changes that were taking place.

Activities

2 Look back again at the sections about the periods in the four bullet points at the top of the page.

a) Now write a slightly longer paragraph on each period, qualifying the simplistic statement in the four bullet points. For example:

'1700–1790 was, in general, a time of continuity because most things stayed the same and any changes were slow or minor. But there were some changes. Based on old heavy cannon, the French developed new, lighter, field artillery, for example. Also, armies generally got bigger; this encouraged countries to have better training for armies and to provide accommodation for them.'

Source A: A 19th-century painting showing the British Royal Horse Artillery using field guns during the 18th century.

Factors causing change

So the pattern of change 1700–1900 is complex. At times change was slow; at times it was rapid.

- What was it that was slowing down change?
- And what was it that was speeding up change?

Several factors were involved. Three examples are:
- attitudes in society;
- industrialisation;
- medical knowledge.

During the period 1700–1850, each of these hindered change. For example, industries were still at an early stage of development. Except in Britain, the Industrial Revolution did not start much before 1850. Most production in the rest of the world was still in small workshops. This limited the changes that could take place in the development of weapons, for example.

But after 1850, each of the three factors speeded up change. For example, attitudes in society changed rapidly. After 1870, British public opinion wanted a more efficient army. Gladstone's government also wanted to create more equal opportunities for all. These views caused the army reforms, led by Cardwell, that abolished the purchase of commissions and introduced promotion on merit.

Source B: An illustration printed in the *London Illustrated News* in 1867; it shows an exhibit at the Paris Exhibition of that year. The exhibit is a heavy cannon, manufactured by Krupps, the Prussian steelworks.

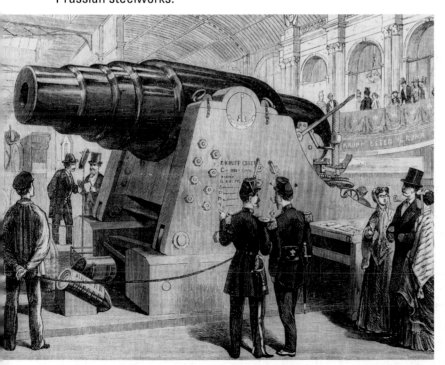

Activities

3 Choose one of the three factors causing change listed on this page. Using the two examples given, write a paragraph explaining how your factor either slowed down or speeded up change in warfare.

 examzone **Build better answers**

What do Sources A and B show about changes in artillery during the period 1700–1900? Explain your answer, using Sources A and B and your own knowledge. (8 marks)

■ **Basic, Level 1**

Answer gives general comments, without support from sources or own knowledge. For example: *It became bigger and more powerful.*
OR
Gives statements based on sources but which don't address the issue of change. For example: *Source A shows artillery pulled by horses. Source B shows the cannon used later.*

● **Good, Level 2**

Answer only describes the changes between the two situations shown in the sources, with limited own knowledge. For example: *The artillery has got bigger between Source A and Source B and it isn't any longer pulled by horses.*

▲ **Excellent, Level 3**

Answer makes an inference about the nature and extent of change during the time of the sources, based on both the sources and own knowledge. For example: *Source A shows the light artillery used on the battlefield in the 18th century. It was mobile and was pulled around the battlefield. But, by the middle of the 19th century, industrialists like Krupps made more powerful cannon which fired much further and helped to make defence more powerful than attack.*

4.1 Warfare 1900-1918

> **Learning outcomes**
>
> By the end of this topic you should be able to:
> - outline the key features of warfare 1900-18
> - explain how far these key features were new.

The First World War 1914-18

Britain and the other Allies went to war against the Central Powers in 1914. Britain, France and Russia were the Allies; Germany was the main Central Power. There were several key features of the war that were new to Britain.

The scale of war

The scale of the war was one new feature. Most of the fighting was in Europe. But, with almost all of the major powers supporting one side or the other, 80 per cent of the world's population were formally at war.

The armies involved were huge. Overall, by the end of the war in 1918, the number of men mobilised was:
- 25 million amongst the Central Powers
- 40 million amongst the Allies.

The type of war

The type of fighting that took place in the First World War was also new. The generals expected a short war that would be won by the overwhelming strength of attacking forces. They expected this because:

- Prussia had won quick victories against Austria (1866) and France (1870–71) with the firepower of rifles, machine guns and artillery. Germany had prepared the Schlieffen Plan for a massed attack and rapid six-week defeat of France.
- Britain had defeated the Boers in South Africa (1900–1902) by using the overwhelming force of an army of 300,000 men.

In fact, the First World War was different. Defenders were more powerful than attackers. They dug into defensive positions and used rifles and machine guns to mow down attacking infantry. The German advance was halted short of Paris. But the French and British counterattack also failed. Neither side could overwhelm the other. It was stalemate. (See pages 72-73.)

Source A: British artillery shells for the Battle of the Somme. Old weapons dominated the war.

The new weapons of war

Some new weapons emerged in this period.

Tanks

The British were the first to use tanks in warfare, at the Somme in 1916. They were effective at times.

- At Cambrai in 1917, 378 British tanks punched five miles through German lines.
- At Amiens in 1918, another 420 tanks successfully protected an infantry attack.

But generals had no experience with tanks; they spread them too widely and linked them poorly with infantry. The tanks often broke down, had a top speed of no more than five miles per hour and were vulnerable to armour-piercing bullets.

In the battles above, half the tanks at Cambrai broke down on the first day and only six tanks lasted the entire battle at Amiens. Tanks eventually became effective weapons – but it took time.

Gas

Gas was another new weapon.

- In 1915, in the second Battle of Ypres, the Germans sent clouds of chlorine gas over the British troops, suffocating hundreds.
- Phosgene and mustard gas were used too.

Both sides used gas. It killed 90,000 men. But it was hard to target and easy to defend against, so had little impact on the war overall.

Aeroplanes

In 1914, British forces sent to fight the First World War had just 63 aeroplanes. They were used mainly for reconnaissance – locating enemy positions.

Later, bigger aeroplanes were built which could drop bombs – first on opposition trenches, then on towns. Next, smaller, quicker planes were built, which could shoot down the bombers. These fighter planes sometimes fought each other in 'dog-fights', using machine guns. By 1918, the RAF had over 20,000 aircraft.

But damage caused by aeroplanes was tiny compared to artillery, and losses were heavy. About 50 per cent of pilots were killed in action and, at times, like mid-1917, the RAF lost 30 per cent of its planes each week. So they had little impact.

The old weapons of war

Familiar weapons, slightly improved, continued to dominate First World War battlefields.

Rifles and machine guns

These were the infantry's main weapons.

Infantrymen were issued with bolt action rifles, which automatically loaded bullets from a cartridge case and gave rapid fire.

The British used Maxim machine guns, invented in 1884. They fired 500 rounds per minute – the fire-power of 100 rifles. A few machine guns could fend off hundreds of advancing infantrymen.

Artillery

Artillery was the other key weapon. During the war, the British developed howitzers which could lob 900kg shells into enemy trenches 20 kilometres away.

Artillery shelling was used on an unprecedented scale.

- British artillery shelling during the Battle of the Somme in 1916 lasted not hours but almost five months.
- Britain used more artillery shells in the 35-minute bombardment at Neuve Chapelle in 1915 than they did in the whole of the Boer War.

It has been estimated that 70 per cent of all casualties in the war were caused by artillery fire.

Activities

1 In what ways was warfare 1900-18 'new'?
2 In what ways was warfare 1900-18 the same as earlier warfare?

Summary

- Warfare during the First World War was of a different scale and type to earlier wars.
- But some old-style weapons remained the most important weapons of the war.

4.2 Trench warfare on the Western Front

Learning outcomes

By the end of this topic you should be able to:

- outline the key features of warfare in the trenches on the Western Front
- identify similarities and differences when compared to earlier periods of warfare.

The First World War began in August 1914, when a German army of a million men attacked France.

By September, they were in sight of Paris. But, in the Battle of the Marne, British and French troops halted the German advance. Troops on both sides spread north and south and dug in, to prevent the enemy outflanking them.

By the start of 1915, Allied and German trenches stretched 600 kilometres, from the Belgian coast in the north to the Swiss Alps in the south. And there they remained, hardly moving, until 1918.

This was the Western Front. It was where most British soldiers were to fight the First World War.

Fighting from the trenches

Rival trenches were normally dug anything from 50 to 800 metres from each other. The space between was known as 'no-man's-land'. This area would be strewn with barbed wire as added protection.

The tactics used by British generals to cross no-man's-land and capture opposition trenches failed.

First, hours of artillery fire were used to weaken opposition defences. This worked in one sense; some 70 per cent of all battlefield casualties in the war were caused by artillery fire.

The trenches withstood the barrage, however, and the shelling ploughed up no-man's-land and made it even harder to cross.

Gas attacks were another feature of trench warfare. At first these struck fear into troops and affected morale. But the wind could disperse gas or even send it back over the attackers. Once gas masks were issued to troops, gas had little effect.

Features of the trenches

- **Front line** trenches were normally two metres deep and wide. These were the first line of defence.
- Support trenches were built further back, for off-duty soldiers and supplies.
- Reserve trenches were further back still; troops could be rested here and rushed to the front line if needed.

Trenches were dug in zigzags so that the enemy could not fire along them if they were captured.

The sides of this British trench were lined with wood.

The mud at the bottom of the trench was covered with duckboards.

Soldiers could stand on the fire step to see the enemy.

Steps enabled soldiers to go 'over the top' when they attacked.

So, in the end, the generals always fell back on sending their infantry 'over the top'. This involved masses of soldiers walking towards enemy fire.

It soon became clear that machine guns could easily mow down attackers. But the generals had no different tactics. They just increased the numbers of men sent over the top.

If troops did reach enemy trenches, fighting reverted to age-old hand-to-hand combat, though flame throwers and hand grenades were also used to clear trenches.

Life in the trenches

Life for British soldiers in the trenches had much in common with infantry through the ages. Day-to-day living conditions were harsh.

- Front-line troops lived in dug-outs, holes in the ground 20 metres behind front-line trenches.
- Daily routines of sentry duty and weapons cleaning were tedious.
- Soldiers complained of the mud, the cold and the lack of sleep.
- Stagnant water, lice and rats spread disease, causing diarrhoea and dysentery.
- Constant cold, damp, unsanitary conditions led to an infection called trench foot.
- Lice were a frequent irritant and caused trench fever. This involved severe headaches and sore limbs; it took a month to recover. About 25 per cent of troops in the trenches caught it.

Source A: Rats were a problem in all the trenches. Here, German troops display rats caught in their trenches.

- Another problem was shell shock – a condition caused by constant shelling. It could cause uncontrollable weeping or shaking, loss of speech or even physical paralysis. Medical treatment was patchy. Shell shock was not well understood; some sufferers were treated as cowards.

Treatment of normal wounds improved.

- Tetanus injections and sodium hypochlorite (a form of bleach) reduced infections.
- Blood transfusions were more successful.
- Even so, about 25 per cent of the wounded died.

Activities

1 a) Why did trench warfare develop in 1914?
   b) Describe the key features of a First World War trench.
2 In a small group, create a list of:
   a) the similarities
   b) the differences between living conditions of infantry in the trenches and infantry in earlier periods of warfare.

You may need to look back through this book to remind yourself about earlier periods.

Summary

- Trench warfare was not new – although trench warfare lasting four years was.
- Artillery and machine guns were the dominant weapons of trench warfare.
- Life in the trenches for infantry had many similarities with earlier periods of warfare.

4.3 The Battle of the Somme 1916

Learning outcomes

By the end of this topic you should be able to:

- outline events at the Battle of the Somme
- evaluate Earl Haig's tactics
- explain the role of tanks, first used at the Battle of the Somme.

The first months of the war had shown the dominance of defensive machine guns and artillery. But generals persisted with massed infantry attacks. The Allies planned a new one, along the River Somme, in 1916. The German positions were strong there; they had deep dug-outs as protection from artillery fire and dense barbed wire. Furthermore, the British infantry were raw volunteers from 1914 and 1915.

The British general commanding the British Expeditionary Force was Earl Haig. One of his generals, Sir Henry Rawlinson, argued for new tactics – a series of small attacks, on selected targets, by independent mobile groups of men. Haig, however, chose the more traditional strategy:

- a seven-day heavy artillery bombardment of 1.7 million shells, to destroy German defences
- a massed attack by 120,000 infantry, at walking speed, following an advancing shield shelling.

So at 7.30a.m. on 1 July, over an 18-mile front, Allied soldiers went over the top and advanced on German lines.

It was soon clear that German defences were intact. The attackers were shelled and mown down by machine-gun fire. As the advance slowed, it fell behind its artillery shield and was even more vulnerable.

By the end of the day, 20,000 British infantry were killed, 2,000 missing, 36,000 wounded and 600 captured. Half the attackers had become casualties, yet only in a handful of places had they reached the enemy lines. The attack had been a disaster.

Source A: From Henry Williamson, a junior British officer, in the first wave of infantry at the Somme.

I see men arising and walking forward; I go forward with them. Some seem to pause, with bowed heads, then sink carefully to their knees, roll over and lie still. Others roll and roll on the ground and scream. As I pass, they grip my legs in fear. I go on… up and down across pitted ground like a huge honeycomb. And my wave (of men) melts away, and the second wave comes up, and also melts away, and then the third wave merges into the ruins of the second. And after a while the fourth blunders into the writhing remnants of the others. We slow and have to run to catch up with the barrage.

The Somme offensive continued for five months. Haig made no changes to his strategy. However, he did allow some British generals, such as Rawlinson, to vary their tactics; they used smaller, carefully targeted attacks. In one assault, on 22 July, Rawlinson's men pushed three miles past the German front lines before being forced to withdraw.

Stung by such setbacks, the Germans tried attacking to regain lost ground. Eventually, when fighting died down in November, losses were about even. British casualties were about 400,000, French 200,000 and German 500,000.

Source B: An artist's impression of fighting at the Battle of the Somme in July 1916.

Tanks

The British used 49 tanks to support the infantry attacks at the Somme in September 1916.

They had a big psychological impact. A German soldier wrote, 'Our blood chilled. Mysterious monsters were crawling towards us over the craters. The word went along the line, "The devil is coming".'

But the tanks were few in number and scattered along the line of attack. Generals had little experience of them and therefore did not yet know how to use them most effectively. They had little physical impact.

General Haig

Haig's defenders say:

- Generals from every army in the war believed that massed attacks would work.
- Haig could not just defend. He was under pressure to regain land lost to Germany.
- The Allies also needed to win in the west before Germany defeated Russia in the east, releasing about 1 million extra German troops.
- The cold calculation was that these deaths were tragic for the Allies, but for Germany, as a smaller power, they would eventually be disastrous.
- Haig had to use the weapons he had. New weapons, such as gas, aeroplanes and tanks, were not effective enough by 1916.

His critics say:

- Haig failed to learn from mistakes and explore new tactics.
- He used new weapons badly and too little.
- He ignored the advice of younger generals, such as Rawlinson.

Summary

- In the Battle of the Somme, Earl Haig persisted with the tactic of massed infantry attack.
- Little ground was gained, with huge casualties, but the battle badly weakened Germany.
- Tanks made a modest appearance at the Somme, but had little initial impact.

Activities

1 Using the text, pictures and written sources in this topic and the previous one on trench warfare, make a list of key features of warfare on the Western Front.

2 Write a paragraph in support of each of the following phrases:

   a) The Battle of the Somme was a failure for the Allies.

   b) The Battle of the Somme was a success for the Allies.

3 Look back at page 71. How much change did tanks make to warfare between 1916 and 1918?

exam zone

Build better answers

Why did Haig keep using massed infantry attacks at the Somme even though the British suffered so many casualties? (12 marks)

You may use the following in your answer.

- Lack of effective new weapons
- Failure to listen to other, younger officers

You must also include information of your own.

 Basic, Level 1

Answer gives a simple, generalised comment, supported by a little knowledge.

 Good, Level 2

Answer makes statements with support from information which is mostly relevant and accurate.

▲ **Excellent, Level 3**

Answer understands the focus on causation. It gives several reasons with accurate information to support the points made. It also explores aspects in addition to those given in the stimulus.

4.4 The Home Front 1914–1918

Learning outcomes

By the end of this topic you should be able to:

- outline how Britain fought the First World War on the Home Front
- understand the concept of total warfare.

Total warfare

From 1914 to 1918, for the first time in British history, the government used all elements of society to help the war effort. This was '**total warfare**'.

Political power

So that it could run the war more effectively, the British Government gave itself extra political powers. The Defence of the Realm Act (DORA, 1914) gave the government the power to:

- control all railways, mines and ships
- re-allocate workers to key industries
- control food prices and introduce rationing
- censor what papers printed about the war.

Motor vehicles

The government also used wartime powers to boost the war effort by using motor vehicles.

Motor cycles, cars and lorries became invaluable for carrying messages, troops, weapons and supplies.

Amongst its efforts to boost army motor vehicles, the government:

- requisitioned 1,200 private lorries
- ordered 7,000 Dennis lorries and 19,000 Model T Ford patrol cars for the army
- shipped a total of 900 London buses to France to transport troops.

Economic power

The government also used Britain's economic might to help the war effort. For example:

- it used the coal, iron and steel industries to produce 170 million shells during the war
- one factory alone – Woolwich Arsenal, in London – employed 100,000 workers.

Manpower

Britain also used all its manpower, adopting new recruitment methods to boost the army.

In 1914, the British Expeditionary Force which was sent to fight the war numbered only 100,000.

So the first step was to appeal for volunteers. The government mounted a powerful recruitment campaign and 2.5 million men volunteered by 1916.

But high casualty rates meant that even this wasn't enough for the government.

- In 1916, **conscription** started. Unmarried men aged 19-40 were called up.
- By 1918, it was married men too.
- By 1918, over 5 million Britons had joined the British Army.

Propaganda

The government also used **propaganda** to fight the war. Propaganda is biased information used to influence people's opinions. It may not be lies; it could be carefully selected facts or opinions.

The government needed people to support the war so that they would:

- volunteer or accept conscription
- help arms production
- accept the high casualty rate
- tolerate the hardships of food shortages.

So, for example, the government issued posters which:

- boosted patriotism – *Your Country Needs You*
- appealed for volunteers – *The Women of Britain say "Go!"*
- demonised the enemy – like Source B, page 77.

War reporting

Government propaganda was successful at first. Unlike William Russell's reports on the Crimean War, First World War reporting tended to support the war effort. Read Source A for an example.

Source A: *The Daily Chronicle* reporting on the Battle of the Somme in 1916.

> Some ground was gained at great loss of life to the enemy, though not without many casualties to ourselves. Fortunately, the proportion of [our] lightly wounded men was wonderfully high.

Actually, only one mile was gained and 20,000 British soldiers died in this part of the battle.

After 1916, reports of shell shortages and rising casualties eroded public support for the war. Lloyd George replaced Asquith as prime minister, but there was little change in military tactics.

Casualties

An unprecedented 10 million combatants died in the First World War. This compares to 1.7 million in the Napoleonic Wars and half-a-million in the Seven Years War of 1756-63.

- About 700,000 British soldiers died, roughly 15 per cent of all British servicemen involved.
- Most died young. Of all men in Britain aged 20-24 in 1911, one-third were dead by 1918.

Source B: A British First World War propaganda poster showing German cruelty to a British casualty.

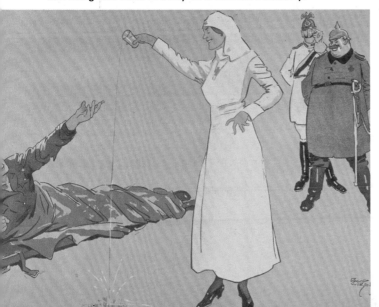

Activities

1. Type First World War posters into a search engine and study the images you get. Select three posters and say what you think they were meant to achieve?
2. a) What were the key features of Britain's war on the Home Front?
   b) Give supporting detail for each key feature.

Summary

- The First World War was Britain's first 'total war'.
- For the first time, men were conscripted and the whole of society was used to wage war.

4.5 The Second World War 1939-1945

> **Learning outcomes**
>
> By the end of this topic you should be able to:
> - identify the key weapons of the Second World War and their effect on combat
> - understand the impact of aerial warfare
> - recognise features of total warfare, e.g. rationing, propaganda and conscription.

Weapons and Technology in 1939

Some weapons and technology that were just emerging in the First World War had been improved by 1939 and dominated battlefields in the Second World War.

Tanks

By 1939, the most effective tanks were:
- relatively light, up to about 20 tons
- lightly protected, by up to 30mm armour
- armed with light guns of about 30mm calibre.

They were also faster – reaching 20 to 40mph on roads, manoeuvrable and reliable. By this time, they could travel hundreds of miles on their tracks. Examples were the British Crusader and the German Panzer III.

Aeroplanes

By 1939, early aeroplanes had developed into effective fighter planes and bombers. A key aeroplane of the early stages of the war was the German Junkers Ju 87 – known as the Stuka. This was a dive bomber – a multi-purpose plane.

- It was fast, reaching almost 240mph and had three machine guns for attacking other aircraft or targets on the ground.
- It also had a long range of almost 500 miles and could carry over 1,000lb of bombs.

Radio and motor transport

Infantry attacks could now be supported by tanks and aircraft by using radio communication and motor vehicles. All German tanks were fitted with radios by 1939; most French and British tanks were not as the Allies were less prepared for war.

Impact on the battlefield

During the First World War, artillery, machine guns and rifle fire had made defence much stronger than attack.

In the early stages of the Second World War, German commanders developed a way of restoring the power of attack. They combined:
- old-style weapons – artillery and infantry
- newer weapons – tanks and aeroplanes
- newer technology – radio and motor vehicles.

> **Blitzkrieg**
>
> The new attacking strategy was called Blitzkrieg. An example is the German invasion of Poland in 1939.
>
> - To weaken enemy defences, the attack started with old-style shelling by artillery, and 1,000 new high-altitude bombers.
> - Then, to penetrate enemy defences, 2,400 tanks, in groups, punched deep into enemy territory.
> - To give aerial cover to attackers on the ground, 300 dive bombers, the terrifying Stukas, dropped 400 tons of bombs on key defences, like airfields.
> - Then, to consolidate these gains, infantry, moved in.
> - To make their attacks difficult to counter, they worked in small, independent groups and moved at great speed, using lorries and parachute drops.
> - The whole attack was co-ordinated by radio.

Using these tactics, in a few months German troops occupied Poland, Denmark, Norway, Belgium, Holland and France. Britain had to evacuate 330,000 troops from Dunkirk in France.

But, at that point, the attack stalled. A period of stalemate followed.

Source A: The Spitfire.

Aerial warfare: the Battle of Britain, July-September 1940

Aerial warfare and new technology decided the next stage, in 1940. Hitler wanted to invade Britain, but he needed to destroy the Royal Air Force (RAF) first, to ensure air cover for his invasion.

Spitfires and Hurricanes

Germany had four times more aircraft than Britain. Britain, however, had the two key aircraft. Working together, they dominated the Battle of Britain.

- The Spitfire was fast. In 1940 it could reach 350mph and outmanoeuvre the German fighter planes sent to protect their bombers. Britain had made 20,000 Spitfires by 1948.
- Britain also had over 2,000 Hawker Hurricanes. Once Spitfires took out the German fighter escorts, the highly manoeuvrable Hurricanes were deadly against the, now unprotected, German bombers.

Radar

Britain also had a technological advantage.

- In 1886, Heinrich Hertz had shown that radio waves would bounce off solid objects.
- In 1935, a British scientist, Robert Watson-Watt, demonstrated that radio waves would bounce back off approaching aircraft.

So the British built Chain Home. This was a series of 110 metre towers stretching from Portsmouth to the Orkney Islands, which sent radio waves towards Europe to detect incoming aircraft. This meant that the RAF always had warning of German attacks and got their planes into the air quickly.

Better weapons and technology won the Battle of Britain and saved Britain from invasion.

Total warfare returns 1940-45

From late 1940, there was stalemate. Both sides used all the powers of society to gain the upper hand – the return of 'total warfare'.

Government power

In Britain, for example:

- **rationing** was started to reduce the need for imported food
- the Ministry of Information censored the press and spread government propaganda (see pages 104-5)
- the government controlled food prices and wages to stabilise the economy
- and took control of key industries, such as mining, shipping and the railways.

Industrial power

The government also ensured that industry made what the armed forces needed.

- Britain made 2,000 RAF aircraft in 1938.
- In 1943, it produced 26,000.

Territorial Army and conscription

The Territorial Army (TA) started in 1920. In the TA, volunteers could earn a small fee of about £3 for becoming part-time soldiers who mainly served within Britain.

- In 1939, the TA doubled in size to 440,000. About 100,000 served as anti-aircraft gun operatives. The rest were infantry.

The government also resumed conscription.

- In 1939, the National Service Act conscripted all men aged 18-41, except those in **'reserved' occupations**.
- From December 1941, this was extended to all men aged 18-51 and women aged 20-30. Women chose to serve in the armed forces or industry.
- In addition, men aged 18-40 had to do six months of military training (called National Service).
- By 1945, 3.5 million had been enlisted.

This 'National Service' in the armed forces stayed in place, in reduced form, until 1960.

Aerial warfare: bombing 1940-45

As the war progressed, bombing changed.

Lancaster bombers

Better bombers were made, like the British Lancaster bomber. First used in 1941, it had a range of 1,660 miles, was protected by 10 machine guns and carried 22,000lb of bombs. Britain built 7,000 by 1945; they carried out 150,000 air raids.

Bombing technology

From 1942, Britain had the oboe system to target bombing. A radio signal was directed from Britain at a target in Germany; radio controllers then guided a pathfinder bomber along a 30 metre wide radio path to the target. Once the pathfinder bomber had hit the target, other bombers could see the target.

Fighter cover

Bombers also got better fighter cover.

- From 1943, British fighter planes had extra petrol tanks. Their range rose to 2,000 miles, giving bombers protection over Germany.
- From 1944, Britain had a jet fighter, the Meteor, which could fly at 600mph.

Source B: A London bus hit in the Blitz.

Missiles

By 1944, Germany was also using missiles.

- The V1 – or 'doodlebug' - carried one ton of explosives; it was like an unmanned aircraft. Its engines were designed to cut out over London.
- The V2 was a rocket; it also carried one ton of explosives. It travelled at over 2,000mph and landed without warning.

8,000 V1s and 1,000 V2s were launched at England. They spread fear amongst civilians, but malfunctioned often and came too late to have much effect on the war.

Effects on strategy

Improvements in bombing changed the way that wars were fought. Bombing became a vital strategy for weakening the enemy.

Strategic bombing

At first, Britain and Germany used strategic bombing of key industries and military sites. However, anti-aircraft guns hit day-time bombers and night-time raids lacked accuracy.

Area bombing

So both sides then turned to area bombing – massive raids on cities to reduce civilian **morale**. This did not require precision, so it could be done at night. In four raids alone, the RAF used 3,000 bombers to drop 9,000 bombs on Hamburg in July 1943.

Effects on civilians

Bombing brought civilians into the front line. In the German 'Blitz' on England, two million houses were destroyed and 60,000 civilians were killed. This was new warfare. By 1942, more British men, women and children died at home than British soldiers in action.

But Allied bombing on German cities killed even more people – over 400,000 by 1945. Area bombing of Dresden for just two days in February 1945 killed 25,000 people.

German industrial output of weapons was hit too. By the D-Day landings in 1944, Britain and her Allies had an aerial superiority of 70 aeroplanes to every German one.

Other new weapons 1940-45

Artillery improved.

- Mobile artillery units evolved, like the Sexton, used by the British army. These looked like tanks, with armour, tracks and muzzles, but could fire shells over long distances and keep up with infantry.
- They sometimes used 'time on target' attacks. Scattered units would use radio to co-ordinate firing, to land all their shells within one second in an area of about 100 square metres, clearing the way for infantry to advance.

Overall, however, the other new weapons used in Europe strengthened defence rather than attack.

- Land mines were mass-produced, mainly to counter tanks. Some were made of plastics, like Bakelite, to foil metal detectors.
- From 1942, the bazooka, fired from the shoulder by a single soldier, could knock out a tank at 400 metres with a 3.5lb rocket.

So tanks had to be protected by thicker armour – anything from 2.5–15cm – and became heavier and slower.

New ways of transporting troops also slowed down attacks. Aeroplanes could parachute attacking troops in, but motor vehicles could quickly move defensive troops to counter them.

Source C: The second atom bomb, dropped on Nagasaki on 9th August 1945. Over 200,000 people were killed at Hiroshima and Nagasaki.

Effects on the battlefield

Advances in defensive tactics meant the attack which finally defeated Germany in May 1945 was not a blitzkrieg attack. It was a long, slow advance.

Aerial bombing: the atom bomb

Things were different in the war in the East. By 1945, the USA had employed 125,000 people and spent $2 billion to develop the atom bomb.

The first atom bomb was dropped on Hiroshima on 6th August. It instantly destroyed everything in a one mile radius. 70 per cent of buildings in the city were damaged. 70,000 people died instantly; within weeks, the death toll had risen to about 140,000. Three days later a second bomb was dropped (see Source C).

The atom bomb ended the Second World War. But no atomic or nuclear weapons have been used since 1945. So the atom bomb did not immediately change warfare, though it has had a dramatic effect on international relations.

Activities

1. During the Second World War, what were the key features of:
   a) Blitzkrieg
   b) bombing?
2. List the ways that improvements in technology affected warfare, 1939-45.
3. List the ways that government policies affected warfare, 1939-45.
4. In a group, debate which of the following was the most important in the Second World War:
   a) the Spitfire
   b) the Lancaster bomber
   c) the atom bomb.

Summary

- Attacking weapons dominated the start of the war.
- Bombing and industrial superiority enabled the Allies to win the war in the West.
- The atom bomb ended the war in the East.

81

4.6 Weapons 1945 to the present day

> **Learning outcomes**
>
> By the end of this topic you should be able to:
>
> - describe the impact of technology, including computers and satellites, on weapons since 1945.

Modern infantry

The infantry still forms the largest part of modern forces like the British Army. However, improved technology means that weapons and equipment have improved hugely since 1945.

A modern infantry soldier is likely to be armed with:

- a pistol, for self defence, accurate over 50 metres; probably semi-automatic (i.e. it automatically ejects the spent cartridge and reloads another, ready for firing)
- a rifle, usually an assault rifle, with telescopic sight and laser aiming, fed from a 30-round magazine, and effective at 400 metres.

They may also have access to:

- a grenade launcher, fitted under their rifle, with an accurate range of about 350 metres
- a mortar, firing explosive rounds up to 5,000 metres
- a machine gun, firing about 1,000 rounds per minute, with an effective range of 800 metres.

They would have body armour, a helmet with night vision glasses and a personal radio.

Infantry soldiers are transported by aeroplanes, helicopters and armoured motorised vehicles.

Modern artillery

Infantry is still supported by artillery. But modern technology has improved this too. For example:

- mobile artillery has replaced cannon pulled into position; rather like tanks, with tracks and muzzles, mobile artillery units can travel at up to 30mph and use GPS (satellite controlled) targeting for an effective range of 25 miles
- air defence systems can launch anti-aircraft missiles from mobile units mounted on trucks.

Modern aerial warfare

Helicopters

Since about 1960, helicopters have been used. Transport helicopters ferry troops and supplies more safely than road vehicles, to areas inaccessible to other aircraft. Attack helicopters use guns and missiles to attack ground targets. The British Army currently has over 500 helicopters.

Jets

Jets were first used in active service in 1944.

- By the 1950s, fighter jets flew faster than the speed of sound – about 760mph. They had on-board radar to spot enemy planes and could fire air-to-air and air-to-ground missiles.
- By the 1960s, Britain had vertical take-off and landing jets, like the Harrier jump jet. It dropped laser-guided bombs.
- From the 1970s, jets had electronic, not mechanical, controls. Pilots had heads-up displays and their jets had 'stealth' features, with low visibility to radar.
- Since the 1990s, jets have had GPS guided missiles and helmet-mounted sights. Today, the British Typhoon fighter jet flies at 1,300mph and at 55,000 feet.

Source A: British troops in Iraq in 2003, with their Chinook transport helicopter.

Bombers and missiles

Technology also improved bombers. For example, by 1956, the British Vulcan bomber could fly 4,600 miles at 65,000 feet, to avoid attack, carrying 21,000lbs of bombs.

Later, stealth bombers were developed which were difficult to spot on radar. But 'stealth' bombers cost $2 billion each. So bombs are now delivered by multi-role fighter jets (see above) or by missiles.

Intercontinental ballistic missiles (ICBMs) have a range of over 3,500 miles. They carry nuclear or conventional warheads and can be fired from land, ships, submarines and even lorries – removing the need to put a pilot and plane at risk.

Drones

Drones are unmanned aircraft, rather like large model aeroplanes, which can be controlled from a communications base. They are used for reconnaissance and bombing missions.

Computers and satellites

Computers feature in all areas of warfare. They:
- provide data about enemy targets
- enable communication between troops
- control weapon targeting and firing.

Network-centric computer systems are used, so all commanders and troops in an operation share identical information on their computers.

Modern forces also use space satellites to:
- take optical, infra-red and radar images of Earth to show enemy troops and military bases
- intercept enemy communications
- give accurate targeting of military weapons through Global Positioning Systems (GPS).

Nuclear weapons

The use of the **atomic bomb**, in 1945, soon led other powers to develop **nuclear weapons**.

- By 1952, Britain had an atomic bomb.
- By 1961, the USA, the **USSR** and Britain all had hydrogen bombs. These became 1,000 times more powerful than the first atomic bomb.
- In 2012, there were about 20,000 nuclear warheads in the world and about ten countries capable of making them.
- Britain currently has about 200 nuclear warheads.

By 1980, the USA had developed mini-nuclear devices as small as a rucksack. Miniaturisation means that nuclear weapons can be secretly transported to their target.

All these changes in technology mean that warfare has changed radically since 1945, as we shall see next.

Summary

- Technology, including computers and satellites, has changed the weapons with which modern wars are fought.

Source B: A British Harrier jump-jet pilot, checking the laser-guided missile fitted to his aircraft.

Activities

1 Type 'modern British soldier' into an image search engine. Choose the three most useful images and list the infantry equipment you find.

2 Explain how the following have improved weapons since 1945:
   a) computers
   b) satellites
   c) other technology.

4.7 Modern warfare

> ### Learning outcomes
> By the end of this topic you should be able to:
> - explain different types of modern warfare
> - describe modern recruitment strategies
> - understand social attitudes to modern wars.

Modern warfare

Modern weapons changed warfare, recruitment and social attitudes towards war.

Nuclear weapons now mean that major powers can no longer wage total war against each other. Both sides would be destroyed. This is called 'mutually assured destruction' (suitably abbreviated as MAD). Since 1945, there have been over 60 years of relative peace between the major powers.

Modern powers still fight wars, however. Britain has been involved in 80 conflicts since 1945; British soldiers have died in combat every year, except 1968. But modern powers now only fight limited wars like those below.

Asymmetrical wars

These are wars where major powers fight limited wars, with limited forces, against weaker countries.

For example, in the Falklands War against Argentina in 1982, Britain fought with limited aims – the return of the Falkland Islands; used a relatively small task force of 28,000 men and 100 ships; and suffered only 255 casualties.

Wars against terrorists

The armed forces of modern powers also combat domestic uprisings or external terrorist attacks.

- Until the 1990s, the British Army was used to combat the IRA, who used arms to destabilise the government of Northern Ireland.
- Terrorist groups use 'guerrilla warfare' – a series of small attacks, by non-conventional forces that can hide amongst the populace. This has proved very difficult for larger armies to overcome, as identifying targets is difficult.

Recruitment

New weapons and different types of warfare have caused changes in recruitment.

What Britain needed for a world war in 1939 was a large, conscripted force. But, since 1945, Britain has fought small, limited wars using sophisticated weapons. This needs a small, well-trained, professional army.

So National Service –military training for all adults - was ended in 1960. Instead, Britain has paid volunteers in the Regular Army, Regular Reserves and Territorial Army.

There is also the RAF (Royal Air Force), the Navy and their reserves (**RNR** and **RAFVR**).

The Regular Army

The Regular Army consists of full-time, well-trained professional soldiers.

- Soldiers normally serve for 22 years.
- A separate force for female soldiers ended in the 1990s and now women serve alongside men in many areas.

Britain currently has an army of about 100,000 soldiers. With the RAF and the Royal Navy as well, Britain has a total permanent full-time military force of 175,000.

In addition, trained troops who have left the forces can be called up in a crisis. Britain has about 175,000 troops in the Reserves.

Territorial Army (TA)

The Territorial Army is a well-trained support for regular forces. They are part-time volunteer soldiers who often serve alongside regular troops. In 2006, about ten per cent of British forces in Afghanistan were from the TA.

TA members are paid whilst on service and train for a minimum of 27 days per year.

Since 1945, the size of the Territorial Army has been steadily reduced. It now stands at about 35,000. Britain has similar forces for the Navy and RAF.

Information about modern warfare

Changes in technology also mean that the flow of information about modern wars is now very different than before.

When the public had to rely upon government propaganda posters and films, and a small number of newspaper and radio companies, information about wars was quite limited. This made the control of information easier. Even as late as the Falklands War in 1982, the main source of news was a daily press conference, broadcast on television, by a government spokesman.

However, people in Britain today have many more sources of information: a host of television and radio channels with live satellite links to war zones, internet sites, social media, even mobile telephone calls from people under fire. In 2003, over 700 embedded reporters travelled with Coalition troops which invaded Iraq.

Even this level of press reporting does not ensure complete freedom of information. Embedded reporters, for example, have contracts which limit what they can report. TV coverage of the Iraq War stressed the success of the invasion and showed footage of attacks, but it took longer for details of civilian casualties to be reported.

Nevertheless, modern technology makes it much harder for governments to control information about warfare. This has had an effect on social attitudes to warfare.

Source A: Live television reporting from Iraq.

FD 99

Live Kuwait Front Line

Social attitudes to warfare

In general, support for warfare has fallen.

- Jingoism and patriotism meant support for wars from 1850-1950 was high.
- Since then, public opinion is much more divided. In 2003, one million people marched in London against the Iraq war.

One reason is that the public are more likely to know when things go wrong.

Source B: A *Guardian* report, 2006.

> A Royal Marine killed in Iraq by a missile fired by British forces was "let down" by the failings of his senior officers, a coroner ruled today. Oxfordshire assistant deputy coroner Andrew Walker listed a series of mistakes by commanders, which led to the death of Marine Christopher Maddison.

Another reason is the financial cost of war.

- Spitfires cost about £6,000 each.
- In 2008, Britain ordered new Typhoon fighters, at a cost of £80 million each.

Growing civilian deaths is another reason. The percentage of civilian deaths in warfare has been rising. It was:
- 10 per cent before 1900
- 50 per cent in the Second World War
- 75 per cent during the 1990s conflicts.

Activities

1 How have new weapons changed:
   a) the types of wars fought
   b) recruitment for the armed forces?
2 How has modern reporting affected public attitudes to warfare?

Summary

Technology has changed the types of war fought.

- Recruitment has changed to suit these types of warfare.
- Technology has increased reporting of warfare; this has affected public attitudes.

4.8 Modern logistics

> ### Learning outcomes
>
> By the end of this topic, you should be able to:
> - explain how modern armies are supplied
> - explain how modern armies are cared for.

Logistics is the term for the supply, movement and care of equipment and troops.

Movement of supplies

Before 1900, armies normally used baggage trains to carry their food and supplies with them. Modern improvements in transport mean that, increasingly, this is no longer necessary. Supplies can be stored centrally and moved quickly when needed. From about 1900, armies created special units to do this.

Army Service Corps

In 1888 the Army Service Corps was created – the first time the army had one unit for the procurement and movement of supplies. It had 6,000 men.

By 1918, they were using steamships, railways and lorries – as well as horse-drawn vehicles. The ASC had increased to over 300,000 men and supplied the Western Front each month with 30,000 tons of meat and 40,000 tons of bread.

During the Second World War, air transport was used to move supplies and, since the 1950s, helicopters have been available to drop troops and supplies right into the heart of the combat zone.

Source A: A military transport aircraft, 1999.

Royal Logistics Corps

In 1993, the purchase, storage and movement of supplies was reorganised under the Royal Logistics Corps. It currently has a force of 16,000, who organise the transport of supplies and troops, catering and the maintenance of army equipment.

This means that, when on active service, troops are now fed in field kitchens or given emergency rations that they carry and cook themselves as best they can.

British troops in Afghanistan in 2009 were issued 4,000-calorie ration packs of pre-packed food such as corned beef, fruit dumplings in custard, chocolate – and even chicken tikka masala.

Movement of troops

Whilst 90 per cent of equipment is normally transported overseas by ship, for rapid deployment 90 per cent of troops are now transported by air. Private contractors are often used.

When 45,000 troops and their tents, food, water, fuel and portaloos were transported to the Iraq War in 2003, 49 per cent of the air transport and 88 per cent of the sea transport was chartered in this way.

The flying time was about seven hours to cross 3,000 miles. In contrast, transporting troops 6,000 miles by sea to the Boer War in 1901 took about one month.

Care of troops

As well as supplying, feeding and equipping troops, army planners have to ensure troops are cared for.

Medical care

As part of the Victorian re-organisation of the army started by Gladstone in 1870, the Royal Army Medical Corps (RAMC) was created in 1898. This, for the first time:

- combined medical officers and medical orderlies into one united army unit
- gave medical officers the same status, pay and conditions as other army officers.

By 1914, it had 9,000 personnel.

The RAMC treated battlefield wounds and looked after the general health of troops on campaign. It brought an immediate improvement. For example, typhus, an infectious disease, killed 8,000 soldiers in the Boer War (1899-1902) and almost none in the First World War (1914-18).

This was a significant change. Before this, more troops normally died from illness than wounds.

- In the Napoleonic Wars (1803-15), 85 per cent of British deaths were due to illness.
- Of 179 British soldiers killed in the Iraq War (2003-09), five died from illnesses.

A second significant improvement was the treatment of war injuries, especially in the prevention of infection of wounds.

- Immunisation against tetanus was available during the Second World War. Of the 17,000 immunised British soldiers wounded at Dunkirk in 1940, none got tetanus.
- Penicillin was discovered in 1928 by Alexander Fleming. It prevents infection. By 1944, the Allies had enough penicillin to treat all the wounded at the D-Day landings in France.

Thirdly, the quality of medical resources improved.

- Today, the Royal Army Medical Corps has a staff of about 3,000 men and women, and levels of training among its staff are equal to those in civilian hospitals.
- The armed forces also have their own hospital facilities. The main one is at the Queen Elizabeth Hospital in Birmingham.

Conditions of service

Modern reporting has put soldiers' conditions of service in the public eye. Society now demands reasonable treatment for its troops.

- Soldiers now have their time balanced between training at base and service on active duty.
- Single soldiers live in barracks in rooms for between one and four people.
- Married soldiers are entitled to houses at subsidised rent.

Pay has also improved.

- In 2008, the average annual earnings of full-time employees in Britain was about £25,000.
- Army privates earned less than this. However, Army corporals, the next rank up, earned more. Higher ranks earned much more.

Finally, during their service, modern soldiers are trained in a host of skills, ranging from combat skills to vocational skills in areas such as communications, administration and catering. Soldiers therefore leave the army well placed to earn a living in civilian life.

Activities

1 How has technology helped, since 1900, with:
   a) the movement of supplies
   b) transporting troops?
2 Describe the key features of improvements, since 1900, in the care of troops.
3 List three key features of modern conditions of service for British soldiers.

Summary

Logistical issues, like:
- the requisition and distribution of military supplies
- the movement and care of troops

are now highly organised.

4.9 The Gulf War 1991

> ### Learning objectives
>
> By the end of this case study, you should be able to explain how the Gulf War is an example of:
> - limited warfare
> - asymmetrical warfare
> - the impact of technology on weapons and warfare.

The Gulf War of 1991 is an example of limited warfare in modern times. The war had limited objectives. Iraq, led by Saddam Hussein, had invaded a neighbouring country, Kuwait. The **United Nations** condemned the attack; it authorised a Coalition of countries, led by the USA, Britain and France, to free Kuwait. Once this had been done, the Coalition left and Saddam was allowed to continue as Iraqi leader.

It is also an example of asymmetrical warfare. Iraq had 250,000 troops, 2,000 tanks and 1,000 aircraft. The Coalition had 750,000 troops, 3,000 tanks and 1,800 aircraft. The Coalition had more troops; they were also better-trained and better equipped.

Operation Desert Storm – air attack

The Coalition began its attack in January 1991 with a five-week aerial bombardment. They flew 100,000 sorties and dropped 88,000 tons of bombs. It was very technologically advanced. One effect was that the bombing was accurate.

Source A: An Iraqi aircraft hangar, hit with total accuracy by a guided bomb.

The Coalition used:
- stealth bombers dropping laser-guided bombs;
- cruise missiles fired from up to 1,500 miles away but targeted to an accuracy of ten metres;
- daisy cutters, bombs that destroyed everything within hundreds of metres of the explosion.

As a result of the bombing:
- The Iraqi air force was destroyed on the ground; only two Iraqi MiG-29s took off, and these shot each other down by mistake.
- Seventeen of Iraq's power stations were disabled; electricity supply fell to 4 per cent of pre-war levels.
- Water pumping stations and sewage plants were destroyed; raw sewage poured into the River Tigris, from which the desperate people of Baghdad were taking their water.

The bombing therefore inflicted military damage and disrupted the whole of Iraqi society. In five weeks, Iraq was reduced from one of the most advanced Arab countries to the most regressive.

> ### FASCINATING FACT
> The Coalition targeted many bombs and missiles by GPS (global positioning system). In 1990, a US officer travelled to the US embassy in Baghdad with a GPS receiver. He took one reading and flew home. This reading enabled the Coalition to use GPS to hit vital targets all over Iraq.

Operation Desert Sabre – ground attack

In February 1991 the Coalition sent in their ground troops. Again, the contest was unequal. The first contact was between rival tanks. Superior technology made all the difference. The British Challenger tank had a top speed of 45 miles per hour, was protected by Chobham armour and was armed with **depleted-uranium** shells. The Iraqi T-72 was 25 years old, had a top speed of only 37 miles per hour, armour half as strong and a gun with a shorter range. Their T-55s were even older. The Coalition tanks fired from three times the distance that the Iraqis could. One Coalition unit of tanks destroyed 50 Iraqi tanks in ten minutes.

After only three days, Saddam ordered his army to retreat. His well-trained and disciplined Republican Guard put up some resistance. But his conscripted troops were poorly trained and lacked morale; they deserted or fled in disarray. Many were killed fleeing across their own minefields. Others fled in any vehicles they could find, down the main road from Kuwait to Baghdad. Without any air cover, they were relentlessly picked off by Coalition aircraft – rather like 18th-century cavalry picking off infantry in retreat.

Casualties

About 20,000 Iraqi soldiers were killed. But since military targets in Baghdad were in the middle of a huge city, there were also about 50,000 civilian deaths. Most deaths were caused by bombing.

In contrast, there were only 350 Coalition deaths.

- About half were caused by Iraqi fire.
- Half were caused by accidents and **friendly fire**.
- Some British soldiers returned with stress-related illness or undiagnosed ailments – known as Gulf War Syndrome.

Accidental deaths and stress-related illness have probably been features of warfare for centuries. But it has only been modern **media** coverage that has brought them to light.

Decisive factors

There were two decisive factors in the war:
- financial superiority – for example, Britain spent over £3 billion on the Gulf War;
- technological superiority, especially Coalition aeroplanes, bombs and tanks.

But Source B suggests that one other decisive factor has also been key throughout the history of warfare.

Source B: From *The Cambridge History of Warfare*, edited by Geoffrey Parker.

> Training, discipline and organisation underpins the efforts of military forces. That has been the essence of western warfare since the time of the Greeks and Romans. In Iraq, the Coalition forces had those advantages. Their opponents did not.

Source C: The wreckage left when Coalition aircraft massacred fleeing Iraqi troops on the 'Highway of Death'.

Source D: A Coalition officer describing bomb victims.

> The **overpressure** was incredible. Blood was coming from their eyes and mouths. They had no will to do anything, their legs wouldn't work, they were paralysed. Groups of soldiers ambled around, and you'd shout at them, but you wouldn't get through.

Activities

1 List the technological advantages of Coalition forces in the Gulf War.

2 There were three decisive factors in this war:
- financial superiority
- technological superiority
- superior organisation and discipline.

In a group, discuss whether:
a) one of these was the most important
b) all of them are inseparably linked.

Summary

- The Gulf War of 1991 was an example of modern limited warfare and asymmetrical warfare.
- Superior technology was a key factor in the victory.

4.10 Summary: Warfare c1900 to the present day

The rate of change

Since 1900 the impact of warfare on society in Britain has been changing.

- From 1900–1914 and from 1918–1939, the impact of war on society grew gradually, as more newspapers, radio and newsreels made the public more aware of the realities of war.
- From 1914–1918 and from 1939–1945, the impact of war on society increased suddenly and significantly because of the effects of warfare, such as conscription and bombing.
- Since 1945, the impact of warfare has continued to grow on society. Television, films and the internet have made the public even more aware of the realities of warfare.

If we were to try to represent these changes on a simple diagram, it might look like this.

Source A: A graph showing the impact of warfare on society 1900–present.

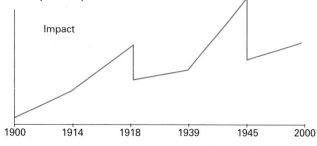

Activities

1 Now you can do a diagram. Here is a simple description of changes in recruitment since 1900:
   - from 1900 to the present day, Britain has relied upon a small army of volunteers, except
   - from 1916–1918 and 1939–1945, when there was conscription
   - and 1939 to 1960 when there was National Service.

   How would you represent these changes on a simple diagram?

Activities

2 a) Write a simple description of the rate of change in weaponry since 1900.
   b) Draw a diagram that gives a simple picture of this rate of change.
   c) What other key features of warfare since 1900 would it be possible to represent in this kind of way?

Factors affecting change

Two factors that have shaped Britain's experience of warfare since 1900 have been:
- social attitudes
- technology.

For example, the positive attitude of the British public at the time of the First World War:
- helped recruitment in 1914
- meant conscription was tolerated from 1916
- kept morale high despite hardships.

Activities

3 Write a list of ways in which social attitudes have changed the treatment of troops since 1900.

Technology also affected the British experience of warfare.

For example, during the First World War, the dominance of machine guns accounted for many British casualties on the Western Front.

Activities

4 Write a list of ways in which technology changed the civilian experience of war during the Second World War.

Significant factors

Some factors are more important than others because they have more impact or significance.

For example, in the First World War, the use of gas attacks was new, but it was not significant. Wind made them unreliable and gas masks were an easy solution.

Activities

5 Write a brief explanation of why tanks were not a significant factor in the First World War.

Nuclear weapons were a significant factor in shaping warfare after 1945.

Activities

6 Write a brief explanation of why nuclear weapons were a significant factor in the type of wars fought by major powers since 1945.

Source B: A British convoy moving troops and supplies during the First World War.

 examzone
Build better answers

What do Sources B and C show about changes in the way troops are moved since 1900?
Explain your answer using Sources B and C and your own knowledge.   (8 marks)

■ **Basic, Level 1**
Answer makes general comments about change, but gives no supporting evidence from the sources or own knowledge.
OR
Answer ignores the idea of change and just describes features of troop movement.

● **Good, Level 2**
Answer describes changes and illustrates these from the sources or own knowledge.

▲ **Excellent, Level 3**
Answer makes an inference (explains a change which is not obvious from the sources) and supports this from the sources and own knowledge.

Source C: Troop movement during the Iraq War in 2003.

Warfare timeline

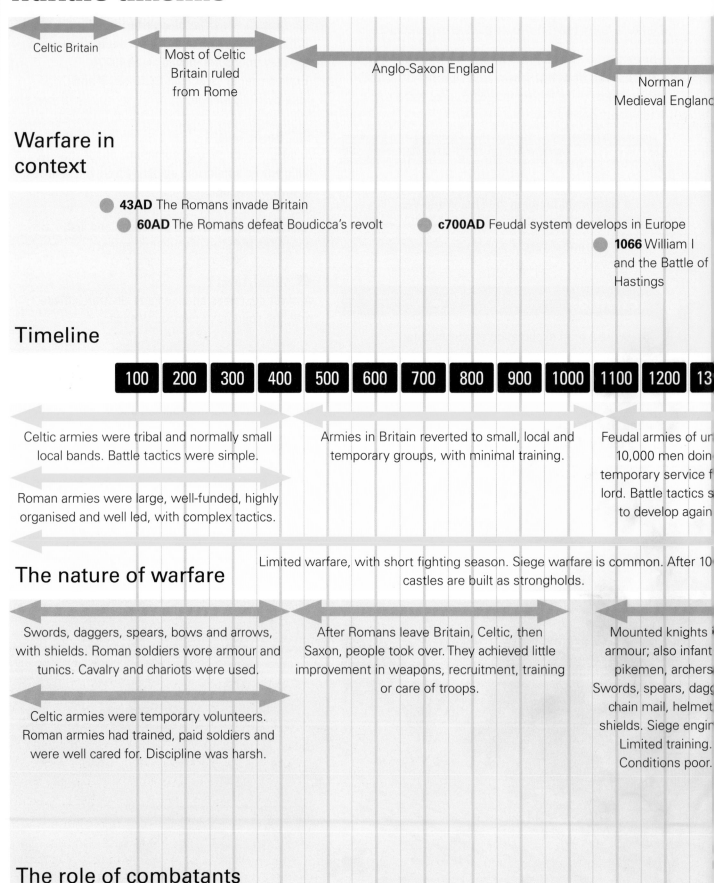

Celtic Britain

Most of Celtic Britain ruled from Rome

Anglo-Saxon England

Norman / Medieval England

Warfare in context

43AD The Romans invade Britain

60AD The Romans defeat Boudicca's revolt

c700AD Feudal system develops in Europe

1066 William I and the Battle of Hastings

Timeline

| 100 | 200 | 300 | 400 | 500 | 600 | 700 | 800 | 900 | 1000 | 1100 | 1200 | 13 |

Celtic armies were tribal and normally small local bands. Battle tactics were simple.

Armies in Britain reverted to small, local and temporary groups, with minimal training.

Feudal armies of un 10,000 men doin temporary service f lord. Battle tactics s to develop again

Roman armies were large, well-funded, highly organised and well led, with complex tactics.

The nature of warfare

Limited warfare, with short fighting season. Siege warfare is common. After 10 castles are built as strongholds.

Swords, daggers, spears, bows and arrows, with shields. Roman soldiers wore armour and tunics. Cavalry and chariots were used.

After Romans leave Britain, Celtic, then Saxon, people took over. They achieved little improvement in weapons, recruitment, training or care of troops.

Mounted knights armour; also infant pikemen, archers Swords, spears, dagg chain mail, helmet shields. Siege engin Limited training. Conditions poor.

Celtic armies were temporary volunteers. Roman armies had trained, paid soldiers and were well cared for. Discipline was harsh.

The role of combatants

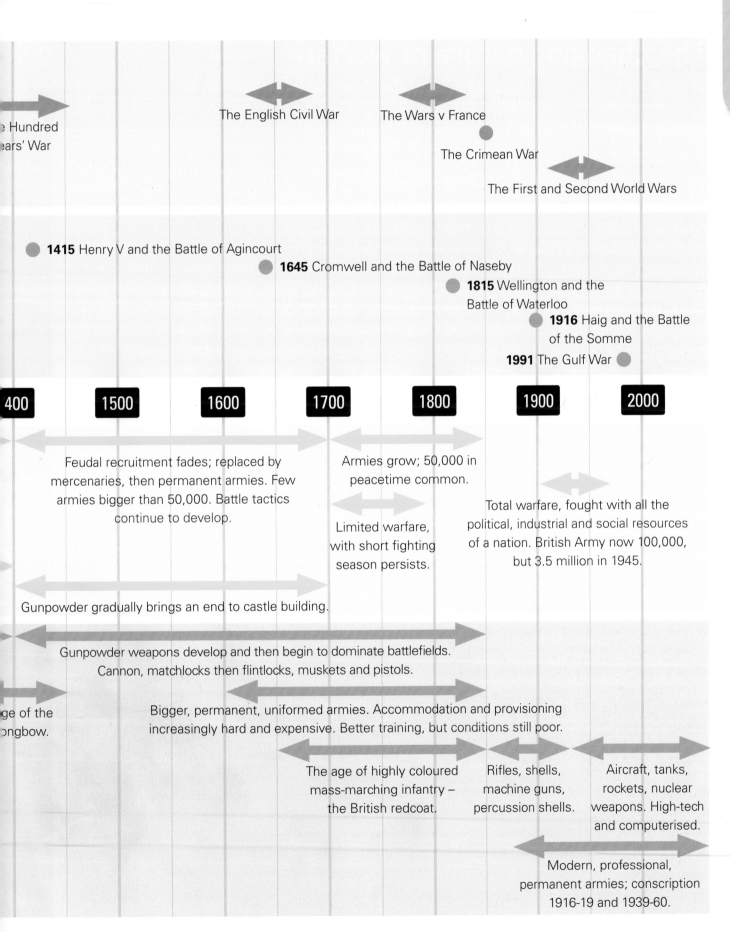

The English Civil War

The Wars v France

The Crimean War

The First and Second World Wars

e Hundred
ears' War

1415 Henry V and the Battle of Agincourt

1645 Cromwell and the Battle of Naseby

1815 Wellington and the Battle of Waterloo

1916 Haig and the Battle of the Somme

1991 The Gulf War

400 **1500** **1600** **1700** **1800** **1900** **2000**

Feudal recruitment fades; replaced by mercenaries, then permanent armies. Few armies bigger than 50,000. Battle tactics continue to develop.

Armies grow; 50,000 in peacetime common.

Limited warfare, with short fighting season persists.

Total warfare, fought with all the political, industrial and social resources of a nation. British Army now 100,000, but 3.5 million in 1945.

Gunpowder gradually brings an end to castle building.

Gunpowder weapons develop and then begin to dominate battlefields. Cannon, matchlocks then flintlocks, muskets and pistols.

ge of the
ongbow.

Bigger, permanent, uniformed armies. Accommodation and provisioning increasingly hard and expensive. Better training, but conditions still poor.

The age of highly coloured mass-marching infantry – the British redcoat.

Rifles, shells, machine guns, percussion shells.

Aircraft, tanks, rockets, nuclear weapons. High-tech and computerised.

Modern, professional, permanent armies; conscription 1916-19 and 1939-60.

KnowZone
The changing nature of warfare

Introduction

For your Unit 1 exam you answer five questions.

Question 1 will ask you what two sources show about some aspect of change. The two sources will normally be from two different periods

Question 2 will give you a choice of two aspects of warfare. It will ask you to choose one and describe its key features.

Question 3 will give you a source. It will ask you how useful that source is to the historian investigating a certain aspect of warfare.

You then answer **either** Question 4 **or** Question 5.

Both these questions will ask you to consider the causes of continuity or change in warfare.

Finally, you answer **either** Question 6 **or** Question 7. Both these questions will ask you to analyse and evaluate the change which took place in an aspect of warfare. They will also test your spelling, punctuation and grammar.

As there is only a limited choice of questions in the exam, you need to make sure you have good knowledge of all the topics in the specification and that you are prepared for the different types of question that are asked.

Self-evaluation checklist

What you should know for the exam.

Generally, c50 to the present day:

- what changed in warfare; how much it changed; did this bring progress
- the soldiers and weapons used; how this affected the type of warfare fought
- examples of key battles
- the influence of key individuals
- how soldiers were recruited, trained, moved, supplied and cared for
- what factors or developments prevented or caused change, particularly society, governments, industrialisation, technology

c50AD to c1350:

- Boudicca's revolt and the Battle of Hastings; Boudicca and William I
- the weapons and role of infantry, archers and knights
- siege technology and castle design
- how the feudal system affected warfare

1350 to 1700:

- the battles at Agincourt and Naseby; Henry V and Oliver Cromwell

- the longbow, cannon and muskets and their impact
- the decline of feudal armies; mercenaries; the start of professional armies

1700 to 1900:

- the Waterloo campaign and the Crimean War; Wellington and Florence Nightingale
- rifles, cannon, bullets and shells; decline of cavalry
- the impact of industrialisation and improved technology, transport and communication
- impact of war reporting and public opinion
- the beginnings of a professional army; improved medical care

1900 to the present day:

- the Western Front, the Battle of the Somme and Haig; the Gulf War
- tanks, gas, improved artillery, motorised transport, aerial warfare, computer and high-tech equipment, nuclear weapons
- propaganda, conscription, National Service, the professional army, Territorial Army, Royal Logistics Corps, Royal Army Medical Corps
- war reporting; its impact on the public and troops

What do Sources C (page 34) and E (page 53) tell you about changes in the way troops were trained in Britain? Explain your answer, using the sources and your own knowledge. (8 marks)

Student answer

Training became better.

The training in Source C shows knights practising using lances.

The training became more organised. Source C shows knights practising on their own. But, in Source E, the soldiers are being trained to take discipline from an officer and to work as a group. There is more of a plan to training in Source E.

Comments

The first statement is not supported by reference to the sources or own knowledge.

The second statement has nothing to do with change.

The third statement is better. It describes a change and gives evidence for it from the source.

To improve, the student needs to:
- describe more changes shown in the sources
- support statements with own knowledge
- work out the extent of change which the sources infer.

To improve, the student added:

I know that knights, like those in Source C, only trained occasionally in mock fights or tournaments. But regular training like that shown in Source E meant that, by the 18th century, armies used the same drill books and could march into battle in columns at 75 steps per minute and then, without pausing, wheel into firing lines.

I can infer from all this that, from 1700 onwards, training allowed generals to use more complex tactics. Wellington's troops must have been trained to be better disciplined than Henry V's army.

Build better answers

The boxes below show weapons used in warfare. Choose **one** and describe the key features of the weapon and its impact on warfare. (6 marks)

The musket 1450–1700	The machine gun 1860–1918

Student answer

The machine gun was very effective, it fired many bullets.

It helped troops against attack.

It changed the way battles were fought.

Comments

The student has correctly identified some key features of the impact of the machine gun.

However, to improve, the student needs to give more relevant, detailed information which will illustrate each key feature.

Improvements

To improve, the student wrote:

The machine gun was very effective. Gatling guns were introduced from the USA which could fire 150 bullets per minute.

It helped troops defend against attack. By 1914, the British used Maxim machine guns which had the firepower of 100 rifles. A single machine gunner could mow down many attackers.

It changed the way battles were fought. Machine guns stalled attacking troops in 1914; they dug into trenches; the result was stalemate on the Western Front.

examzone

How useful is Source A (page 14) to the historian who is investigating Boudicca's revolt in 60AD. Use Source A and your own knowledge to explain your answer. (8 marks)

Student answer	Comments	Improvements
There's definitely information in here about why Boudicca rebelled – and it's detailed - so the historian would find it useful.	The student says any information is useful whether it can be trusted or not and that all primary sources are reliable. These points are not entirely accurate.	To improve, the student added: The source therefore explains why Boudicca rebelled and I think a historian could trust it.
It is a primary source written at the time so it must be reliable and the historian should use it.	The third statement is better because it shows that the content in the source is relevant to the question the historian is researching.	The reason I think the source can be trusted is that it was written by a Roman. You wouldn't expect a Roman to make up mistreatment of the Britons by Roman soldiers, so it is more likely to be true.
The source is useful because it covers what the historian wants to know – why Boudicca rebelled. It was because she and her daughters were whipped and ravished. The Britons were treated like slaves.	To improve, the answer must also consider questions like the provenance of the source and decide whether it is reliable or not. They should also use of own knowledge.	The source contains relevant information which can be trusted, so it would be useful.

Why was there stalemate for so long on the Western Front in the First World War? (12 marks)
You may use the following in your answer: • Defensive weapons • The tactics used by generals
You must also include information of your own.

Student answer	Comments	Improvements
The German attack on France in 1914 was stopped short of Paris. Neither side could defeat the other so they dug trenches.	The answer mainly describes what happened rather than explains why it happened.	Extract from improved answer: The German attack was stopped because their infantry could not advance; defence was stronger than attack. Attacking infantry were mown down by machine gun and rifle fire.
When one side attacked, the other side fought off the attack with powerful defensive weapons.	To improve, the answer needs to:	Armies could dig in and defend; but neither side had weapons to attack and capture enemy positions, so it was stalemate.
So the two sides just fired artillery shells at each other and launched new attacks with even more men, e.g. when the British attacked at the Somme.	• give reasons why there was stalemate and why it lasted so long • give relevant information from the source to support those reasons • use own knowledge to add to the information from the source.	The stalemate went on so long because generals kept attacking enemy defences with artillery and gas. But they did not work because defenders used dug-outs and gas masks. Generals attacked with more men and tanks, but the tanks were not reliable. New tactics didn't work so the stalemate went on until 1918.
They tried new weapons, such as tanks and gas, but the stalemate went on until 1918.		

How much did the British Army change in the 19th century? Explain your answer. (16 marks + 3 for SPaG)
You may use the following in your answer.
- Improved medical care.
- Cardwell's army reforms.

You must also include information of your own.

Student answer

The British Army changed a lot during the 19th century.

In 1872, the government reformed the army. They started a better way of appointing officers and soldiers were better treated. They were also given better weapons.

Medical treatment for troops improved too. Hospitals got cleaner and nursing got cleaner and nursing got better.

Comments

The first statement is vague, because it is not supported by relevant material.

The second and third statements are correct but still only make general points. There is little supporting detail.

The candidate mentions improvements, but does not say how much of a change they were.

In addition, the candidate has only made points prompted by the stimulus in the question. There are no changes from own knowledge.

To improve we need more:
- changes – including from own knowledge
- detail given for each change, e.g. details of better weapons, details of medical improvements, etc
- analysis of how much of a change these improvements were.

We then need to see a conclusion as to the extent of change shown.

The candidate communicates meaning clearly. There is also good spelling and punctuation. They should continue to take care with spelling, punctuation and grammar.

Improvements

There was little change before 1850. There was no progress in weapons or tactics. Some ideas – like the telegraph for sending messages - were ignored. In some ways the Army went backwards, for example, it got smaller. But there was much more change after 1850.

[Cardwell's reforms explained in detail.]

[Medical reforms explained in detail.]

The weapons of the British Army improved. They began to use the Maxim machine gun and the Martini-Henry breech-loading rifle. This was a very important change. For example, at the Alma river, in the Crimea, British rifle fire killed the Russians before their old fashioned muskets came within range.

Military transport also improved. The British Army in the Crimea used a railway. This was a big change; it moved troops 15 times faster than marching.

So the changes after 1850 in recruitment, organisation and weapons were significant because it made the British Army more efficient and professional.

The impact of war on Britain

Introduction

War changed British society from 1903-1954, especially during the First World War, 1914–1918, and the Second World War, 1939–1945.

Both these wars were different in nature from any previous wars.

Blitz

They changed:

- the impact of war on civilians
- the role of government and the way society was organised
- social attitudes.

You will also look at the factors influencing these developments.

The impact of war on civilians changed. For the first time, the enemy brought the war direct to Britain through air raids, including the Zeppelin raids of the First World War and the Blitz of 1940–1941.

It was total war. The government took a far more active role in organising society to help the war effort. New government measures ranged from rationing to the **evacuation** of schoolchildren and from propaganda to taking over control of whole industries.

As a result of wars, society was reorganised to make social provision such as medicine and education more available to all the people. This was achieved in two bouts of reforms, 1906-11 and 1945-51.

Social attitudes changed, too, particularly about women's role in society, in politics and in the workplace.

Overall, war had a profound effect on Britain between the years 1903 to 1954.

Women

WOMEN OF BRITAIN
COME INTO THE FACTORIES
ASK AT ANY EMPLOYMENT EXCHANGE FOR ADVICE AND FULL DETAILS

1904	1906–11	1914	1915	1916	1918
Official report shows concern about health and fitness of army recruits.	Government social reforms, e.g. to help children and the sick.	Outbreak of the First World War. Government introduces the Defence of the Realm Act (DORA).	Lloyd George becomes Minister of Munitions and encourages the employment of women workers.	Government introduces conscription.	The Representation the Peoples Act gives the vote to women over the age of 30.

Activities

1 Work in pairs.
   a) Sit back to back.
   b) One of you should describe the poster on this page to the other, who should make a sketch based on your description (rather than what you can remember from looking at it in your textbook!).
   c) Compare your version of the poster with the original.
2 Why do you think this poster discouraged waste?
3 How did the artist get his message across?

FASCINATING FACT

During both the wars the government tried to discourage excessive drinking of alcohol because of its effects on the workforce and therefore on the war effort – it caused lateness and frequent absenteeism. Lloyd George was particularly concerned about the impact on munitions workers in 1915. He reduced pub opening hours and had beer watered down. Some workers composed a song, 'Lloyd George's Beer', which criticised these measures. Despite government laws, not surprisingly, beer consumption actually increased during both conflicts.

1920s	1928	1939	1940	1941	1945–51
Some young women known as 'flappers' begin to wear short skirts and smoke and drink in public.	Women over the age of 21 are given the vote.	Outbreak of the Second World War. Government again introduces conscription. Voluntary evacuation of schoolchildren.	Government introduces the Essential Work Order (EWO).	Conscription of women into the labour force.	Following the Beveridge Report (1942), government social reforms, e.g. in health and education.

5.1 Air raids and bombing

Learning outcomes

By the end of this section you should be able to:

● describe the bombing of Britain during the First and Second World Wars

● describe the propaganda and censorship used during the First and Second World Wars

● explain the impact of bombing, censorship and propaganda on British civilians.

British civilians experienced a new threat during the First and Second World Wars – direct attacks from the enemy in the form of bombing raids.

First World War Zeppelin attacks

From January 1915 Zeppelins began to make bombing raids on British cities. These were airships filled with hydrogen that could fly at 4,600 metres (15,000 feet) – well above British fighter planes, which could fly at a maximum height of only 13,000 feet. There were 51 Zeppelin raids between 1915 and 1916. Their main target was London, where strict **blackout** regulations, involving the switching off of lights so that German bombers could not see their targets, and other precautions were enforced.

Source A: A nurse, Ursula Somervell, kept a diary in which she described Zeppelin raids.

We had a pretty terrifying time with Zepps again last night. We were woken at 10.30 by a terrific noise of bombs, aircraft, guns etc. all apparently around us. We rushed on dressing gowns, said a prayer and got downstairs as quickly as we could. There was a tremendous glare in the sky to the west of us, which came from a big fire in Wood Street. I believe most of the damage was done on Oxford Street. A lot of people were killed in a motorbus. It would have been terrifying to be out, as I believe there is a fearful panic in the streets. I am afraid there must have been many casualties.

Source B: Letter, August 1915, describing a Zeppelin raid.

I turned out of bed and looking up above us saw two Zepps. The searchlights were on them and they looked as if they were among the stars. They were very high and like cigar-shaped constellations they kept pulling away from the searchlights, only to be caught again. It was lovely.

Activities

1 What can you learn from Source A about the effects of a Zeppelin raid?

2 Does Source B have the same views? Explain.

The British public soon became angry because of the apparent lack of defence against the Zeppelin. The first Zeppelin was not shot down until 3 September 1916, and the successful pilot was awarded the Victoria Cross.

However, the Zeppelin attacks stopped in 1917 due to improved British defences, including the use of searchlights, which meant that the Zeppelins could be easily spotted. Moreover, if a Zeppelin was hit, it burst into flames. The crew had little chance of surviving (see Source C). In all, 57 Zeppelin raids on Britain killed 564 civilians and injured a further 1,370 people.

Source C: A painting of 1917, based on eyewitness accounts, of the shooting down of a Zeppelin.

Source D: Sybil Morrison describes the shooting down of a Zeppelin, in an article in a local newspaper, 3 September 1916.

> It was like a big cigar I suppose and all of the bag part had caught fire. And it seemed to come floating down slowly instead of falling down with a bang. We knew there were about 60 people in it and that they were being roasted to death. Of course, you weren't supposed to feel any pity for your enemies. Nevertheless, I was appalled to see the good, kind-hearted British people dancing about in the streets at the sight of 60 people being burned alive – clapping and cheering and singing.

Activities

3 What can you learn from Source D about the shooting down of the Zeppelin?

4 Devise two different propaganda captions for the painting Source C:
   - one for use in Germany
   - one for use in Britain.

5 Work in a group for the following task. Study Sources A–D. Put together a newspaper report on a Zeppelin raid. Include:
   a) a catchy headline
   b) a description of the damage caused
   c) different eyewitness accounts from civilians of the raid and the shooting down of a Zeppelin.

German bombing raids, 1916–1917

In May 1917 the Germans began to use aircraft known as Gotha IV bombers (see Source E) and by the end of the war there had been 57 raids. These did not cause as much damage as the ones during the Second World War would because the bombs they carried weighed only 100 kilograms and were capable of destroying only a few houses.

Nevertheless, the raids did have a dramatic effect on British civilians, as they had not experienced anything like this before. Moreover, the loss of life was high, as there were few ways that people could protect themselves since there were no shelters. For example, in June 1917, 20 Gothas carried out a bombing raid on London in which 162 civilians were killed and 432 injured. In total, 850 people were killed in Gotha raids during the First World War.

The public outcry against these raids forced the government to bring into operation better searchlights, balloons and anti-aircraft guns. As a result, 7 out of 19 Gotha bombers were shot down in the raid of 19 May 1918. The Germans could not afford such losses and called off further raids.

Source E: A photograph of a Gotha IV bomber, 1917.

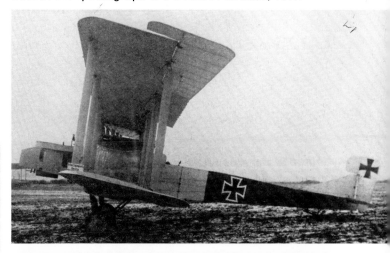

Activities

6 In pairs, study Sources A–E. Make a copy of the following table.

	Value	Limitations
Diary (Source A)	First-hand account that gives immediate reactions to the attack. Evidence of panic caused.	Only one account of one reaction. May not be typical.
Letter (Source B)		
Painting (Source C)		
Newspaper report (Source D)		
Photograph (Source E)		

- One of you should give examples of the value of these different types of sources.
- The other should give limitations. An example has been done for you.
- Try to use evidence from the sources themselves not from your knowledge of the topic.

5.2 The Blitz

During the Second World War the German bombing raids were far more serious than in the First World War because advances in technology meant that more powerful bombers and more destructive bombs could be used. These attacks were known as the Blitz, which is a shortened version of the German word *blitzkrieg*, which means lightning war. The German raids, which began on 7 September 1940, targeted British towns and cities with the aim of destroying civilian morale, forcing the British into submission (see Source A) and undermining British armaments production.

Source A: Field Marshal Kesselring explained, in his memoirs written in **1957**, the aims of the Blitz.

> Our main assignments now were the disturbance of production and incoming supplies. The underlying purpose was to slow down British armament production and begin a full-scale economic war. To destroy civilian morale we began 'reprisal raids' at the same time.

British towns and cities suffered heavy bombing from the autumn of 1940 to May 1941, with the targets usually military or industrial centres.

From May 1941 the attacks became less and less frequent as Hitler diverted resources to the invasion of the Soviet Union.

- The primary target was London, which was bombed every night from 7 September to 2 November 1940, especially the docks and factories of the East End. Some 12,500 people died during December 1940.
- In the south, Bristol, Southampton and Plymouth were also targeted. The naval base at Portsmouth was the target for a massive attack on 10 January 1940 where 930 civilians were killed and 3,000 injured.
- Coventry was badly hit by a series of raids in November 1940, with the Germans using incendiary bombs to increase the damage caused. People were so terrified that they fled from the city each night, sleeping with relatives or in open fields in nearby countryside (see Source B and Source C).
- In the north, Manchester was attacked in December 1940 while Liverpool suffered its worst raid – from over 500 bombers – in May 1941.
- Glasgow and the Clyde shipyard towns were hit hard in the spring of 1941.
- Belfast suffered badly in April and May 1941. At least 1,000 people were killed and 150,000 were made homeless.

Source B: A street in Coventry the morning after the raid of 14 November 1940.

Source C: From *Mrs Milburn's Diaries*. She describes Coventry about six weeks after the November 1940 raids.

> It was not long after we reached the outskirts of Coventry that we saw the evidence of the raiders' visit, and as we drew nearer the damage became greater. We went along Trinity Street and the devastated Rex Cinema, bombed twice over, and the other buildings near with all the windows blown out and boarded up. The old stone Grammar School had lost its windows, too, and was pitted and blackened and the Hospital seemed much more damaged than we expected. It was deliberate bombing of non-military objectives guaranteed, as the German brutes think, to terrify the ordinary citizen into fright and submission.

Source D: A photograph of damaged houses in a street in Walthamshaw, London, September 1944 after a V1 attack. This photograph was censored.

Activities

1 What can you learn from Source A about the aims of the Blitz?

2 Many people were more upset by the later V1 and V2 raids than the Blitz of 1940–1941. Give two reasons for this.

3 Study Source D. Why do you think it was censored?

V1 and V2 raids

There were further air attacks in 1944–1945 from V1 and V2 missiles. About 6,000 V1 bombs reached targets in Britain, causing 20,000 casualties and great damage to houses (see Source D). The V1 was a flying bomb powered by a rocket engine and was nicknamed the doodlebug because of the noise it made. It flew towards the target area and then came down wherever it ran out of fuel. People on the ground could hear the engine cut out and then a shriek as the bomb hurtled to the ground.

The V2 was a more serious threat because it was so fast, flying at supersonic speed, and it could not be shot down or seen. It was the first guided missile. About 500 V2s hit London between September 1944 and March 1945, causing over 9,000 casualties.

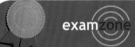
Build better answers

What impact did German bombing have on civilians in Britain during the Second World War? Explain your answer, using Source C and your own knowledge. **(10 marks)**

■ **Basic, Level 1**
Simple statements with no detail, either from Source C or from own knowledge. E.g. *Source C describes the damage in Coventry* or *Thousands of people were killed in the Blitz*.

● **Good, Level 2**
Statements supported by detail from Source C and/or own knowledge. E.g. *Public facilities were damaged, for example, Source C says the cinema, school and hospital were damaged in Coventry*.

▲ **Excellent, Level 3**
Answer gives a sustained explanation of the impact of bombing, using relevant details from the source and precise own knowledge: e.g. it mentions damage to munitions factories, industry, public facilities, houses, and casualties and morale, with lots of relevant detail.

103

Effects on industry

Bombing of industrial targets was generally not effective because precision was needed. Some factories were isolated, unlike housing estates, and they could easily be missed at night. Most factories were able to resume production within two to three days of being hit.

Effects on civilians

The bombing affected everyday life, especially the blackout and the use of air raid shelters. Homes, shops, businesses and even trains and cars had to 'black out' to avoid providing a target for the German bombers. People did eventually get used to operating in the blackout, although the number of car accidents doubled during this period.

The government gave out air raid shelters before and in the early months of the war. Some 2 million **Anderson shelters** were provided. These definitely saved thousands of lives by protecting people from shrapnel and flying glass. However, they offered little protection from falling masonry and many poorer people did not have gardens in which to build them.

In 1941, therefore, 500,000 Morrison shelters were provided, which could be set up indoors.

Only 27 per cent of people used these private shelters. The rest used public shelters or 'self-chosen' shelters, such as the London Underground (see Source E). At the beginning of the war, the government had rejected the use of the Underground for shelter, but the force of public demand made them change their mind. In September 1940 they opened up 80 stations. People felt safer in these stations and enjoyed the comradeship and shared sacrifices.

Surveys suggested that only 40 per cent of Londoners regularly took shelter. This accounts for the high casualty rates. By June 1941, 43,000 civilians had been killed and 1.5 million homes lost due to German bombing raids.

On 10 September 1940 a bomb hit Buckingham Palace while the king and queen were at Windsor. Even though the damage was slight, people were impressed with the attitude of the Royal Family who insisted on staying at Buckingham Palace throughout the war.

Source E: People sleeping in an Underground station in London during the Blitz.

Activities

4 Source E was used for propaganda. Write a suitable caption for the photograph.

The 'Blitz Spirit'

The Blitz provided the media, especially newspapers, with the ideal opportunity to portray the Nazis as evil murderers who must be defeated (see Source C on page 103). Moreover, at first sight, the bombing appears to have been a failure. Far from destroying morale and bombing Britain into submission, it had the opposite effect and made the British people even more determined to stand up to Hitler. People seemed cheerful in the face of great hardships and determined to get on with everyday life. The underground was full of people singing as they sheltered from the bombs.

However, high morale was not felt by everyone, everywhere. **Censorship** and propaganda was very effective in playing down the negative (and quite understandable) reactions of individuals or groups who were badly affected by the bombings (see Source G).

Source F: A cartoon from the *Daily Express*, November 1940.

"IS IT ALL RIGHT NOW, HENRY?"
"YES, NOT EVEN SCRATCHED."

Source G: Extract from a local government report on the East End of London, September 1940.

The whole story of last weekend has been one of unplanned hysteria. The newspaper versions of life going on normally in the East End are greatly distorted. There was no bread, no milk, no telephones. There is no humour or laughter. There was thus every excuse for people to be distressed. There was no understanding in the huge government buildings of central London for the tiny crumbled streets of massed populations.

Source H: Extract from an official report into the effects of the bombing of Portsmouth, January 1941.

By 6.00 p.m. all traffic is moving northwards. The movement begins at 3.30 p.m. and continues to dusk. The people are making for the bridge on the main road out of Portsmouth in order to sleep in the northern suburbs, the surrounding hills, or towns and villages in the radius of twenty miles. One night it was estimated that 90,000 people left the city. Looting and wanton destruction have reached almost alarming proportions. The effect on morale is bad and there is a general feeling of desperation.

Source I: From the autobiography of T. Clarke, a special constable in the Blitz, published in 1974.

Of the Blitz Spirit I shall write little. We in 'S' Division were luckier than many London police, but we had our fill of its cruelty and horror, and its sickening destructiveness, its white dusty filth, and its peculiar stink of fresh decay. Just these few words and it begins to depress me again.

Activities

5 Study Sources G, H and I. Do they support the idea of the 'Blitz Spirit'? Explain your answer.

6 'Although less in number, the Zeppelin raids of the First World War were more devastating for the British people than the Blitz of 1940–1941.' Discuss.

5.3 Civilian volunteers

Thousands of men and women, alarmed by the threat of war and then by its outbreak in 1939, volunteered to defend the Home Front.

Air Raid Precautions (ARP)

As early as 1937, as the danger of war increased, the Air Raid Precautions Act was passed. This gave local authorities the responsibility to:

- build air raid shelters
- provide gas masks
- recruit and train volunteer wardens.

By the end of the Second World War, 1.4 million civilians had volunteered to become ARP wardens, to help defend the Home Front from the horrors of German bombing. ARP wardens:

- built air raid shelters
- distributed 38 million gas masks to the public
- enforced blackout regulations
- kept order in air raid shelters and at bomb sites
- reported fires and unexploded bombs.

Some were full-time and paid - £3 per week for men, £2 for women. Most were unpaid, part-time volunteers. At first, each warden was issued only a tin helmet, a gas mask, a whistle and, for gas attacks, a rattle. But, from 1940 onwards, they had uniforms.

In 1941, the ARP was incorporated into the **Civil Defence** along with fire-fighting services.

At first, ARP wardens were figures of derision, enforcing regulations nobody thought necessary. However, during the Blitz, they became heroes. By 1945, almost 7,000 Civil Defence staff had been killed on duty.

Emergency services

Civilians also joined other wartime emergency services. For example:

- the Auxiliary Ambulance Service, whose youngest member was Ennis Smith, aged 16
- the Auxiliary Fire Service, mostly unpaid volunteers, also heroes of the Blitz
- reserve policemen and policewomen.

Source A: British Government circular entitled 'Air Raid Warnings', 1939.

> When air raids are threatened, warning will be given in towns by sirens, or hooters which will be sounded in some places by short blasts and in others by a warbling note, changing every few seconds. The warnings may be given by the police or air-raid wardens blowing short blasts on whistles.
>
> When you hear the warning, take cover at once. Remember that most of the injuries in an air raid are caused not by direct hits by bombs but by flying fragments of debris or by bits of shells. Stay under cover until you hear the sirens sounding continuously for two minutes on the same note which is the signal "Raiders Passed".

Source B: An ARP warden and his horse, both wearing gas masks, 1940.

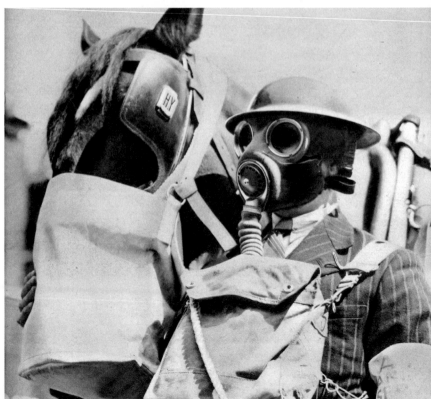

The Home Guard

By 1940, there was serious danger of a German invasion. Anthony Eden, the Secretary of State for War, launched an appeal for a volunteer military force to help defend the country. See Source D.

Within 24 hours, 250,000 men had volunteered to join Eden's Local Defence Volunteers (LDV). Within 6 weeks, 1.5 million men had volunteered.

It was an unpaid, part-time force. At first, there were no uniforms and few weapons. The public were asked to volunteer whatever weapons they had. Within months, 20,000 weapons were offered.

But the weapons were a motley collection; so were some of the volunteers. Volunteers had to be between 17 and 65 years old and unfit for regular military service – because they were medically unfit, in a reserved occupation or just too old. As a result, the LDV was soon dubbed 'Dad's Army'.

However, in July 1940, Winston Churchill changed the name to the Home Guard. Weapons started to arrive from the USA and from Canada. Uniforms were issued, military ranks organised and a code of discipline issued.

By June 1941, 1.6 million men were under arms in the Home Guard. By 1943, they had their own anti-aircraft batteries and some were credited with destroying German aircraft and V1 flying bombs.

Women were not admitted to the Home Guard. However, the Women's Home Guard Auxiliaries was formed in 1942 to perform administrative Home Guard Duties and unofficial Women's Home Defence units were formed in many areas.

Source C: A member of the Home Guard, c1943.

Source D: Anthony Eden, radio broadcast, 14 May 1940.

> We want large numbers of men in Great Britain, who are British subjects, between the ages of seventeen and sixty-five, to come forward now and offer their services. The name of the new Force which is now to be raised will be 'The Local Defence Volunteers'. This name describes its duties in three words. It must be understood that this is, so to speak, a spare-time job, so there will be no need for any volunteer to abandon his present occupation.

Source E: Anthony Eden, Memoirs, 1965.

> I had expected the response to this appeal to be prompt. In fact it was overwhelming, the first recruit arriving within four minutes of the end of the broadcast.
>
> The Local Defence Volunteers acted as a catalyst, giving point to the nation's will to resist. The volunteers recorded long periods of service… with only one reward, the knowledge that 'The Home Guard', as it was re-christened, closed a gap in our defences which must have been dangerous and could have been fatal.

Activities

1 What was the difference between the ARP and the Home Guard? Use details to explain your answer.

2 In the Second World War, the call to volunteer in the defence of the nation impacted on the lives of hundreds of thousands of British civilians.

Collect together five pieces of information to support this statement.

5.4 Propaganda and censorship

One way in which the First and Second World Wars impacted the lives of citizens in Britain was the use of propaganda and censorship.

From 1914 to 1918, and again from 1939 to 1945, the British public were submitted to a campaign of propaganda and a regime of censorship the like of which had never been seen before.

Propaganda

Propaganda is information which is used to promote certain ideas or attitudes.

- The information which is used may be lies, but this is not always the case.
- It may be limited or one-sided information.

Sometimes propaganda is used by governments to get public support for what they are doing.

Sometimes propaganda is spread by private individuals or organisations, such as newspapers, which have strong views of their own that they want to spread.

During the First and Second World Wars, the British government used propaganda to influence civilian attitudes to the wars. For example, government propaganda:
- encouraged people to volunteer to fight or to help in essential industries, in order to boost the war effort
- masked the scale of casualties and the defeats they suffered to stop people becoming discouraged
- tried to keep morale high during the hard times caused by bombing, rationing and evacuation.

Traditional media for propaganda included newspapers and posters. However, new media developed during the twentieth century which could be exploited for propaganda. These included cinema films and the radio.

Hate campaigns

One way that propaganda was used to persuade people that they were fighting for a just cause was to stir up hatred against the enemy. These 'hate campaigns' could be done either by publishing information or by starting rumours and leaving them to spread. For example, during the First World War:

- The government produced many posters that showed acts of brutality or atrocities supposedly carried out by the enemy. These were often exaggerations or outright lies. See Source A for an example.
- Government propagandists started hostile rumours about the enemy. For example, they invented the rumour that the Germans sent corpses to a factory that then used the human fat to make soap, candles and boot polish.

Such campaigns were used by both sides in the war.

Source A: A British poster from 1914.

HOW THE HUN HATES!

THE HUNS CAPTURED SOME OF OUR FISHERMEN IN THE NORTH SEA AND TOOK THEM TO SENNELAGER. THEY CHARGED THEM WITHOUT A SHRED OF EVIDENCE WITH BEING "MINE LAYERS". THEY ORDERED THEM TO BE PUNISHED WITHOUT A TRIAL.
THAT PUNISHMENT CONSISTED IN SHAVING ALL THE HAIR OFF ONE SIDE OF THE HEAD AND FACE.
THE HUNS THEN MARCHED THEIR VICTIMS THROUGH THE STREETS AND EXPOSED THEM TO THE JEERS OF THE GERMAN POPULACE.

BRITISH SAILORS! LOOK! READ! AND REMEMBER!

Censorship

Censorship was another way the First and Second World Wars impacted upon the lives of British civilians.

Censorship is limiting the flow of information to the public.

- It may involve preventing the release of any information about something.
- It may involve limiting information or keeping some information completely secret.

During the First and Second World Wars, the British government controlled information about the war which could reach the public in:

- soldiers' letters
- newspapers and magazines
- films in the cinema
- (Second World War only) radio broadcasts.

The reason for all this censorship was:

- to prevent bad news reaching the public which might have reduced morale
- to prevent information reaching the enemy which could have been used against us.

Sometimes the government directly censored information. For example:

- private letters were censored. During the Second World War, the British government employed about 10,000 people to censor information going through the Royal Mail. They would use scissors to cut out censored parts.
- the letters which soldiers sent home were all read and some information was taken out. For example, any information which mentioned casualties, revealed troop positions or gave information about intended attacks by British forces was deleted.
- newspapers which printed information which the government disapproved of could be shut down.

Sometimes the government indirectly censored information. For example, Britain entered the First World War in August 1914, but no British journalists were allowed to be at the war front until November 1916. This obviously limited the information which they could send home (see page 160 for details).

Sometimes the government urged the public to 'censor' themselves. For example, the public could accidentally give away information which might be helpful to the enemy – information about troop movements or factory production. So, during the Second World War for example, there was a campaign to persuade the public to be careful what information they passed on to others.

Source B: A British Second World War poster warning people to be careful what they said to others.

Activities

1 What is propaganda?
2 What is a hate campaign?
3 What is the purpose of propaganda like Source A?
4 What is censorship?
5 Is Source B a form of censorship?

5.5 Propaganda and censorship during the First World War

Censorship

In the first month of the First World War, August 1914, the Defence of the Realm Act was passed. Amongst other things, this gave the government the powers of censorship throughout the war.

This had an immediate impact upon civilians. For example, the only news about the war which newspapers could publish was news issued by the British Army headquarters or by government departments.

- Any newspaper using unauthorised information could be taken to court.
- Police sometimes threatened to confiscate the presses of printers who published anti-war papers. Pacifist newspapers, such as *The Call* and the *Tribunal*, were forced to close several times in 1917 and 1918.

Source A: An article from *The Nation*, May 1916. This journal was later banned.

> It is a domestic tragedy of the war that the country which went out to defend liberty is losing its own liberties one by one, and that the government which began by relying on public opinion as a great help has now come to fear and curtail it.

Censorship also meant that letters written by soldiers from the battlefront were censored by officials in the armed forces. The government felt that they just could not afford to let the British public know the full extend of bad news – or to risk information falling into enemy hands.

Source B: The prime minister, Lloyd George, in a private conversation with the editor of the *Manchester Guardian*, December 1917.

> If the people really knew the truth about the war, the war would be stopped tomorrow.
>
> But of course they don't – and can't – know. The correspondents don't write, and the censors would not pass, the truth.

Propaganda

Civilians were bombarded with propaganda in the early months of the war. The government was concerned that people would not support the war effort if they didn't believe it was a just war which could be won in a reasonable time. So, propaganda concentrated on criticising Germany and encouraging men to join the armed forces.

Rumours

The British government spread stories that the Germans were evil and had to be stopped. Often these were wildly exaggerated. For example, by the end of 1914, it was widely believed in Britain that the German armies in Belgium were bayoneting babies and murdering innocent civilians.

Newspapers

Even the newspapers which civilians read published wild stories. Several published artists' impressions of women being crucified and many others depicted Germans as evil.

Source C: An article in the *Accrington Observer*, 19 September 1914.

> In the towns and villages where the German army stop they begin by requisitioning food and drink, which they consume till they are drunk.
>
> Then… they seize the opportunity to decimate the population, pillage the houses, and then set them on fire. After a preliminary attack and massacre, they shut up the men in the church, and then order the women to return to their houses and to leave their doors open all night.

This campaign to turn the British against the Germans was so successful that Germans living in Britain were attacked and shops with German names were looted.

Posters

The government used posters for a range of reasons. For example, in 1917, German U-boat attacks seriously reduced Britain's imports. Posters urged the public to cut down, especially on food, and avoid wastage.

The government also used 'conscience posters', which were designed to shame young men into joining up. See Source D for an example.

Source D: A poster of December 1914. It followed a German naval raid on Scarborough.

Film

In 1914, a new means of informing and influencing the masses was provided by the cinema. By 1917, there were 4,500 cinemas in Britain.

A group of film companies formed The British Topical Committee for War Films and made films about the war to sell to the War Department. In 1916, their patriotic film *For the Empire* reached an audience of 9 million Britons. Their most famous film was called *The Battle of the Somme*. By this time, there was no hiding the reality of war from the public. So, amongst some staged shots, it also showed real scenes from the battle, including real casualties. By October 1916, it had been shown in 2,000 British cinemas. Sources E and F show its effect on civilians.

Source E: *Extract from How I Filmed the War by Geoffrey Malins, 1920.*

> The Somme film has caused a great sensation. I really thought that some of the dead scenes would offend the British public. And yet, why should they? They realised that it was their duty to see for themselves. Yes, the truth has at last dawned on the British public.

Source F: From the diary of Henry Rider Haggard, 27 September 1916.

> Today I went to see the Somme War Film. It is not a cheerful sight, but it does give a wonderful idea about the fighting at the front, especially of shelling and its effects. Also, it shows the marvellous courage and cheerfulness of our soldiers in every emergency.

Impact on civilians

Censorship and propaganda were very successful until 1916. Civilians generally supported the war, hated the Germans and believed that the war would soon be won. Men joined the armed forces in their droves.

Attitudes changed after 1916. Most were not against the war, but they were more critical. For example, they were angry about the tactics of generals on the Western Front.

This change was due to several factors:
- Soldiers brought home news of hardships on the Western Front.
- Casualties at the Battle of the Somme in 1916 – 58,000 on the first day alone – hardened attitudes.
- Stalemate on the Western Front meant that the war dragged on.

Activities

1. Explain how censorship affected civilians in the First World War.

2. List the different kinds of propaganda used in the First World War. Give one detailed example of each type.

3. What was the impact on civilians of the film *Battle of the Somme*?

5.6 Propaganda and censorship during the Second World War

The civilian experience of the Second World War was also shaped by propaganda and censorship.

On 4th September 1939, just one day after Britain joined the Second World War, the Ministry of Information was formed. It was the government's mouthpiece, its ministry of publicity and propaganda.

This prompt action showed how important it was to the government to take control of all forms of public information.

Censorship

The government again took emergency powers to ensure that the press did not publish and the BBC did not broadcast any information that might be helpful to the enemy or might lower morale.

Newspapers were carefully controlled and had to submit their articles to the censor before they were printed.

The BBC was never directly censored by the government, but it did take care to censor itself. Weather reports and the movements of the prime minister, Winston Churchill, for example, were never broadcast.

One newspaper, the *Daily Worker*, was banned in 1941 because it claimed that employers were making a lot of money out of the war by exploiting their workers.

Letters from soldiers at the front to loved ones in Britain were also carefully censored. Despite this, during the Second World War, some servicemen and women devised coded messages to avoid censorship.

- Some soldiers managed to send secret messages about where they were. The mention of 'yellow' meant North Africa and 'grey' meant Iceland, and so on.
- They also hinted when they might be going on leave. A letter to a girlfriend suggesting that she pick the cabbages meant that her husband or boyfriend was coming home.

Propaganda

Perhaps informed by the success of the film, *The Battle of the Somme*, during the First World War, the Ministry of Information decided against a policy of exaggerating victories or enemy activities.

Instead, the Ministry tried to get across the truth about the horrors of war and avoid giving the public any false hopes of victory.

Posters

Some early efforts by the Ministry seemed to be lecturing the public and were rather dull. See Source A for example. Government propaganda was most effective when it appealed to British humour. For example, there was a series of posters to stop people giving military information to spies. Posters were also used, as they had been in the First World War, to encourage people to conserve food or fuel. See Source B.

Source A: An early Second World War propaganda poster.

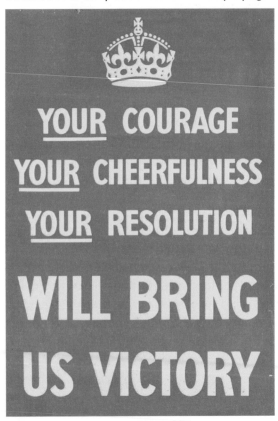

BETTER POT-LUCK

with Churchill today

THAN HUMBLE PIE

under Hitler tomorrow

DON'T WASTE FOOD!

Source B:
A humorous propaganda poster.

In addition, wartime propaganda made use of pictures of the prime minister, Winston Churchill, to inspire support for the war effort and boost morale. This was particularly important in the months after the defeat of France, when Britain's troops had to be evacuated from French soil at Dunkirk.

Radio and cinema - information

For civilians, the BBC was a key source of information. At first, only the Home Service was broadcast. But, in February 1940, a second channel began, the Forces Programme. By 1945, an estimated 25 million people were listening to the BBC's programmes worldwide.

The BBC had a reputation of reporting defeats as well as victories. But it sometimes put an optimistic slant on news. Some reports described Dunkirk as a heroic escape rather than the result of a defeat, for example. The BBC relied on the government for its information. In the Battle of Britain, in August 1940, the BBC first reported that 144 enemy aircraft were destroyed. This figure was later reduced to 69.

The cinema was also popular during the Second World War and was an important way for the government to publicise information about the war.

The Ministry of Information set up the Crown Film Unit to make official propaganda films, which were meant to boost the war effort and keep up morale. It made short, ten-minute documentaries such as *Fires Were Started* and *Listen to Britain*.

Film companies also made films like *In Which We Serve*. These generally showed heroic British troops or brave civilians working on the home front.

By the end of the war, cinemas were selling 25 million to 30 million tickets every week.

Radio and cinema – entertainment

Entertainment did a similar job to propaganda. Propaganda kept morale high; and so, by keeping the nation entertained, so did radio and cinema. It all helped the war effort.

- The radio was used to entertain workers in factories. Many programmes featured British and American singing artists, a favourite being *Music While You Work*.
- Dance programmes were also popular. In 1941, there were 21 on the radio every week – the most popular being Victor Sylvester's *Dancing Club*.
- Humour was also an important method of keeping up people's morale, especially humour that poked fun at the home front and government rules and regulations. For example, *It's That Man Again* (ITMA) enjoyed a huge following. It starred Tommy Handley, who played the Minister at the Ministry of Aggravation and Mysteries – a dig at the Ministry of Agriculture and Fisheries.

The cinema was also a useful escape from the harsh realities of wartime life. Many women, for example, needed to escape from thoughts of absent loved ones. Hollywood movies were shown because they generally provided glamour and romance.

The government also encouraged live entertainment through organisations such as ENSA (Entertainments National Service Association), which provided entertainment not only to the armed forces but also to the civilian population, including people at work and families sheltering from the Blitz in the London Underground.

Activities

1 Explain how censorship impacted on civilians during the Second World War.

2 List the different kinds of propaganda that were used in the Second World War. Give a detailed example of each type.

3 What purpose did entertainment perform for citizens in the Second World War?

5.7 Representations of the Blitz

Representations in history

Evidence of the past can come in many forms. For example, you could find, in an antique shop, a First World War medal issued for bravery, showing the head of the King on one side.

This would be a random source of evidence about the First World War. It would be up to you to decide what the medal told you. For example, it might tell you that Britain had a king during the First World War or that the British Army issued medals.

But the King's head on the medal is not random. *It is there for a purpose.* The government chose an image of the King for the medal in order to:
- give it official status
- emphasise the link between service in the Army and patriotic service for your country
- make it more desirable for soldiers.

In other words, *the King's head on the coin is a representation* – it is a source about the past which was created for a purpose.

Representations of the Blitz

Many sources of evidence about the Blitz are representations – sources in which the creator of the source had a distinct purpose in mind when they created the source. Look at Source A for example.

Source A is a photograph of people after a bombing raid during the Blitz.

Some of the information which you can find in the photograph is there by chance. You can see what houses were like in 1940, for example. This is called 'unwitting testimony'.

But some aspects of the photograph are included *for a reason*. The people shown are not burly men, for example; they are two women, two girls and a young boy. This makes it more likely we'll feel sorry for them.

Some aspects of the photograph are *excluded* for a reason. There is no damage to the houses shown, for example, no fires, no casualties.

Finally, the *tone* of the photograph is created. The children are shown as cheerful; the women as resolute, determined. They do not look like bomb victims; they have clean clothes and faces. This makes it more likely that the photograph was posed.

In other words, this is not random evidence of the past. It is a carefully constructed representation created for a purpose.

To help you determine the purpose of a source/ representation, you also need to use your own knowledge. We know that German bombing was going on at this time, so the purpose could be to show that the bombing is not destroying morale – civilians remain cheerful and resolute despite the bombing.

Source A: A newspaper photograph showing a family giving the 'thumbs up' sign and their bombed Anderson shelter in 1940.

Source B: A photograph used in a national newspaper showing the King and Queen outside Buckingham Palace the day after the raid of 10 September 1940.

Activities

1 Look at Source A. Take brief notes to answer the following questions:

*   What content has been carefully chosen to be included?

*   What content has been carefully excluded?

*   What tone has been carefully created for this photo? How has it been created?

*   Look at page 104. What knowledge does that give you about the air raid of 10th September 1940 which is relevant to this representation?

*   Do you think it is relevant that this photo was being shown in a newspaper?

These are important questions for deciding the purpose of a representation. You are now ready to tackle the Build Better Answers exercise, which relates to Source B.

Build better answers

Study Source B. What was the purpose of this representation? Explain your answer, using Source B and your own knowledge.   (8 marks)

◼ **Basic, Level 1**

A valid purpose stated, but with no support from the source or own knowledge.

● **Good, Level 2**

A valid purpose stated with support from the source and own knowledge.

▲ **Excellent, Level 3**

A valid purpose explained, using an analysis of the representation and supporting evidence from the source and own knowledge.

Summary

*   Bombing was a feature of the First World War and a major factor, including the Blitz, in several British cities in the Second World War.

*   Propaganda and censorship were used by the government to control the information civilians received during the wars.

*   Propaganda, censorship and bombing had a big effect on the lives and the morale of civilians during wartime.

6.1 Government organisation for war

Learning outcomes

By the end of this section you should be able to:

- describe some of the effects of government action on society during both world wars
- explain the part played by women in the armed services and workforce
- understand the part played by rationing and evacuation
- evaluate sources for reliability.

Activities

1 Study Source A, which was used for propaganda.
   a) Why was it chosen to be used for propaganda?
   b) Write a caption for the photograph.
2 What do DORA and EPA stand for?
3 Give two examples of the powers used by the government during the two wars.

Overview

The powers of the British government were greatly extended during the course of the two world wars.

Government powers

The government had very wide-ranging powers during both conflicts. The Defence of the Realm Act (DORA), August 1914, allowed it to take over industries and control what the public knew about the war. The Emergency Powers Act (EPA) of May 1940 gave the government almost unlimited powers. From then on, civilians could be told to do anything and be sent anywhere.

Rationing

In both wars Britain suffered from food shortages, mainly due to the sinking of merchant ships by German U-boats, and had to bring in rationing. This meant that the government controlled what people could eat and drink. Although at first voluntary, rationing was soon made compulsory.

Evacuation

Evacuation was brought in just after the German invasion of Poland, in September 1939, due to the fear of air attack. About 1.5 million people, mainly children, were evacuated from towns or cities to live with families in the 'safer' countryside.

Source A: Children being evacuated by train.

Mobilisation of women

In both wars, women were used to cover the shortages of male workers as a result of conscription and war casualties. During the First World War, women's armed forces were set up for the first time, and they played an important part in both conflicts. Moreover, women were also employed in jobs previously done only by men, especially in heavy industry.

Role of Government

Conscription

Conscription is the system of forcing men and sometimes women to serve in the armed forces. It was first brought in by the government in 1916 to cover the heavy losses on the Western Front and the decline in men volunteering. It was reintroduced in May 1939, just before the outbreak of the Second World War.

6.2 Government powers

During both wars, the role and powers of the government were greatly extended.

The Defence of the Realm Act 1914

People's lives were greatly affected by the passing of the Defence of the Realm Act, which gave the government special powers. During the First World War, the government added extra powers, which included the right to take possession of any factory, workshop or piece of land and also to censor newspapers.

Here are some of the things people were not allowed to do according to DORA:

- talk about military affairs in public places;
- spread rumours about military affairs;
- light bonfires or fireworks;
- buy binoculars;
- buy whisky or brandy in a railway refreshment room;
- ring church bells;
- fly a kite;
- use invisible ink when writing abroad;
- melt down gold or silver;
- trespass on railways or bridges.

As the war progressed, the government brought in many other measures. These included:

- introducing British Summer Time (putting the clocks forward an hour) to provide more daylight for work in the evening;
- controlling the consumption of alcohol, to try to reduce absenteeism from work due to drunkenness, by cutting down on pub opening hours, giving instructions for beer to be watered down and not allowing customers in pubs to buy rounds of drinks;
- appointing special constables to help maintain law and order;
- making strikes illegal in certain vital industries;
- not allowing workers in certain occupations, such as mining and farming – known as reserved occupations – to join the army because their skills were needed at home in Britain.

Activities

1 Working in pairs, choose four regulations from DORA telling people what they could not do and give reasons why they were introduced. Why did the government want to control this behaviour?

Conscription in the First World War

One of the important powers used by the government during the First World War was conscription. At first the government was reluctant to force men to join the armed forces. Instead, they encouraged them to volunteer through the use of conscience posters and peer pressure. However, the number of volunteers began to slow down during the course of 1915 due to news of the conditions at the war front and the high numbers of casualties, which were published in local newspapers. Moreover, conscription became necessary because Britain was unable to cover the heavy losses incurred, especially on the Western Front.

As early as August 1915 the government introduced the national registration of all single men. This was later extended to married men. It gave the government a list of men who could be called upon to fight if necessary. However, in January 1916 the Military Service Act made all unmarried men between the ages of 18 and 41 liable for service in the armed forces.

In May 1916, the act was extended to include married men. From 1916 to 1918 a total of 3,500,000 men were conscripted into the armed forces.

There were only four exceptions:

- men in reserved occupations, i.e. in important industries such as mining;
- men with ill health;
- men with family responsibilities, i.e. in situations where someone else in the family would suffer if they were conscripted;
- conscientious objectors.

Emergency Powers Act 1940

The Emergency Powers Act was introduced by the government in May 1940, after the British Army had been forced to retreat from Dunkirk and there was a real threat of invasion. This was a time of desperation, with France on the verge of defeat and every likelihood of a German invasion.

The Act gave the desperate British government almost unlimited powers over people and property. From then on, civilians could be required to do anything and be sent anywhere.

Conscription in the Second World War

In April 1939, as war became increasingly likely, the government passed the Military Training Act. This conscripted all men aged 20-21 for six months compulsory military training.

In September 1939, when war broke out, this limited measure was extended and the National Service Act was passed. This made all men aged 18-41 liable for conscription.

From October 1939, the first men, aged 20-23, were sent their call-up papers. Those in reserved jobs, essential to the war effort, were excused.

By the end of 1940:
- 200,000 men from reserved occupations had been excused conscription
- over 1 million men had volunteered or asked for their call-up to be speeded up.

Source A: Men volunteering to serve in the Royal Navy, 1939.

Source B: From the memories of James Palmer written in 1994. He was called up for Military Training in May 1939.

> It was with mixed feelings that I sat down on the platform bench waiting for the train. Dad and my girlfriend Muriel had come along with me and both looked terribly upset. I felt both excitement and anxiety. I knew that I would not like being in the army, yet I felt pleased at being one of the first to go. I was looking forward to the experience. It was only for six months, so the papers said, and I would come home before Christmas.

Gradually, as the war dragged on, more and more men were called up to the armed forces. Some people objected to conscription (see page 119), but these were a small proportion of those called up.

Indeed, there was some criticism of the government for the slow pace with which it was brought in. It was only gradually that conscription was extended.

- In December 1941, conscription was extended to men aged 18 to 51 and women aged 20 to 30.
- From December 1943, some conscripted men were sent into key jobs vital to the war effort, like coal mining. Men sent into these jobs were sometimes known as 'Bevin Boys', in reference to Ernest Bevin, the Minister of Labour and National Service.(see pages 120-121 and 160-162).

After the Second World War

In 1948, conscription was scaled down – but not abolished. All men aged 17 to 21 were required to:

- complete 18 months of National Service in the Armed forces
- serve in the Army Reserve for a further four years.

Conscription finally ended in Britain in 1960.

Conscientious objectors

One group of civilians who objected to conscription by the government during both wars were 'conscientious objectors'. These were people who refused to fight because of moral grounds, such as pacifists, or religious beliefs, such as Quakers.

First World War

Some 16,100 men refused to fight in the First World War. They had to appear before a military **tribunal** to prove that they deserved to be exempt from military service.

Of these, around 9,500 helped the war effort by working behind the lines in non-fighting roles or by doing essential work connected with the armed forces.

The remaining conscientious objectors were sent to prison camps where they were often treated with great cruelty. For example:

- at a Home Office Works Centre in Dyce, near Aberdeen, conditions were so cold and harsh because tents were the only form of accommodation that many caught pneumonia and several died
- at another centre, the prisoners' job was to handle the rotting corpses of animals. In total, ten died in prison, 63 died soon after release and 31 suffered a mental breakdown because of their experiences.

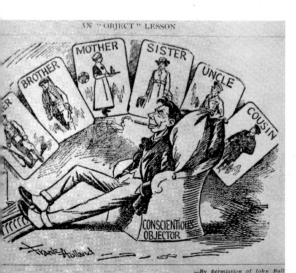

Source C: A cartoon from 1918 illustrating the opinion some people had of conscientious objectors.

Source D: From an interview in the 1960s with Percy Wall, who was sent to a prison camp because he refused to fight in the First World War.

> The attitude of the soldiers at the camp varied. A small minority told us they would like to see us shot. Others wished to know exactly what we were standing for and some of them told us they would be conscientious objectors next time. Another group seemed to think we were simply trying to get out of going to the trenches.

Second World War

About 60,000 men and women claimed exemption from military service in the Second World War. Once again, they had to justify their stance to a tribunal.

About 3,000 were given full exemption.

But about 18,000 claims were dismissed as false and the men obliged to serve or be imprisoned. About 6,000 went to prison.

The rest, almost 40,000 people, were given non-combatant roles, for example:

- Almost 7,000 joined the Non-Combatant Corps, set up in 1940. Members were put to work in military work jobs not directly involved in fighting. Of these, 465 volunteered for bomb disposal.
- Other conscientious objectors were required to work in jobs like farming, mining, fire-fighting or ambulance work.

Activities

2 What emergency powers did the government take in the First and Second World Wars?

3 Who was conscripted in the First and Second World Wars?

4 What happened to citizens who were conscientious objectors in the First and Second World Wars?

5 What were the public reactions to:

a) increased government powers

b) conscription

c) conscientious objectors?

6.3 Reorganisation of industry

Changes during the First World War

In the First World War, the government made many changes to harness industry to the war effort. For example, in 1914, with the Defence of the Realm Act (DORA), it took more powers. It could:

- take control of key industries
- allocate labour to key industries.

The government made full use of these powers.

For example:

- The railway network was taken over. In 1914, there were 120 different railway companies. During the war, the government made a unified system to ensure transport was more efficient.
- Coal mines were taken over. Miners were paid a national minimum wage, set by the government. Production rose to an all-time high of 262 million tonnes per year.
- Shipyards were taken over to ensure that enough vessels were built to replace the many being sunk by German U-boats.

Munitions production was particularly important. So, by 1915, the Ministry of Munitions had tight control of the steel and chemicals industries, which were needed for weapons manufacture. By the end of the war, the munitions industry had produced:

- 4 million rifles
- 250,000 machine guns
- 52,000 aeroplanes
- 25,000 artillery pieces and 170 million rounds of artillery shells.

Assuming control of all these industries meant that, by 1918, the government ran over 20,000 places of work.

Finally, in 1916, the Ministry of Labour was set up to organise the nation's labour force. It introduced directed labour, which gave the government the power to direct workers – both men and women - into the jobs which the country most needed them to do.

Source B: A diary entry for 25 April 1917.

> There is great pressure put on men in this district to go munition-working. George Stokes, blacksmith, has to go this week. H.W. Thorogood, landlord of the 'Dog and Partridge', has also to go. James Humphreys has obtained exemption from military service on condition of munition-working.

Source C: From a report by the government's medical officers, 1919.

> Most women enjoyed the more interesting, active and hard jobs, and in many cases their health improved rather than deteriorated. Women have with success undertaken work involving the lifting of weights, heavy machine work, and even forge and foundry work. This shows that light work is not by any means the most suitable for women. The conditions under which women worked before the war, long hours, low wages and poor diet, resulted in poor physical health.

Source A: Munitions workers at Woolwich Arsenal working over the Easter holiday in 1918.

Changes during the Second World War

The government again reorganised industry for the Second World War.

Even before war broke out, the government built "shadow factories" next to motor car plants. When war came, these were put into military production, with managers and workers drawn from the motor industry. This harnessed companies like Austin, Morris, Daimler and Ford to the war effort.

Ernest Bevin, the Minister of Labour, worked closely with employers and with the trade unions to make Britain's wartime production as efficient as possible. But the needs of the country always came first, before those of employers or the unions.

For example, to ensure that there were enough workers in essential industries, such as engineering and shipbuilding, the Control of Employment Act (1939) was passed. This gave the government control over hiring and firing of workers in key industries. It also enabled them to employ semi-skilled and unskilled workers where there were not enough skilled workers.

Workers had to accept jobs which the war effort needed doing. For example:

- Coal supplies were a problem throughout the war, so some men were sent down the mines.
- Women were, for the first time, conscripted into the labour force. From Spring 1941, every woman in Britain aged 18-60 had to be registered, and their family occupations were recorded. Each was interviewed and required to choose from a range of jobs.

Employers could not just produce what they wanted either. They had to produce what was needed.

- In 1940, the Limitation of Supplies Order cut the output of consumer goods like toys and jewellery to two-thirds of the 1939 level.
- It worked. From 1940 to 1943, yearly production increased for:
  – tanks from 1,400 to 7,500
  – warplanes from 15,000 to 26,000.

Source D: Women working in a steel factory in January 1944.

Activities

1 Find two examples of each of the following ways in which government reorganised industry during wartime:
   a) taking over production
   b) controlling working practices
   c) controlling the labour force.

Build better answers

How reliable are Sources B and C as evidence of the effects on workers of government reorganisation of industry. Explain your answer, using Sources B and C and your own knowledge.
(10 marks)

■ Basic, Level 1
Answer assumes reliability on the basis of the content and/or the origin of the sources. E.g. *It's detailed* or *It's official, so it's reliable.*

● Good, Level 2
Answer evaluates reliability based on either content of source (e.g. compares information in Sources B or C with sources A or D and own knowledge) or origin of source (e.g. discusses possible bias in Sources B or C). Answer also uses some own knowledge.

▲ Excellent, Level 3
Answer uses sources and own knowledge to evaluate reliability on basis of source content *and* origin.

6.4 The mobilisation of women

Women played a key role during both world wars, in the armed forces and in the workforce.

First World War

During the First World War women were recruited into the armed forces for the first time. At first, in 1916, they were used as volunteers in Voluntary Aid Detachments (VADs), where they worked behind the lines as nurses (see Source A).

Source A: A VAD volunteer describes her experiences, after the First World War.

> Looking back at my time as a VAD in hospital, I think that it was the happiest time I ever spent, for it was all so worthwhile. The men who suffered did so because of their terrible heroism, not just because they had pneumonia or had been run over in the street. And no matter how tired one was, what terrible things one had to do, it was worthwhile to work until one could work no longer.

However from 1917–1918 women were recruited as full-time members of the armed forces:

WAAC	WRNS	WRAF
The Women's Auxiliary Army Corps was set up in January 1917. It took over many of the office jobs in the army, which freed the men to fight (see Source B).	The Women's Royal Naval Service was set up in 1917. Women did not go to sea or fight. As with the army, they took over office duties.	The Women's Royal Air Force was set up in 1918. Women did not fly the planes or fight. Instead, they carried out routine office and domestic duties.

From the early stages of the war, British industry began to suffer a desperate shortage of labour. By early 1916, Britain had up to 2 million workers fewer than were necessary to keep the country going. This was due to the number of men who had volunteered for the armed forces between 1914 and 1916. Gradually, more and more women were employed to do 'male' jobs (see Source C).

Source B: A recruitment poster for the WAAC.

QUEEN MARY'S ARMY AUXILIARY CORPS.

The GIRL behind the man behind the gun.

ENROL TO-DAY FULL PARTICULARS AND FORMS OF APPLICATION FROM THE NEAREST EMPLOYMENT EXCHANGE. ASK AT POST OFFICE FOR ADDRESS.

- Women were soon employed in place of male clerks. By the end of the war half a million women had replaced men in office jobs.
- At first, employers and unions resisted the employment of women in manufacturing industries. Employers believed they did not have the skills, and unions believed employing women would bring down wages. However, by 1916 the shortages were so great that women had to be employed. By 1918 almost 800,000 women were working in engineering, especially in **munitions** work.

- Women were also employed in other jobs previously regarded as exclusively for men. They worked in transport as paid bus conductors and drivers, and as grave diggers, postal workers, fire fighters, chimney sweeps, blacksmiths and welders.
- There was a Women's Voluntary Police service in most major cities.
- About 260,000 women worked in the Women's Land Army where they took the place of male farm workers.

Source C: A table showing the work of women during the First World War from B. Walsh, *Modern World History*, Murray, 1996, p. 77.

Area of work	Women in 1914	Women in 1918	Women replacing men
Metals	170,000	594,000	195,000
Chemicals	40,000	104,000	35,000
Food and drink	196,000	235,000	60,000
Timber	44,000	79,000	23,000
Transport	18,000	117,000	42,000
Government	2,000	225,000	197,000

Activities

1 What do the following abbreviations stand for?
   a) VAD
   b) WAAC
   c) WRNS
   d) WRAF
2 What can you learn from Source A about the VADs?
3 Study Source B. How does the poster get across its message?
4 Study Source C. In which area of work was there the greatest change?

Second World War

From late 1941 women, unless they were pregnant or had small children, were sent to work in industry or the **auxiliary** armed services. By 1943, 90 per cent of single women and 80 per cent of married women were doing work of national importance.

The women's armed services included the WRNS, the WAAF (Women's Auxiliary Air Force) and the ATS (Auxiliary Territorial Service). The WRNS was the most popular service followed by the WAAF – many women thought that the uniforms of these services were more exciting than the dull khaki of the ATS. By 1944 there were 450,000 women in these services, with 212,000 in the ATS. As during the First World War, the women did the routine office, driving and domestic duties and freed the men to do combat duty.

Despite not being involved in combat, women did hard and often dangerous jobs too. They worked as mechanics, welders, pilots, carpenters and even gunners on anti-aircraft guns – though they were not allowed to fire the guns. A total of 335 women were killed in the ATS and another 300 wounded.

Source D: A booklet prepared by the War Department in 1942. It was given to American soldiers coming to Britain.

British women officers often give orders to men. The men obey smartly and know it is no shame. For British women have proved themselves in the war. They have stuck to their posts near burning ammunition dumps, delivered messages on foot after their motorcycles have been blasted under them. They have pulled aviators from burning planes. There isn't a single record of any British woman in uniformed service quitting her post, or failing in her duty under fire.

Activities

5 Study Source D. What is the purpose of this booklet? How does it get this message across?

Once again, as in the First World War, women worked in a variety of jobs.

By September 1943 there were:

- nearly 8 million women in paid work (3 million more than when the war started)
- 1 million women working in voluntary services.

Source E: From an advert for Hoover in 1944.

HOUSEWIFE 1944

The Hand that held the Hoover helps the Bombed!

When an "incident has occurred," nobody is more welcome to 'bombed out,' wardens, and demolition workers, than the W.V.S. with their mobile canteens. Now there is a bite to eat, and a cup of tea to hearten them. That's only one of the many jobs W.V.S. do, voluntarily, and without pay, and they nearly all have homes to run and families to look after as well. As a token of our very heartfelt admiration for this splendid Service we say —

Salute! FROM HOOVER

Hoover users know best what improvements they would like in the post-war Hoover. Suggestions are welcome.

BY APPOINTMENT TO H.M. KING GEORGE VI AND H.M. QUEEN MARY
HOOVER LIMITED, PERIVALE, GREENFORD, MIDDLESEX

Source F: A painting by an official war artist. It shows a woman working in an engineering factory.

WOMEN OF BRITAIN
COME INTO THE FACTORIES
ASK AT ANY EMPLOYMENT EXCHANGE FOR ADVICE AND FULL DETAIL

Activities

6 What is the message of Source E? Use examples from the source in your answer.

7 Why was Source F produced? Use examples from the source in your answer.

Factory work

By 1943 women occupied 57 per cent of the jobs in factories and, when they were in direct competition with men, often showed that they could do a better job. For example, the Ministry of Information published details of women's achievements. It included the information that a woman welder 'produced 120 pieces of equipment a day, compared to 100 by her male colleagues'.

Source G: A factory worker interviewed in 1942.

> Working in the factories is not fun.
>
> To be shut in for hours on end without even a window to see daylight is grim. The noise was terrific and at night when you shut your eyes to sleep all the noise would start again in your head. The work was often monotonous. I think boredom was our worst enemy.

Land Army

The Women's Land Army was revived in 1939, and 80,000 women volunteered for work.

They had no choice where they worked and were often billeted in remote areas in very basic conditions.

They proved themselves more than capable of coping with tough jobs and handled animals particularly well.

Source H: From an interview with Lily Halford who served in the Women's Land Army.

> I was called up in 1942. I did not mind being called up. I think all of us were eager to do some kind of war work. I chose the Land Army because I liked gardening and decided to apply for a job to do with the horticultural side of the Land Army.

Source I: Iris Walters, referring to life in the Land Army.

> The girls came from all walks of life and various parts of the country.
>
> We had some from Yorkshire and London. It must have been quite a culture shock for them. I, having been born in the country, didn't feel quite so bad.

Voluntary services

Many women entered the voluntary services.

By September 1943, more than one million had joined the Women's Voluntary Service (WVS).

They fulfilled a variety of roles. By this time there were:
- 180,000 in civil defence
- 47,000 in the fire services
- 130,000 serving as messengers and dispatch riders for the post office.

Many others ran nurseries and hostels, drove ambulances or worked in medical centres, first aid posts, mobile canteens and rest centres.

exam zone
Build better answers

What part did women play in the war effort in the Second World War? Explain your answer, using Source E and your own knowledge.　　(10 marks)

■ Basic, Level 1
Answer makes simple statements based on the source or own knowledge. E.g. *Women worked in the WVS or Women served in the armed forces and worked in factories.*

● Good, Level 2
Answer supports statements, using Source E and/or own knowledge. E.g. *Women worked in the WVS. For example, Source E says how much their mobile canteens were appreciated and that they did lots of other unpaid jobs.* Better answers give support from Source E and own knowledge.

▲ Excellent, Level 3
Answer gives a developed explanation, using **both** Source E and own knowledge. E.g. uses supported statements like the one in the Good answer above, together with other supported statements to come to an overall conclusion.

6.5 Rationing

One key role of government in both wars was to control food supplies through **rationing** to prevent Britain from being starved out of the war.

First World War

One of the aims of DORA was to prevent food shortages. By 1917 the Germans were using their submarines to stop supply ships from getting through to Britain from America and the continent. In April 1917 Britain had only six weeks' worth of wheat stores left. Food was so scarce that prices rose sharply and queues to buy food grew. Coal was also in short supply and, in October 1917, it was rationed.

In 1917 the government was, at first, reluctant to bring in compulsory rationing. Instead, it asked people to voluntarily limit themselves each week to:

| Two and a half pounds of meat | Three-quarters of a pound of sugar | Four pounds of bread |

But voluntary rationing did not work; the food shortages continued and the queues for food grew longer. Moreover, the rich seemed to have access to as much food as they wanted through the black market and this caused widespread resentment. Therefore, in January 1918, the government introduced compulsory rationing. Everybody was issued with a ration card, and had to register with a local butcher and grocer. Every person could have the following ration each week:

| Fifteen ounces of meat | Five ounces of bacon | Four ounces of butter |

Rationing worked. Queueing more or less stopped, and the system was seen as fair. Indeed, many poorer people became healthier because they got a better share of healthy food.

Source A: A ration card of 1918.

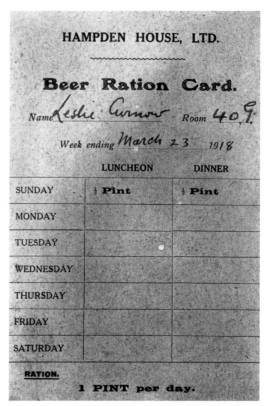

Activities

1 At home, weigh 15oz (425g) meat. Compare it to your week's meat.

2 Give two reasons for compulsory rationing and two achievements of rationing.

Second World War

The government was much quicker to introduce compulsory rationing during the Second World War. In January 1940 the Ministry of Food under Lord Woolton worked out fair food rations. At first only butter, sugar and bacon were rationed. Eventually, almost all food except seasonal fruit and vegetables was rationed. Rationing soon went beyond food. Almost every other essential article could only be bought with coupons. In other words, even if you were rich, you could not legally get extra rations because you had the same number of coupons as everyone else. Even the Royal Family had ration books.

Source B: The average weekly ration for each adult each week.

meat	1 shilling to 2 shillings and a pennyworth
bacon	4 oz to 8 oz
cheese	1 oz to 8 oz
fat	1 oz to 8 oz
eggs	1 to 2
tea	2 oz to 4 oz
sugar	8 oz to 16 oz + 2 lb for jam making
sweets and chocolate	3 oz to 4 oz
dried milk	1 tin
dried eggs	one-eighth of a packet

Rationing was a success, although there were some shortcomings.

Achievements

- It was a fair system that ensured that the poorer people were adequately fed with generally healthy food.
- It helped to unite people as they were all, rich and poor, sharing the same rations.
- The quality of rationed clothes was guaranteed by the government's utility mark.

Shortcomings

- The rich could buy extra rations on the black market.
- Very large families with several ration books were better off than small families with one or no children.
- Food supplies were more plentiful in certain areas. For example, vegetables were in greater supply in rural areas and pork and bacon were not rationed in Northern Ireland.

The government used other measures to control food supplies too:

- The 'Dig for Victory' campaign encouraged people to grow vegetables and keep chickens and pigs. Private gardens were turned into vegetable patches. Playing fields and railway embankments were ploughed up (see Source E).
- There were campaigns to avoid waste. For example, boy scouts and girl guides collected scraps for pigs.

Activities

3 Compare the message of Sources C and D. How similar are they?

4 What can you learn from Source E about the Dig for Victory campaign?

5 In what ways was food rationing better organised during the Second World War?

Source C: From a government leaflet of 1918.

I am a crust of bread. I am wasted once a day by 48,000,000 people of Britain. I am 'the bit left over'; the slice eaten absent-mindedly when really I wasn't needed. I am the waste crust. If you collected me and my companions for a whole week you would find that we amounted to 9,380 tons (9,530 tonnes) of good bread.

WASTED! Nine shiploads of good bread.

SAVE ME, AND I WILL SAVE YOU!

Source D: A Ministry of Food announcement, 1941.

Nearly half of our food comes across the sea. The U-boats attack our ships. Now, here is your part in the fight for Victory. When a particular food is not available, cheerfully accept something else – home-produced if possible. Keep loyally to the rationing regulations. Above all – whether you are shopping, cooking or eating – remember, 'FOOD IS A MUNITION OF WAR, DON'T WASTE IT'.

Source E: A British government poster of 1942.

DIG ON FOR VICTORY

6.6 Evacuation

Evacuation – the process of moving people from towns and cities into the countryside for safety – was brought in during the Second World War.

Reasons for evacuation

The British government believed that the Germans would bomb British towns and cities in order to destroy the morale of the people and force Britain to surrender. Therefore evacuation measures were put in place to protect civilians from bombings and gas attacks. Children were to be protected by being moved from the likeliest targets, the cities, to the countryside where it was thought they would be safe.

The organisation of evacuation

The first evacuation was announced on 31 August 1939, the day before Hitler invaded Poland. Many parents were reluctant to be separated from their children but accepted they would be safer in the country. Parents were told what the children needed to take with them and where they were to assemble for evacuation. The evacuation began on 1 September 1939. Many city schools were closed, and teachers went with the children to the countryside to carry on teaching them (see Source A).

Source A: From a government leaflet *Evacuation: Why and How?*, 1939.

> The government has made plans for the removal of schoolchildren from what are 'evacuable' areas to safer places. Householders have offered homes where the children will be most welcome. The schoolchildren will have their teachers and other helpers with them. The transport of 3 million children is an enormous undertaking. Of course it means heartache to be separated from your children, but you can be sure that they will be looked after.

Activities

1. What was the main reason for evacuation?
2. What can you learn from Source A about the organisation of evacuation?

At their destinations the evacuees gathered in village halls or schools where they were chosen by the foster family they were to live with. However, homesickness and the 'Phoney War', when little fighting took place and there were no enemy bombing raids, meant that many children had drifted back to the cities by Christmas 1939.

When German bombers began blitzing London in 1940, a second evacuation from the cities took place. There was a further wave of evacuations in 1944 when the Germans used their V1 flying bombs and V2 missiles to bomb Britain.

Source B: A government poster of 1942.

Experiences of evacuees

The children had varied experiences of evacuation, some pleasant and some unpleasant, as the sources describe.

Source C: The memories of Rita Wright, written in 1989. She was evacuated at the age of nine from the East End of London.

One really good thing about being evacuated to the countryside was the fact that my health improved so much. Although my parents had fed me well, I suffered from pneumonia every winter because of the crowded living conditions at home. From the time I was evacuated I never suffered from it again. The abundance of locally produced fruit and vegetables kept me very healthy.

Source D: An interview with the actor Michael Caine, who remembers life as an evacuee.

The woman said, 'Here's your meal' and gave us a tin of pilchards between the two of us and some bread and water. Now we'd been in a rich woman's house before, so we said: 'Where's the butter?' And we got a sudden wallop round the head. What we later found out was that the woman hated kids and was doing it for the extra money. So the meals were the cheapest you could dish up.

Source E: Beryl Hewitson describes what happened to her when she was evacuated.

We were told to sit quietly on the floor while villagers and farmers' wives came to choose which children they wanted. Eventually only my friend Nancy and myself were left. A large, happy-looking middle-aged woman rushed in asking: 'Is that all you have left?' A sad, slow nod of the head from our teacher. 'I'll take the poor bairns.' We were led out of the hall and taken to a farm where we spent two years.

Source F: Ted Cummings, who was evacuated from Manchester to Sandbach in 1939, remembers his experiences in the 1960s.

We left feeling sad for our parents and afraid that they would be killed by bombs. When we arrived in Sandbach we were chosen for a variety of reasons. For the extra income they received for us, to help on the farm or with the housework. A very few were lucky because they lived with families who really cared for them. For those, life was like a holiday.

Activities

3 Was evacuation a success?
- Evacuees were not used to rural life and there was a clash between city and country values.
- Evacuation saved many lives.
- The organisation was sometimes poor, especially the way in which the evacuees were chosen by their foster parents.
- Evacuees often found themselves in much wealthier homes and had to cope with different standards of behaviour.
- It meant that some children, from poor inner city areas, saw the countryside for the first time.
- Many evacuees stayed with better-off people and were given a better standard of living, for example, better food.
- Evacuation also showed better-off people in the countryside the social problems of families living in inner city areas and increased the demand for change.
- There is evidence that some people tried to avoid taking evacuees.

Working in pairs, make a copy of the scales and organise achievements on the left and shortcomings on the right. Include evidence from Sources C – E.

Overall, do you believe that evacuation was a success?

6.7 The Second World War legacy

The economic legacy of the war

The Second World War left Britain in a sorry economic state in 1945. Britain:

- lost 500,000 homes through bombing
- had infrastructure, like railway tracks, trains and roads, which were all worn out
- had factories which were converted to producing weapons not consumer goods
- had exports which had shrunk to tiny figures
- had lost £1,000 million of overseas investments
- owed £3,300 million in debts to other countries.

Then things got worse.

US loans and aid

Britain had equipped itself for war largely through 'Lend Lease'. Under this scheme, the USA gave Britain goods, such as aircraft and ships, for the war effort. In theory, the goods were to be returned after the war. But, in September 1945, after the war ended, the USA also ended Lend Lease.

Anglo-American Loan

The end of Lend Lease gave Britain a problem. It could not return the goods or do without goods already in transit. Britain had to quickly negotiate a $5 billion loan from the USA and Canada to ensure it that it could pay for goods it needed, without running out of money.

The loan was quite generous. The interest was only two per cent and Britain had 60 years to pay it off. But, even so, Britain was now even further in debt.

Marshall Aid

Even more aid was needed later. In 1947, the USA was so worried that a bankrupt Europe might fall to a series of Communist revolutions, that it announced the Marshall Plan.

This was a scheme to prop up European states with loans, machinery, raw materials and fuel.

In all, $13 billion of aid went to Europe. $3 billion went to Britain, the most for any single country.

Source A: George Orwell became a famous author. In 1945, he was a journalist.

> We have lost most of our markets and overseas investments, twelve million tons of our shipping have gone to the bottom, much of our industry is hopelessly out of date and our coal mines are in such a state that for years it will be impossible to get enough coal out of them. We have ahead of us the enormous job of rebuilding industry and recapturing markets in the teeth of overwhelming competition from the USA.

Age of economic austerity

So, by 1947, Britain was in dire economic straits. The government decided that special measures were necessary. The Chancellor of the Exchequer, Stafford Cripps, said that Britain needed a period of 'austerity'.

Source B: A British government poster explaining the need for 'austerity'.

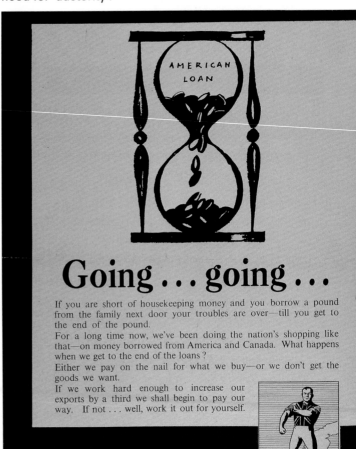

AMERICAN LOAN

Going … going …

If you are short of housekeeping money and you borrow a pound from the family next door your troubles are over—till you get to the end of the pound.

For a long time now, we've been doing the nation's shopping like that—on money borrowed from America and Canada. What happens when we get to the end of the loans?

Either we pay on the nail for what we buy—or we don't get the goods we want.

If we work hard enough to increase our exports by a third we shall begin to pay our way. If not … well, work it out for yourself.

WE WORK OR WANT

Exports and full employment

As part of this age of 'austerity', the government decided that there were two essential steps on the road to recovery.

The first was exports. Britain had to earn money to pay back its loans, so it had to start selling more goods abroad. The government used a number of measures to boost exports. For example:

- car manufacturers were only allowed to buy steel if they made cars for export
- the pound was devalued. The government announced that, instead of $4 dollars, the British pound sterling would be devalued to $2.80. This meant that people abroad paid less for British goods.

The second step to recovery was full employment. The government said that people had to put off the time when they could relax and spend money. Instead, they had to roll their sleeves up (see Source B) and get to work. Only by producing things at home would Britain keep down her imports and make things to export.

The government used a number of measures to ensure full employment. For example, it used building licences to ensure that all new factories were located where the country needed jobs. As a result, in the years after the war, Hoover went to Merthyr Tydfil, Ford went to Liverpool and Chrysler went to Scotland.

Gradually it worked. By 1950:

- exports were 77 per cent higher than 1946
- there was full employment.

Nationalised industries

The government also had another strategy for recovery: nationalisation.

During the war, the government had taken key industries out of private control so that they could be organised to benefit the war effort. By 1945, many of these key industries were very run down.

The Labour government decided that the best way to regenerate these industries was to keep them in public hands. As a result, in the years after the war, the coal, gas, electricity, transport and steel industries were nationalised.

Private owners were bought out by the state and they were run by publicly appointed Boards.

Nationalisation was a useful strategy at a time when national recovery was being planned.

For example:

- The 500 separately owned, private power stations could now be harnessed to the national grid instead of competing against each other.
- The National Coal Board could settle the ongoing disputes between the miners' unions and countless mine owners and concentrate efforts upon production.
- A single Transport Commission could make overall plans for the nationalised road, rail, air and sea transport providers.

Nationalisation was also a success for Britain's most out-of-date industries, like coal and the railways. Government money could be invested in modernising these industries without the necessity of making a profit. Working conditions for miners also improved. So opposition was mild and most remained nationalised until the 1980s.

Nationalisation was less popular in industries like iron and steel, which were already making profits.

Source C: A miner arrives at work at a nationalised coal mine, 1947.

The social legacy of the war

The 'age of austerity' was also a social legacy of the war. Some social features of wartime lingered until 1954 and beyond.

Rationing

Rationing had been a big social change during the war. When the war ended in 1945, rationing continued.

Domestic supplies of food and other consumer goods were still limited and Britain could not afford a rapid increase in imported goods.

Indeed, rationing became worse before it became better. The allowed ration of meat was reduced just after the war finished, and rationing for bread and potatoes was introduced in 1946.

So rationing lingered on and on, even though the public became impatient. Eventually, rationing was ended in: 1948 for flour, 1949 for clothes, 1950 for soap, mincemeat, petrol and canned and dry fruit, 1952 for tea and 1953 for sugar and sweets. In July 1954, the removal of restrictions on the sale of meat finally brought rationing to an end.

Age of social austerity

It wasn't just rationing. The period from 1945 to 1954 was a time of much wider social austerity.

- Bomb sites lingered for years, undeveloped.
- Britain still had conscription.
- Even when food wasn't rationed, it was in short supply. People queued in the shops to buy popular goods before they ran out. Some foods we regard as common now – e.g. bananas – were so rare as to seem exotic then.
- Material for clothes was in short supply too. So styles remained severe and drab.

From the mid-1950s, output and employment improved. But recovery from the war had been a long process.

Activities

1 What were the key features of the economic and social legacy of the Second World War?

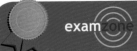

examzone

Build better answers

How reliable are Sources B and D as evidence of the age of austerity? Explain your answer, using Sources B and D and your own knowledge.

(10 marks)

■ **Basic, Level 1**
Answer assumes reliability on the basis of content or provenance (e.g. nature, origin, time).

● **Good, Level 2**
Answer evaluates reliability either on the basis of its content or its provenance. Answer also uses some own knowledge.

▲ **Excellent, Level 3**
Answer evaluates reliability of sources on the basis of both their content **and** provenance, and also uses own knowledge of the historical context.

Source D: Cartoon showing Herbert Morrison, a Labour politician, inviting the public into austerity Britain.

Reliability of sources

Reliability is how much you can trust what a source tells you. So how can we tell if a source is reliable?

You can't be certain

You can never be totally sure if a source is reliable.

- There are some sources which, on balance, you can be pretty sure you can trust.
- There are other sources which you can be pretty sure you can't trust completely.

Since you can't be sure, it's better to say:

- *Source A* **seems** *reliable because…*
- *Source B is* **unlikely** *to be reliable because…*

Ask yourself 'reliable about what?'

A source can be reliable and also unreliable at the same time. Confusing? Well, read this source.

Source E: Extract from the Labour Party Manifesto for the 1950 general election.

> The choice for the electors is between the Labour Party – the party of positive action, of constructive progress, the true party of the nation – and the Conservative Party – the party of outdated ideas, of unemployment, of privilege.

Is Source E reliable? Well, yes and no.

- This is a word for word extract. So it is reliable as information about the Labour Party and what was in their 1950 Manifesto.
- It also tells you about the Conservative Party. But it is not such a reliable source for this. The Labour Manifesto is not likely to give you an unbiased picture about the Conservative Party.

So you can see how a source can be reliable and unreliable at the same time. This means, if you're trying to decide if a source is reliable, it's vital to ask yourself the key question – 'reliable about what?'

Evaluate reliability by content

- One way to decide the reliability of a source is to ask questions about its content.
- What type of content is it? If it is facts, which you can check, you might be more likely to believe it. But not if it is opinion, unsupported by facts.
- Is the content typical? Do other sources provide similar kinds of content?

Evaluate reliability by provenance

The provenance of a source is its origin – where it comes from. Asking questions about the provenance of a source might help you decide whether you trust it or not. For example, you might ask:

- Is it a primary source?
- Is it a secondary source written by a historian or a reporter?
- Is it a source which is likely to be biased or a source which is likely to give you a balanced picture?

You can't just make simple assumptions about reliability based on what kind of source it is.

- Primary sources can be biased. For example, Source E, the Labour Party Manifesto, may give you a biased picture of the Conservative Party.
- You can't believe everything historians say, either. Historians often disagree about their interpretations of events.

So judging reliability based on the provenance of a source is not easy.

However, asking the question 'reliable for what?' and thinking about the content and the provenance of a source should help you make a considered assessment of whether a source is reliable or not.

Summary

- Government intervention in society was needed to fight wars effectively.
- Examples of government intervention are DORA, conscription, re-organising industry, conscription, mobilising women, rationing and evacuation.
- Government intervention was also necessary to deal with the after-effects of the Second World War during the Age of Austerity.

7.1 War and social change: the Boer War

Learning outcomes

By the end of this section you should be able to:

- describe how the Boer War affected British society
- describe how wars affected health and welfare 1900-54
- describe how wars affected women 1900-54
- describe how wars affected social divisions in Britain.

Social attitudes to war

In the early twentieth century, the British public:

- took great pride in Britain's achievements
- expected the government to protect Britain's interests abroad
- wanted strong, efficient military forces
- supported an aggressive foreign policy
- showed an eagerness for war.

This attitude has been called **jingoism**. It is a term which originated from a popular British music-hall song (dating from about 1877):

> We don't want to fight, Yet, by jingo, if we do,
> We've got the ships, We've got the men,
> And got the money too.

Jingoism was one of the reasons the British public supported the Boer War. But it turned out differently than they expected.

The Boer War (1899-1902)

In the Boer War of 1899-1902, Britain defeated Dutch settlers known as Boers, rising against the Empire, in two small states in the south of Africa.

The public expected a quick victory. Boer troops were made up of only 35,000 farmers, not professionals like the British Army.

But the war dragged on.

British troops suffered three embarrassing defeats at Stormberg, Magersfontein and Colenso, in December 1899; the British press called it 'Black Week'.

Another defeat followed at Spioenkop in January 1900. Increased press reporting of foreign wars made problems like these impossible to hide.

Eventually, Britain deployed 450,000 soldiers and spent over £200 million on the war. Despite the eventual victory, well over 5,000 were killed in action and a further 16,000 died of disease.

Source A: A magazine cover showing a British defeat in the Boer War in 1901.

Society calls for military change

As a result of Britain's poor performance in the Boer War, pressure began to build up for reform. This pressure took several forms.

First, the public began to fear that Britain's army was falling behind other countries, like Germany – an impression other countries enjoyed (see Source B).

Then two royal commissions, set up to investigate military performance, reported in 1903 and 1904. They suggested change.

As a result, there were several military reforms.

In 1905, the Royal Navy began work on a powerful new battleship, the Dreadnought, to reassert British control of the seas. It was launched in 1906.

In 1905, Lord Haldane became Secretary of State for War. He introduced a series of changes called the Haldane Reforms. The two main ones were:

- the creation of a rapid response force, later called the British Expeditionary Force (BEF), which could respond to crises abroad
- the Territorial Force, trained, but part-time, soldiers who supported regular troops.

Both these reforms put Britain in a much stronger position for the First World War. The BEF was Britain's first response to the outbreak of war in 1914. One of the first two Territorial Units, the 55th West Lancashire Division, earned 12 Victoria Crosses during that war.

In addition, in 1908 Robert Baden-Powell, a senior army officer, set up the Boy Scouts movement. This was not overtly military, but he boasted that the Scouts were 'a potential recruiting ground' and that 70 per cent of scouts went into the army.

Source B: Britain's reputation abroad suffered. This is how a French magazine portrayed the Boer War in 1901.

LE LION ANGLAIS ET LE TAUREAU BOER

Society calls for social change

However, concern about Britain's performance in the Boer War was soon to have much more far-reaching effects. This is because blame eventually fell on the quality of army recruits.

Social reformers, like Charles Booth in London and Seebohm Rowntree in York, had shown widespread poverty amongst Britain's working class, from which most soldiers were recruited.

Then army reports showed that about 40 per cent of army recruits for the Boer War were unfit for service. It was worst in the cities; in some, nine out of ten recruits were rejected.

Fearing that Britain's military and economic efficiency were being undermined by the condition of the poor, the government set up an investigation by senior military and political figures. It was called the Committee on Physical Deterioration.

The Committee reported in 1904. It called for a whole raft of social reforms to tackle poverty and improve the quality of Britain's army recruits. In particular, it suggested:

- nurseries for the children of working mothers
- free school meals for the very poor
- medical inspections in schools
- training in cooking and mothering skills
- an end to sales of tobacco to children
- an end to overcrowded slum housing
- an end to smoke pollution in towns.

So, by the time a new Liberal government was formed in 1906, there was an irresistible pressure for social reforms to tackle poverty.

Activities

1 What was 'jingoism'?
2 Why did the Boer War worry British society?
3 Describe the military reforms resulting from worries about the Boer War.
4 Describe the mounting pressure for social reform after the Boer War.

7.2 Liberal Party reforms 1906-1911

Liberal social reforms

The Liberal government elected in 1906 contained politicians, like David Lloyd George, who were determined to tackle Britain's problems. They passed a series of radical reforms (see page 137). There were several reasons why the reforms were passed. Some of these were related to public opinion about the Boer War and some were not.

Reasons for the reforms

- The Boer War suggested that Britain was losing its military lead in the world. The Committee on Physical Deterioration showed that many recruits were not healthy or well-fed enough to create an efficient army. This was not good enough for jingoistic social opinion.
- People realised that they could not just sit back and wait for the poor to solve their own problems. The poor could not solve their poverty if they were children, aged, sick or unemployed, for example. They needed help.
- People also realised that, if the urban poor were unfit for the army, they were probably also unfit for work. Without a good workforce, Britain could also lose its place in the lead of world economic progress.
- Liberals feared that, if they did not help the poor, they might turn to their rivals, the Labour Party, or trade union action – or even revolution.

Source A: A school medical inspection, 1912.

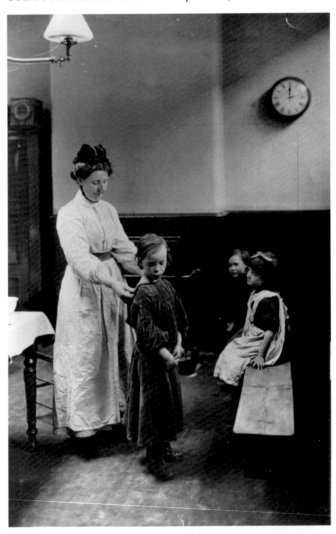

Source B: Free school meals being served to children in London, 1910.

Reforms to help children and families

1906	Local authorities were allowed to provide free school meals for children, part-funded by the government, so that the poor were better fed and healthier. By 1914, 150,000 children were getting one free meal per day. But only half the councils offered the scheme, so, in 1914, it was made compulsory.
1906	The Workers Compensation Act gave compensation for workers injured at work, making it less likely that injury would condemn them and their families to poverty and ill-health.
1907	School medical inspections began. These diagnosed problems which could then be tackled.
1908	The Children and Young Persons Act was a set of regulations which became known as the Children's Charter. For example, it: • made it a crime to neglect children and sell children cigarettes, alcohol or fireworks • set up separate juvenile courts for children, so they were not treated as harshly as adults, and borstals, which were prisons which provided training for young people.
1909	Labour exchanges were set up to help unemployed people find work. By 1914, they were placing 3,000 people in jobs each day. The Trade Boards Act made it possible to prosecute employers who paid less than the Board's minimum wage in 'sweated industries' – workplaces with long hours and low pay. A tax allowance for children was introduced, so workers with children paid less tax.
1910	The Education (Choice of Employment) Act was passed, enabling local authorities to give careers advice to help children get work. From 1911, grants were given by central government to help local authorities with the cost.
1911	The National Insurance Act was introduced to help families during times of hardship. It provided: • medical insurance to prevent illness causing poverty. Workers paid 4d per week (employers 3d and the state 2d). In return, workers got free medical treatment and sick pay of 9s per week for 26 weeks. • unemployment insurance to prevent loss of work causing poverty. Workers paid 2.5d per week. In return, they got unemployment pay of 7s a week for up to 15 weeks.

Other Liberal social reforms

1906	The Trades Disputes Act said that unions would no longer be liable to pay for damages caused by strikes.
1908	Eight hour working day set for miners.
1908	Pensions were introduced for the over 70s. They received 5s per week (25p) or 7s 6d per married couple (37.5p).
1910	The Merchant Shipping Act – improved working conditions for sailors.
1911	Pay for MPs – enabled working men to stand for election to parliament.

Activities

1 Look at Sources A and B and the reforms which were passed. How would the reforms reassure those members of the public who were worried by Britain's performance in the Boer War?
2 Look at the reforms which were passed and the reasons for these reforms described on page 136. How far did the impact of the Boer War help to cause the Liberal reforms?

7.3 Wars, welfare and health

First World War

Medical advances

During the years 1914 to 1918, there was little direct improvement in medical services for civilians in Britain. There were very few civilian casualties in the First World War, so there was no new need for medical improvements at home. Indeed, the huge cost of the First World War meant there was little money left for improving medical care at home.

However, in the *longer* term, the First World War did bring medical improvements to Britain, because governments and medical firms co-operated to help medical knowledge in wartime (see Source A).

Source A: From a book on warfare, edited by Sir Zacharay Cope, 1953.

> Surgery and war have always been linked…the chief school of surgery was the battlefield. In war, the surgeons of many nations are united in a common effort… Manufacturing firms will devote their whole resources [to medical improvements]… Supplies, transport, equipment are all [made] available.

Particular progress was made in areas of medical need which were common in warfare, for example:

- wounds, using sodium hypochlorite and tetanus injections to avoid infection
- disfiguring injuries, using plastic surgery or the manufacture and fitting of prosthetic limbs
- mental disorders, for example treatment of soldiers with 'shell shock'.

Source B: C Spry, Medicine at War, 1970.

> X-rays of bones became commonplace. Despite steel helmets, 10% of all injuries were to the head. Surgery of the eye, face, ear, nose and throat and the brain and plastic surgery developed rapidly under the stimulus of war. Many surgeons gained new knowledge and experience and later set up as 'specialists'.

After the war, these innovations were used in civilian services, improving medical provision for all.

Blood transfusions

Blood transfusions became more common after the First World War. Doctors treating battlefield wounds were desperate for ways of replacing lost blood. But blood transfusions were risky before 1914.

A breakthrough came with the discovery of anti-coagulants, first sodium citrate in 1914 and then heparin in 1916. Adding these to blood meant that it didn't clot in tubes and bottles. Surgeons could now store blood ready for use when needed.

From 1921, voluntary blood transfusions were used in some hospitals and Britain's first blood bank opened in Ipswich in 1938.

Welfare provision

As with medical services, the First World War brought no real improvement in welfare provision during the war itself. However, the war did cause longer-term improvements.

A land fit for heroes

At the end of the war, David Lloyd George, leader of the new Liberal government, promised "to make Britain a fit country for heroes to live in". So they introduced a series of new measures which included:

- **The Education Act (1918)** This required council schools to provide education up to the age of 14.
- **The Housing and Town Planning Act (1919)** This gave councils subsidies to help them provide new council houses. In Dagenham, the council built the Becontree estate, the largest council estate in the world. By 1932, 25,000 houses had been built there and over 100,000 people moved in.
- **The Unemployment Insurance Act (1920)** This extended the 1911 Act, raising the benefit paid and insuring an extra 11 million workers against unemployment, so that 75% of workers were now covered.

Second World War

New medical treatment

As in the First World War, the treatment of millions of casualties during the Second World War prompted a number of improvements in medical treatment which also came to benefit civilians. Mass immunisation and burns treatments are examples.

However, the best-known example is penicillin, which can fight infection. It was discovered by Alexander Fleming in 1928. However, it was very difficult and expensive to manufacture for use as a drug.

Eventually, the US government was persuaded, after they entered the war in 1941, to finance the development of penicillin. They spent $75 million and it took two years. But, by 1943, it was issued to British and US troops in North Africa and it soon became available for use by all.

New medical provision

The Second World War also brought a very different benefit to British civilians.

Until this time, there was no National Health Service. People who had enough money to pay for a doctor or hospital, or who were insured, could do so. But many people who were injured or fell ill could not afford to pay for medical treatment.

Source C: Working Class Wives, by Margery Spring Rice, 1939.

> Fathers and children come under the National Health Insurance… It is the mother who gets left out. She may get the family doctor for herself and the children if she pays into a medical club. If she does not pay in she carries on as long as she can without advice or treatment.

By 1939, it was clear to the government that the war would involve the bombing of British cities and thousands of civilian casualties. Existing medical services could not cope.

It was also clear that Britain could only rely upon its soldiers and workers if they were healthy. Again, the existing medical services could not ensure this.

So, when the war broke out, the government took responsibility for overseeing a national system of emergency and medical care for everybody.

This new medical provision included:
- a national network of air raid wardens trained in first aid and ambulances assigned to medical posts
- free or cheap medical treatment for everyone who needed it
- a new national blood transfusion service.

New welfare provision

The government also realised that only a well cared for nation could win the war, so it improved the national welfare provision. From 1940, this included:
- an Assistance Board to help bombed-out families and the sick and aged
- free meals for more school children
- a National Milk Scheme for all children and expectant mothers. A year later, free cod liver oil and orange juice were added to the scheme.

Letting the genie out of the bottle

But the real long-term benefit was that the government had taken responsibility for:
- the welfare of the nation
- affordable health care for everyone.

Once they had done this *during* the war, there was no way of going back *after* the war. This was the thinking that lay behind the Beveridge Report.

Source D: Children queuing for cod liver oil during the Second World War.

Beveridge and Labour reforms

Shared suffering, work and benefits

Both world wars caused suffering for the whole nation and were won because the whole nation worked together for victory. As a result, both wars created a demand for greater social equality.

The First World War, for example, accelerated the process leading to wider suffrage – giving those that had worked and fought for victory a say in the running of their country.

The Second World War created even stronger feelings of unity. Partly this was because the shared suffering was so much greater – from bombing, for example.

It was also because the government did so much to ensure fairness in the nation's war burden.

- Rationing was seen by the British public as both necessary and fair. Rich and poor alike were given the same rations.
- Evacuation often involved more fortunate people in the countryside taking responsibility for those escaping hardship in the cities.

As a result, there was a growing feeling that this kind of fairness and benefit for all should be a feature of society during peace as well as war.

The Beveridge Report

In 1941, this desire for a fairer society led the government to set up a Royal Commission under Sir William Beveridge to consider how Britain could rebuild after the war.

The Beveridge Report of 1942 recommended that the government should set up a system which protected people:

- from the 'Five Giant Evils': Want, Ignorance, Disease, Squalor and Idleness
- throughout their lives, 'from the cradle to the grave'
- whoever they were, whatever their income.

The published Report was a best-seller. Long queues formed outside His Majesty's Stationery Office to buy it. From 1944, a series of reforms were introduced to implement the report, mostly by the new Labour government.

Together, these reforms became known as the 'Welfare State'.

Source E: A cartoon from 1942, showing Beveridge setting out to defeat the 'Five Giants'.

TACKLING THE FIRST GIANT

" WANT is only one of the five giants on the road of reconstruction." — The Beveridge Report.

The attack on ignorance

The 1944 Education Act was brought in by Churchill's wartime government. It applied to England and Wales and abolished the idea of elementary education, ending at age 14.

Instead, it said that primary schools would take children until they were eleven. These schools continued to provide milk, meals and dental checks.

Then there would be secondary education for all, with the leaving age raised to 15 as soon as possible; this was done in 1947.

Labour welfare reforms 1945-51

It fell to the new Labour government to introduce measures to achieve the rest of the Beveridge proposals.

The attack on want

The 1946 National Insurance Act made insurance compulsory for everyone of working age except married women. The scheme started in 1948.

In return for a weekly contribution, there were:
- sickness and unemployment benefits
- retirement and widows' pensions
- maternity benefits
- a funeral grant.

It was supplemented by the payment of Family Allowance, which had started in 1946. Five shillings per week was paid to parents for every child after the first one, until the age of sixteen.

The attack on disease

The 1946 National Health Service Act was introduced by Aneurin Bevan, the Minister of Health. Under this act, everyone was entitled to free:
- medical care by GPs and hospitals
- dental care
- eye treatment.

This scheme also started in 1948, but it was financed, not from insurance, but from national taxation.

The attack on squalor

There were serious housing shortages due to the effects of bombing and the lack of building during the Second World War. The Labour Government adopted three solutions.

- As a short-term measure, homeless families were housed in emergency accommodation – army huts, converted aircraft factories and thousands of 'pre-fabs' (pre-fabricated, factory-built sections of houses bolted together on concrete bases).
- Secondly, there was a campaign of council house building. Britain built more council houses in the five years after the war than any other country in Europe.
- Then there was the 1946 New Towns Act. This provided government money for a series of new towns, like Harlow and Milton Keynes, to be built close to London and other cities. These reduced overcrowding in older urban centres.

The attack on idleness

Finally, there was the attack on idleness. The Labour Government declared that Britain needed to work its way out of economic trouble and started a series of schemes to boost jobs. (See page 131 for details).

By 1950, they had achieved virtually full employment.

Activities

1. Look at pages 138-141 and list three detailed examples of the following:
   a) war boosting medical improvements for the public
   b) war boosting welfare benefits for the public.
2. Why did the two world wars prompt a demand for a fairer, more equal society?
3. List two ways in which society was made fairer by:
   a) the First World War
   b) the Second World War.

7.4 Women in the early 20th century

At the start of the twentieth century, the rights and role of women in society were slowly improving. Some of the improvements are described on pages 144-45. However, progress was slow.

This is because many of the views which held women back in Victorian times were still very powerful in 1900. For example, the view of some people was that women were less capable than men (see Source A, for example).

Source A: Leading scientist, Thomas Huxley, 1851.

> In every characteristic, whether mental or physical, the average woman is inferior to the average man.

Many people believed that women were not intelligent enough, or were too emotional, to be involved in important matters, such as politics or business. As a result, women did not have the vote in national elections and there were no women MPs. Women seen by many as second-class citizens who should play a limited role in society.

Role and status in the family

Some women in poor families had to work to make ends meet. But in middle class homes, the primary role of women was generally restricted to the house. Girls were prepared for domestic duties until they could marry a man who would provide for them. Then they would have a role overseeing the home and the family.

In many homes, women were also raised to think of themselves as inferior to the men in the family (see Source B for example).

Source B: From the biography of Joseph Ashby, a farm worker.

> Their mother would teach them, by action and words, that girls and women find it best to submit to their husbands and brothers. Their duty was to feed them well, run their errands and bear all the burdens except the physical ones.

Source C: 'The Daydreamer', produced in 1894, showing a seamstress watching a wedding and daydreaming about when she can get married.

Activities

1 Look at Sources A, B and C and make a list of the attitudes towards women which they illustrate.

Education

Some progress in education for girls had been made (see pages 144-45). But most girls were held back by their schooling. Their education prepared them for a future domestic role. It was generally confined to reading, writing, some arithmetic and subjects such as needlework and cookery.

As Source D shows, attitudes to women also reduced their opportunities for higher education. Views such as this regarded women as unsuited and harmful to the education of other students.

Source D: A statement made by students at a hospital in London in 1861.

> We consider that the mixture of sexes in the same class is likely to lead to results of an unpleasant character. Lecturers are likely to feel some restraint through the presence of females in giving explicit enunciation of some facts which is necessary. The presence of young females in the operating theatre is an outrage on our natural instincts and feelings and is calculated to destroy those sentiments of respect and admiration with which the sex is regarded by all right-thinking men.

examzone

Build better answers

What can you learn from Source E about women and work at the start of the twentieth century?

(6 marks)

■ **Basic, Level 1**
Simple comprehension of the source, e.g. *Most women workers were unmarried.*

● **Good, Level 2**
Answer makes a valid inference, but it is unsupported. E.g. *Most women who worked only got low pay.*

▲ **Excellent, Level 3**
Answer gives a valid inference supported by evidence. E.g. *Most unmarried women who worked must have given up their jobs when they married. I can tell this because Devon had 3,442 women teachers who were unmarried, but only 336 who were married.*

Social life

Attitudes to women also limited them socially.

- Single women were expected not to go out without an older escort or **chaperone**, and not to smoke or drink.
- They were also expected to dress in a conservative way, wearing long dresses or skirts, and to have long hair, tied back. Make-up was frowned upon.

Employment

Since most men and many women believed that a woman's place was in the home supporting her husband and bringing up their children, many married women were not expected to work.

Some married working-class women worked in order to supplement the family income. This was often in unskilled, low-paid jobs, especially in the textile industry and the sweated trades, such as tailoring. However, by 1911, only ten per cent of married women were in paid employment. Where women did the same job as men, they were almost always paid less.

For unmarried women, job opportunities were limited to doing domestic work as maids or cooks in wealthy households, or working as shop assistants, telephonists, typists and nurses. Better paid professions such as the law, medicine and accountancy were generally closed to women, who, in any case, usually lacked the necessary qualifications to enter these professions.

Source E: Extract from the 1901 Census in Devon, showing numbers of women in certain roles.

	Unmarried	Married
Domestic servants	37,558	7,611
Dressmakers	12,698	3,293
Teachers	3,442	336
Nurses	811	851
Lawyers, accountants, engineers	0	0
Doctors	3	0
Managers in companies	4	0

As we shall see later, the First World War brought changes in the position of women in British society. But it is important to note that attitudes towards women were already slowly changing even before the First World War started in 1914.

Developments in education

There had been some progress in education. For example, in 1872 the Girls' Public Day School Trust was set up to raise money for girls' grammar schools.

In 1886, Oxford University raised the status of Higher Education for women by the foundation of St Hugh's and St Hilda's Colleges there.

In 1904, Hertha Ayrton became the first woman to present a paper to the Royal Society, Britain's most prestigious academy of science.

Developments in work

More women were making their mark at work.

- Rosa Lewis started work in domestic service. She worked her way up to become head of the kitchen for the Duke of Orleans and then went into business. In 1902, she bought her own hotel, The Cavendish, in London. It is still a top class hotel today.
- Beatrix Potter published her first book in 1902, became a renowned author and also went on to become a leading breeder of livestock.
- Gertrude Jekyll was probably the country's foremost garden designer by the 1900s.
- Mary Howarth became the editor of a new newspaper, the *Daily Mirror*, in 1903. It was aimed particularly at women.

Women in medicine

There was also progress in professions, such as medicine.

- In 1865, Elizabeth Garrett Anderson overcame immense difficulties to qualify as the first female doctor. There were 477 by 1911.
- In 1902, the work of midwives was properly recognised by the Midwives Act. This created a Central Midwives Board which ensured high standards of training and practice.
- In 1907, the First Aid Nursing Yeomanry was set up to nurse soldiers at field hospitals in wartime.

Women in local politics

There was slow progress in local politics.

- In 1907, the Qualification of Women Act allowed women to be elected to county and town councils and as town mayors.
- In 1908, Elizabeth Garrett Anderson became the first woman to be elected mayor, at Aldeburgh in Suffolk.

Growing independence

Some enterprising women became pioneers of exciting new ways of life.

- In 1903, Dorothy Levitt became the first British woman to take part in an organised motor car race.
- In 1908, Dolly Shepherd, a parachute stunt artist, made the first mid-air rescue of a fellow parachutist in difficulty.
- In 1912, American Harriet Quimby became the first woman to fly an aeroplane across the English Channel.

Source F: A march, in London in 1913, by the NUWSS, which campaigned for votes for women.

The campaign for the vote

Some people were also beginning to contemplate a role for women in national politics.

Up to this time, women could not vote or stand for election to parliament. There were many arguments for this.

- Many men claimed that women were emotionally unsound and would be unable to vote sensibly.
- Others said that, as women could not fight for their country, they should not be allowed to vote.
- Even many women believed it would be wrong. For example, Queen Victoria called giving women the vote a 'mad, wicked folly'. Nevertheless, the campaign for women to vote was stepped up in the years before 1914.

There were two main groups of campaigners:

The suffragists

Suffragists believed that women should campaign peacefully. All they had to do was keep on the right side of the law, and do all they could to persuade the general public and parliament that women ought to be given the vote.

One such group was the National Union of Women's **Suffrage** Societies (NUWSS) led by Millicent Fawcett. This group organised marches (see Source F), posters and petitions. They tried to demonstrate that women were sensible enough for the vote.

The suffragettes

In contrast, suffragettes believed in using militant or extreme methods. They were prepared to break the law in order to get the vote as this would get them publicity and force the government to give way. They were led by Emmeline Pankhurst, who set up the Women's Social and Political Union (WSPU) in 1903.

During 1906–1914, their methods became more militant. They began by interrupting the meetings of leading Liberals and moved on to going on hunger strike after being arrested, smashing windows, cutting telephone wires, setting fire to derelict buildings and assaulting leading Liberals.

Source G: The UK Parliament website, describing the NUWSS.

> They were led by Millicent Garrett Fawcett (1847-1929). She published widely on women's issues and was a frequent public speaker on women's rights. She was married to an MP, Henry Fawcett, and regularly sat in the Ladies' Gallery of the House of Commons to watch the debates. Her tactical and determined leadership of the NUWSS made it a substantial and influential force in the campaign for women's votes.

Source H: Richard Lloyd George, son of the Chancellor of the Exchequer.

> The militant suffragettes showed their hysteria by planting a bomb in our home, which wrecked four rooms. One of the women threw a steel spike through the window of father's cab. It missed his eye by a fraction and pierced his cheek.

Why did women not get the vote?

Despite all this activity, women did not have the vote by 1914.

- This was partly due to the militancy of the suffragettes which had convinced many people, including MPs, that women were not responsible enough for the vote.
- Moreover, the two leading political parties, the Liberals and the Conservatives, were unable to decide which groups of women to give the vote to, since many men did not yet have the vote either.

Activities

2. What can you learn from Sources F and G about the methods used by the suffragists to campaign for the vote?

3. What can you learn from Source H about the suffragettes?

4. Using the following headings, outline what progress had been made by women before the 1914-18 war in their quest for a more equal place in society?

   Education, Work, Politics

7.5 Women in the First World War

The position of women in society was already changing before the First World War. But the war accelerated those changes. Women played a vital role on the home front, especially in employment and the women's armed forces. First, this changed the lives of the women. Second, it also did much to change some people's attitudes to women in general.

Women at work

Once men began to volunteer for armed service and then conscription took still more from their jobs, Britain needed women to do the jobs vacated by the men.

At first, employers seemed only happy for women to do light work, like office jobs. But the government led the way in employing women in a much wider range of jobs, for example, making munitions.

The Women's Land Army

From 1915, women could join the Women's Land Army, to help fill jobs in farming. By the end of the war, there were 23,000 women serving in the Women's Land Army. Altogether, there were over 260,000 women working on the land.

Munitions work

One place where munitions were made was Woolwich Arsenal, in London. In 1914, it employed only 125 women. By 1917, the government employed 27,000 women there.

Indeed, by the end of the war, about 60 per cent of all workers in the munitions industry were women. Almost 800,000 women worked in engineering. The work was hard.

- They worked 12-hour shifts, seven days a week, packing explosives and cordite charges into bullets and shells.
- Sometimes they developed lead poisoning, or illnesses from the chemicals, which caused their hair to fall out and turned their skin yellow. This earned these women the nickname 'canaries'.
- Some workers were even killed when munitions factories blew up. In 1917 a fire in Silvertown munitions works in East London caused an explosion that killed 69 people and injured 400.
- Overall, between 1914 and 1918, about two million women replaced men in employment and the percentage of women in work rose from 24 per cent to 37 per cent.

Source A: Women working in a munitions factory in 1917.

The armed forces

From 1917, women could work in the armed forces in support roles. Typically, these roles involved work as nurses, cooks, clerks, telephone operators and typists. Although these were non-combat roles, they were often performed in war zones.

By 1918, about 100,000 women had joined:
- the Women's Army Auxiliary Corps (WAAC) – formed in 1917
- the Women's Royal Air Force (WRAF) – formed in 1918
- the Women's Royal Naval Service (WRNS) – formed in 1917.

Growing independence

All these developments in the types of work women did brought other changes to the lives of Britain's women as well.

For example, some women appeared in uniform, in roles ranging from railway porters to ambulance drivers. Others took to having their hair cut short or wearing trousers, for example, as it was more practical.

Women also gained much greater freedom. With fewer men around, chaperones for wealthier girls became less common.

In addition, full wage packets meant that women had money to spend. They now smoked, drank in pubs, went to the cinema, on bicycle trips and on shopping trips in town unsupervised.

Source B: An article from the *Daily Mail*, September 1916.

> The wartime business girl is to be seen at night dining out in restaurants in London. Before, she would never have had her evening meal in town unless in the company of a man friend. But now, with money and without men, she is dining out more and more. The meal, of course, is accompanied by a cigarette.

Source C: A historian writing in 1965.

> Women became more independent. Women munitions workers paid for their round of drinks at the pub. Fashion changed for practical reasons. Never again did skirts sweep the ground. The petticoat disappeared. Women's hats became neater. A few women cut their hair.

Activities

1   List three detailed examples of the following effects of war on women:
    a)   women doing different work
    b)   women in the armed forces
    c)   changing behaviour of women
    d)   changing attitudes towards women.

Attitudes to women

Opinions on these changes for women varied. Some people were scandalised; some troops returning home from France were amazed. But everybody noticed.

Source D: An article called 'The New Woman' from The Sphere, May 1918.

> She has entered practically all the professions. A postwoman brings you the letters and a girl brings you the milk for your morning tea. There are girls, uniformed or not, at the wheels of half the cars that pass. If you go by train, women will handle your luggage. If you choose a bus or tram, the conductress in her smart uniform has long become a familiar figure. You can even be shaved by a woman.

Source E: From a letter to the Glasgow Herald sent by a woman in 1916.

> To observe how men speak and write about women today is vastly amusing to us. We have not changed with the war. It is only that the scales have fallen from men's eyes. In the hour of Britain's need her sons have realised that if victory was to be won they could not afford to hem women in with the old restrictions.

Source F: A report by the National Employers' Federation (all men), 1918.

Quality	
Sheet metal	Women's output better than men's output
Aircraft woodwork	Women's output equal to men in most areas
Cartridge production	Women's output equal to men's output
Shell production	Women's output poorer than men's output

7.6 Women 1918-1939

The First World War clearly changed the role of women in society. It seemed to change people's attitudes too, but how far did these changes last after the war ended?

Political changes

A big step forward came in 1918.

The Representation of the People Act was passed in 1918, just before the end of the war. This gave the vote to all women property owners aged 30 and over, together with all men over the age of 21 (and those 19-21 who had been on active service in the war).

This was in recognition of the role that women had played during the war, though it's not clear that everybody agreed with it. See Sources A, B and C.

Source A: From a speech made in **1917** by Herbert Asquith, Prime Minister from 1908-1916.

> My opposition to women's rights is well known. However, for three years now the Suffragettes have not restarted that horrible campaign of violence. Not only that, they have contributed to every service during this war except of fighting. I therefore believe that some measure of women's suffrage should be given.

Source B: Written by an MP in 1922.

> The vote was won, not by burning churches, slashing pictures or damaging pillar boxes but by women's work during the war. It was not giving way to violence but a reward for patriotic service.

Source C: From M. Pugh, *Women's Suffrage, 1867–1928*, 1992.

> A very simplified view would see the vote as a reward for wartime service. However, careful study shows little change resulted from the war, not how much. In the newspaper reports of the time women received a warm welcome; but in farms, hospitals and factories they were greatly resented.

Following this new law, in 1919 Nancy Astor became the first woman MP to take her seat in parliament.

However, younger women, in their twenties, were disappointed with the age limit. Many of these women were the very ones who had done such arduous and useful work in the munitions factories and on farms during the First World War. But some people considered them too young and immature to cope in a responsible way with a vote. Others feared that a female majority in voters, due to the death of so many men during the war, would elect a great number of female MPs.

However, their disappointment was short-lived. In 1928, women aged 21 and over were given the vote. At last, they had equal voting rights to men.

Source D: A flapper from the 1920s.

Social changes

The social position of women continued to improve in some ways too. Labour-saving devices, such as washing machines, allowed women more leisure time. Better contraception gave women more control of when to have children and how many. The war also gave women the confidence to change their appearance and social habits.

- Young women no longer had chaperones. They went out with boyfriends without having to take another female with them.
- Women's clothes were less restrictive and make-up became acceptable. Some women even wore one-piece swimming costumes, instead of costumes with sleeves and skirts.

The 'flappers' were the most extreme example of these social changes. They were young women who challenged old ideas about fashion to express their independence. They wore more revealing clothes, with short skirts, used a lot of make-up and had shorter hair. They drank and smoked in public and adopted American dances, like the Charleston.

Women also made progress in their legal rights.

- In 1923, they were given the same right as men to seek divorce on grounds of adultery.
- The 1925 Property Act allowed married women to own property on the same terms as men.

Employment changes

When the war ended in 1918, most women wanted to keep their jobs. For example, one survey asked 3,000 women: 'Do you wish to return to your former work or stay in the job you are doing now?' 2,500 wanted to stay. But, in fact, women were expected to give up their war work for the returning men.

Women who tried to hold onto their jobs were criticised. It was argued that women who stayed in these jobs were depriving men of jobs.

Source E: From the *Southampton Times*, 1919.

> Women have still not brought themselves to realise that factory work, with the money paid for it, will not be possible again. Women who left domestic service to enter the factory are now required to return to their pots and pans.

Women were therefore forced to return to their more traditional, lower paid, roles or household duties. By the 1930s, women's wages were only half those of men, even if they were doing the same job.

Source F: From a report by the Chief Inspector of Factories, 1919.

> The first year after the end of the War has been a very important one for industry. It is remarkable how complete has been the changeover from war to peacetime production. The first step was the gradual and now almost complete withdrawal of women from the men's industries.

Source G: Graphs comparing women's employment in 1914 and 1931.

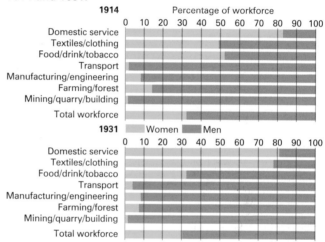

However, even in employment, there was some progress.

- The Sex Disqualification Removal Act of 1919 meant that *single* women could no longer be barred from any job because of their sex. In theory, this meant that they could now enter the professions, such as the law and architecture.
- In 1925, the Civil Service admitted women to government service for the first time.
- Overall, therefore, it was a mixed picture.

Activities

1. List the improvements in the position of women which took place 1918-1939.
2. List the ways in which things went back to how they were before the First World War.
3. Overall, do you think that improvements during the First World War continued or stalled?

7.7 Women in the Second World War

Women's role in the war

The return of war, in 1939, again put Britain in a national emergency. Once more, the role of women changed to meet the country's needs.

- Women were again needed in jobs which were traditionally done by men. By May 1945, there were over 6.5 million women in paid work.
- Women joined voluntary groups. By the end of 1943, there were over a million women in the Women's Voluntary Service (WVS).
- Women also volunteered for, or were conscripted into, the armed forces. Altogether, by May 1945, there were 460,000 women in non-combat, support roles in the women's army, navy and air force, and over 190,000 more in the Auxiliary Territorial Service (ATS).

Overall, by 1943, almost 90 per cent of single women and 80 per cent of married women were doing some kind of work of national importance. Once again, as well as changing the lives of women, this also changed attitudes about women.

Women's attitudes

The war changed the attitudes of some women about their role in society. War work gave many women far more freedom. They enjoyed the independence this gave them. It also gave some women much more confidence about themselves and their abilities (see Sources A and B).

Source A: An interview with Mona Marshall in the 1960s. She worked in the steel industry during the war.

> To be quite honest, the war was the best thing that ever happened to us. I was green as grass and terrified if anyone spoke to me. I had been brought up not to argue. My generation of women had been taught to do as we were told. At work you did exactly as your boss told you and you went home to do exactly as your husband told you. The war changed all that. The war made me stand on my own two feet.

Source B: An interview with Pat Parker, in the 1980s, about her three and a half years in the Women's Land Army.

> Those years were absolutely fantastic. They were complete freedom, where I'd never known it before. I'd always had my father standing on the corner of the street saying, 'You should be indoors.' …And that went on until I was sixteen. Whereas, being away, I could do as I liked. All of a sudden my life was my own.

Source C: A WREN operating a Holman projector on the ranges.

Men's attitudes

The attitudes of many men began to change too. Men in influential positions, for example in business, politics or trade unions, were impressed with the contribution to the war effort made by women.

Source D: Clement Attlee, the Deputy Prime Minister, writing in 1943.

> This work the women are performing in munitions factories has to be seen to be believed. Precision engineering jobs which a few years ago would have made a skilled turner's hair stand on end are performed with deadly accuracy by girls who had no industrial experience.

The **trade unions** began to accept women workers much more readily than they had done in the First World War. The Trades Union Congress (TUC) campaigned to make sure that women were treated the same as men. For example, the TUC successfully complained about the fact that women were paid 25 per cent less and received lower accident compensation than men in the Rolls-Royce armament factories.

Source E: A woman shop steward interviewed in 1941.

> We have no objections to working in the factories but we do object to the conditions we have to work in. Women in industry are called upon to bear burdens that are beyond imagination. Many are soldiers' wives who are obliged to go to work to keep their homes together as their allowances are so inadequate. We have to work up to ten hours a day but we still often only earn half the man's wages.

The government also showed support for women workers. They started to help women with childcare commitments.

- They provided nurseries and encouraged employers to allow women with children to job share.
- By 1944 there were 1,450 nurseries, compared to 104 before the war.

Women's pay

Women's pay, however, continued to lag behind. They were paid less than men for doing the same job, especially in factory work, where they usually received about 75 per cent of a man's wage (see Source F).

Source F: Average weekly wages for men and women in July 1943.

Adult male	Approx £6
Adult female	Approx £3.30
Teenage male	Approx £2.40
Teenage female	Approx £1.70

Based on M. Chandler, *Britain in the Age of Total War*, Heinemann 2002, page 21.

In 1943, the government set up the Equal Pay Commission, to persuade employers to pay women better. But it had no powers to force changes. So, by the end of the war, women were no nearer equality with men in pay than they had been in 1939.

But at least women were earning more than before the war. In 1939, the average woman's wage was about £2 a week. During the war, some women doing dangerous munitions work were earning as much as £10 a week. However, the belief that men should be paid more than women lingered: even amongst women (see Source G).

Source G: A 1942 interview with a woman by the research group Mass Observation.

> I do feel that equal pay would upset the relations between the sexes. Personally, I like a man to have more money than me. It gives me twice as much pleasure to have a dress bought for me by a kindly man than to buy it myself, and this is because I am feminine.

Activities

1 List three examples of how women's roles in the war changed each of the following:
   a) women's attitudes about themselves
   b) men's attitudes towards women
   c) women's conditions of work.
2 Give a detailed example of something which did not change.

7.8 Women after the war

During the Second World War, the lives of women changed; so did the attitudes of many people towards women. But, did that last, after the war ended? What was the situation by the mid-1950s?

Back to the old days?

In some ways, the role of women and attitudes about women seemed to go back to the way they were before.

- Most women willingly left their wartime jobs because they wanted to return to the home. A government survey of 1947 revealed that 58 per cent of women believed that married women should not go out to work. Many had delayed having children during the war and now decided that they wanted to start families.
- Women's career opportunities weren't drastically improved by the war. For example, the new opportunities in areas such as metal manufacturing and engineering only lasted as long as the war. The shutting down of nurseries after the war meant the end of jobs for women with children.
- Women made only slow progress in professions such as medicine and law. As late as 1961 only 15 per cent of doctors and 3 per cent of lawyers were women.
- The Equal Pay Commission, set up in 1944, reported in 1946 that the average male manual worker's wage was £5.70 a week, while the average wage for a woman was £3. The Commission did not recommend any changes, suggesting that women did different jobs from men, so equal pay was not an issue. The male was still seen as the main breadwinner.
- The media continued to portray women in their stereotyped domestic role (see Source C).

Source A: A woman recalls life after the war.

> After a while we settled to some sort of married life but there were times when I thought it was hell on earth, I was living in. Many of us felt as though we were going back to prison.

Source B: Professor Ruth Watts, 2008.

> ...despite the increased educational opportunities from 1944 and full employment in the 1950s, female career choices were restricted by the seemingly universal opinion that woman's place would be in the home, an expectation much confirmed by a younger age of marriage and motherhood. The vast majority of girls left school at 15 and, after a brief training period, entered employment only to leave once married.

Source C: A 1947 advert for new cookers.

Handsome is and handsome does - that's the GAS idea!

The new gas cookers make you a better cook because they are so easy to use — and a prouder housewife because they are so attractive to look at.

BRITISH GAS COUNCIL · 1 GROSVENOR PLACE · LONDON · SW1

Continued progress

But, although most women did leave their wartime jobs and return to a more familiar lifestyle after the war, things didn't quite return to the way they were before.

- The war gave many women more confidence and self-respect. They had shown that not only could they do the same jobs as men but, in many cases, they could do them better.

- The number of married women in paid work stayed above pre-war levels. (See Source D). This shows that there was some change in attitudes towards married women working.
- There was some progress in equal pay. In 1953, equal pay for teachers was agreed and, in 1955, equal pay for civil servants – though, in both cases, this was introduced over time.
- Some women continued to pioneer new ground. The 1950s saw the first female bank manager, television news reader, managing director of an advertising agency and senior permanent secretary in the civil service.

Since the beginning of the twentieth century, the role of women and attitudes towards women had been gradually changing. The two world wars accelerated these changes. After the Second World War, things were never quite the same.

Source D: Married women in paid work (%) from N. DeMarco, *The Second World War,* Hodder 1997, page 54.

1911	1921	1931	1951
10%	9%	10%	22%

Activities

1 Give three detailed examples of ways in which the role of women in society in the 1950s went back to the way it had been before the Second World War.

2 Give three detailed examples of ways in which the role of women in society in the 1950s had improved since before the Second World War.

examzone
Build better answers

[You may find it useful to look at pages 154-155 before attempting this Exam Zone exercise.]

Source B suggests that, after the Second World War, attitudes to women and the role of women in society reverted to the way they had been before the War. How far do you agree with this interpretation?

Explain your answer, using your own knowledge, Sources A, B, C and D and any other sources you find helpful. (16 marks)

■ **Basic, Level 1**
EITHER the answer makes valid comments but with no support from the sources or own knowledge – e.g. *Many women left the jobs they had in wartime.*
OR the answer selects information from the sources but does not relate these to the question asked – e.g. *From 1952, women teachers were paid the same as men.*

● **Good, Level 2**
Answer makes a simple judgement agreeing or disagreeing with the interpretation and links this to relevant evidence in the sources or own knowledge – e.g. *I agree with the interpretation. By 1961, only 15 per cent of doctors and 3 per cent of lawyers were women.*

▲ **Better, Level 3**
Answer makes a developed evaluation of the interpretation, agreeing or disagreeing. It considers a variety of information from the sources and own knowledge to support a case, but mainly puts only one side of the argument.

▲ **Excellent, Level 4**
Answer gives a sustained argument, using sources and own knowledge to evaluate the case for and against the interpretation, finishing with a balanced overall judgment. The best answers will take into account the relative strength of the sources and will recognise the difficulty of coming to a 'true' interpretation.

Make sure you write accurately – there are three marks available for spelling, punctuation and grammar in these questions.

7.9 Using sources to make a case

You may need to use sources to make a case for a specific proposition. Consider this question:

Source D suggests that women loved their time at work during the world wars. How far do you agree with this interpretation? Explain your answer, using your own knowledge, Sources A, B, C, D and E and any other sources you find helpful.

Source A: An official painting of women working in a munitions factory in the First World War.

Source B: From the Southampton Times, 1919.

> Women have still not brought themselves to realise that factory work, with the money paid for it, will not be possible again. Women who left domestic service to enter the factory are now required to return to their pots and pans.

Source C: A woman shop steward interviewed in 1941.

> We have no objections to working in the factories but we do object to the conditions we have to work in. Women in industry are called upon to bear burdens that are beyond imagination. Many are soldiers' wives who are obliged to go to work to keep their homes together as their allowances are so inadequate. We have to work up to ten hours a day but we still often only earn half the man's wages.

Source D: An interview with Pat Parker, in the 1980s, about her three and a half years in the Women's Land Army during the Second World War.

> Those years were absolutely fantastic. They were complete freedom, where I'd never known it before. I'd always had my father standing on the corner of the street saying, 'You should be indoors.' And that went on until I was sixteen. Whereas, being away, I could do as I liked. All of a sudden my life was my own.

Source E: A woman recalls life after the Second World War.

> After a while we settled to some sort of married life but there were times when I thought it was hell on earth, I was living in. Many of us felt as though we were going back to prison.

154

The way to tackle your answer

Outline the answer

The key words in this question are:
- How far do you agree....?

And the way to answer is:
- There is evidence to agree...
- But there is evidence to disagree...
- Overall, I agree (or) disagree because...

Make the case for and against

In the first section, you should find evidence from the sources and your own knowledge to agree with the interpretation in the question.

- Source D puts forward the interpretation.
- Source B seems to support the interpretation.
- Source A seems to support the interpretation.

In some ways, I agree with the interpretation. Source D suggests that women enjoyed their work. In fact, Pat says her work years were 'fantastic'. Pat and the woman in Source E both enjoyed the freedom. Source B supports this too. It suggests that women liked the money paid for factory work and they didn't want to 'return to their pots and pans'. Source A supports the idea too. The women look content and well dressed and the factory looks clean and safe. From my own knowledge, I know that one million women volunteered for the WVS, so they must have enjoyed that work.

In the second section, you need to find evidence from the sources and your own knowledge to challenge the interpretation.

- Source C seems to express reservations about enjoying the work.
- Also, some of the other sources – like Source E – seem a bit half-hearted.

But there are also reasons to disagree. In Source C, a shop steward doesn't enjoy the work. She says that women had to carry heavy burden of maintaining their homes on top of their paid work. She also says 'We have to work up to ten hours per day, but we still often only earn half the man's wages.' She says women don't object to the work, but this is not really enjoying it. Also, Sources B, D and E don't really say they enjoyed the work, they just say they liked the freedom and wages. I don't trust Source A, the official painting, and I know from my own knowledge that the Land Army girls often worked 12 hour days.

Write a conclusion

It doesn't matter whether you decide to agree or disagree with the proposition in the question. The key thing is to:
- support one side or the other
- explain what made you decide.

Overall, I agree with the interpretation. I think most women did enjoy their work in wartime. It was long and arduous and they didn't get the same money as men. But I think the key is in Sources B, D and E. Compared to their lives before, women enjoyed the freedom and independence work gave them. One woman, Mona Marshall, worked in a steel factory. She said war work was the best thing that ever happened to her.

7.10 War and social divisions

A divided society

British society at the beginning of the twentieth century was clearly divided.

There were class divisions.

- The upper class owned most of the land in Britain, much of which was farmed.
- The middle classes were mainly business and professional people, many of whom lived in the cities.
- The working classes were the poorest in society.
- The quality of life varied hugely between these classes and there was very little movement between them.

There was also a clear gender division.

- Women were widely regarded as inferior to men and their role in society was narrow.
- The opportunities available to men and women varied greatly.

War reduced social divisions

We have looked at the effects of several wars:
- the Boer War of 1899-1902
- the First World War of 1914-1918
- the Second World War of 1939-1945

In each case, these wars resulted in improvements for the poor in the provision of health, financial security and educational opportunities.

We have also seen how war brought changes in the lives of women and attitudes towards women.

As a result, social divisions in Britain began to break down.

Social mobility

By the 1950s, men born into working class surroundings were much more able to improve themselves. And this social mobility was even greater for women than for men (see Source A).

Source A: Percentage of men and women born to working class fathers who remained working class.

Born	before 1900	in 1920s	in 1940s
Men	76%	67%	53%
Women	68%	57%	41%

Source: Twentieth Century Trend in Social Mobility in Britain, Heath and Payne, 1999.

This meant that social divisions in Britain were much less rigid. A key reason for this was that improved education raised the ambitions of bright working class children and enabled them to get better qualifications. These two things gave them a chance to get better paid jobs.

Dame Caroline Haslett

Caroline Haslett was the kind of woman who benefited from the social changes brought by war in the twentieth century.

She was born in 1895, the daughter of a railway fitter. Her first job was as a secretary for a boiler company. But, during the First World War, she worked in their factory and trained as an engineer.

Between the wars, she used these skills to pioneer electrical products for the home. She also founded the Women's Engineering Society, was a magistrate and was made a Dame of the British Empire in 1947.

But did war make the difference?

It is, of course, possible that social divisions would have been broken down even if there had been no wars at all in the twentieth century. We can't know.

However, war certainly united the social classes in a common effort to defeat the common enemy. This meant that the social classes felt less divided.

Source B: A.H. Halsey, Reith Lectures, 1977.

> We do well to remind ourselves of the integrating aspects of war. It is a paradox of conflict that it promotes equality and fraternity within the nation. This is true especially of modern 'total' war. If all must be called upon to fight for their country, all must be brought to believe that they have a stake in it.

Most historians agree that war was a key factor in improving the lot of women and the poor, and reducing the divisions in society.

Source C: Paul Addison, a modern historian.

> Most historians detect in the war years a modest levelling process which redistributed income and influence in favour of the working classes.
>
> We only need to glance at the period to see looming up before us those two giant landmarks, the Beveridge Report of 1942 and the Labour victory at the 1945 general election.
>
> There may be ingenious arguments which appear to divorce these events entirely from the war effort, or the pattern of welfare; but there are also ingenious conjurors who appear to saw the lady in half.

Social divisions had not disappeared by 1954, but, partly because of the impact of war, they had been reduced.

Summary

Between 1900 and 1954, the Boer War, First World War and Second World Wars changed:

- the lives of the poor
- the health and welfare of Britain
- the role of women in British society
- social divisions in Britain.

Inference

Historical sources can provide information about the past. Sometimes, they tell us that information directly.

For example:
- Source A on page 156 tells us that 76 per cent of men born to working class fathers before 1900 remained working class throughout their lives.
- Source C tells us that the Beveridge Report was dated 1942 and the Labour Party won the general election in 1945.

This is useful information. But all you need to do in order to find out this information is understand – or comprehend – the source. That is not inference.

An inference is something:
- which the source *does not tell you directly*
- which *you can work out* from the source.

For example:
Source C *tells us* that there was 'a modest levelling which redistributed income and influence in favour of the working classes'. The working classes became better off and more influential. That's not an inference, because the source directly tells us.

- However, based on that information, we can *infer* that at least one of the other classes, the upper and middle classes, must have become *worse off or less influential* in comparison with the working class. The source does not tell us this directly, but we can work it out.
- You can *support* this inference from information in the source, because it tells us that the Labour Party – the party of the working class – won the election in 1945. This *supports* the idea that the working class was now *more powerful* than the other classes.

You may be asked what you can learn from a source. As well as saying what the source *tells* you, you should also try to say what you can *infer* from the source and find information in the source to *support your inference*.

8.1 The role of the government

> ### Learning outcomes
>
> By the end of this section you should be able to explain how the following three factors shaped changes in the lives of British citizens during wars 1900-1954:
>
> - the government
> - the media
> - industry.

We have seen how Britain's problems in the Boer War prompted the Liberal Reforms of 1906-11. This was an example of government intervening in society to make things fairer and improve the war effort. Even greater government intervention would follow during the First and Second World Wars.

Leadership and organisation

Both world wars in the twentieth century involved 'total warfare'. This meant harnessing all the assets of the nation to the war effort.

So, in both world wars, the government took the role of leading and organising this war effort. This meant an expansion in the role of government and a huge impact on the lives of citizens.

- To strengthen Britain's armed forces, the government changed recruitment to the armed forces. Conscription – the forced recruitment of young men and women into the armed forces – was adopted in both world wars.
- To harness industry to the war effort, the government took a strategic oversight of some industries and even took over direct control of others, taking direct responsibility for the work of millions of workers.
- To protect food supplies, the government prevented the free sale and purchase of food by introducing rationing and other measures to ensure that the country was not starved into submission.

- To maintain morale and increase support for the war effort, the government used propaganda and censorship: government censorship deprived people of some information and its propaganda shaped and controlled the flow of all other information.

Key individuals in government also shaped the war effort.

David Lloyd George

Lloyd George transformed and greatly expanded the role of government during the First World War.

- He became Minister of Munitions in 1915. His department had 'no staff, no tables and too many mirrors'. By 1918, as a result of his efforts, the ministry had a staff of 65,000 and directed the efforts of over 3 million workers.
- He championed the policy of employing women in munitions factories.
- As prime minister, 1916–1918, he led the re-organisation of society for 'total war'.

Source A: A 1915 Punch Magazine cartoon, featuring Lloyd George.

DELIVERING THE GOODS.

Winston Churchill

Churchill's role, as prime minister during the Second World War, was slightly different. Like Lloyd George, his government did increase its role in the organisation of society. However, Churchill also emphasised the importance of leadership by the government.

- He used his skills as a speaker to maintain the morale of the British people during times of hardship, such as the Blitz. He also united the nation during the times of greatest danger, for example, after the evacuation of British troops from Dunkirk, when there was a risk of invasion (see Source C).

Source B: A 1940 poster featuring Churchill.

Source C: Churchill speaking to the House of Commons in June 1940, after the evacuation from Dunkirk.

We shall defend our island. We shall fight on the beaches, we shall fight on the landing grounds, we shall fight in the streets, we shall fight in the hills. We shall never surrender.

Big government

Because of wars, important social changes were introduced by:

- the Liberal government after 1906
- the governments during and after the First and Second World Wars.

These huge changes showed that, when government played a bigger role in society, it made a real difference to people's lives.

This had a lasting affect on Britain. A government which took responsibility for the welfare of the people and exerted a degree of control over all the assets of the nation became a lasting feature of Britain.

However, there are dangers in big government (see sources D and E).

Source D: The 1939 Emergency Powers Act.

Such persons may be detained whose detention appears to the Secretary of State to be expedient in the interests of public safety or the defence of the realm. The Secretary of State for Labour has the authority to oblige any person in the United Kingdom to perform any service required in any place.

Source E: Walter L. Arnstein, a modern historian.

At the same time, the government had transformed Britain into one of the most regulation-ridden and **bureaucratic** of lands; by 1951, more than 26 percent of its people worked for the government at a time when 17 per cent of Americans and 11 per cent of West Germans did so.

Activities

1 Look at Sources A, B and C. How do they show the impact of Lloyd George and Churchill on the role of government?

2 a) Make a list of the ways in which 'big' government expanded its role in society due to war, 1903-54.

   b) What were the benefits of this?

   c) Look at Sources D and E. What do they suggest are the dangers of 'big' government? Can you add any more?

8.2 The use of the media

The impact of the media

One factor which shaped the impact of war on Britain between 1903 and 1954 was the media.

The Boer War

Newspapers had a big impact after the Boer War. This was Britain's first major war in the age of mass literacy, following Foster's Education Act of 1870. Improvements to the telegraph service also helped war reporters.

For example, newspapers:

- sent over 300 reporters to South Africa to cover the war. The *Times* alone sent twenty. The public were kept fully aware of Britain's poor performance. Afterwards, newspapers campaigned for reform of the army to improve Britain's fighting forces.
- publicised reports putting the blame for Britain's war performance on the poor fitness of recruits. A 1903 headline in the Nottingham Evening Post rang out '*Why We Are Deteriorating?*'; it was an advert for medicine.
- joined the campaign for reforms to help the poor, so that the British people would be stronger in the future.

All this contributed to the Liberal Reforms of 1906-11.

The First and Second World Wars

The media were used by the government during the First and Second World Wars for censorship, propaganda and entertainment.

A range of media was involved, including letters and the press. New media, like radio and film, were particularly powerful. Government market research carefully monitored their effect on people. See pages 108-113 for details.

Propaganda

Propaganda was the spread of information – using posters, newspapers and film, etc – to help the war effort. During both the First and Second World Wars, the use of propaganda was prolific.

Censorship

Censorship was the control of information to protect the war effort. During the First World War:

- in 1914, the only journalist allowed to report the war was an army officer, Colonel Swinton, working under the code name *Eyewitness*
- in January 1915, five selected journalists from a variety of newspapers were allowed to report
- it was November 1916 before they were allowed up to the battle front.

Entertainment

Entertainment was used to keep morale high and strengthen the war effort. Radio and film kept up the spirits of millions of Britons and ENSA tours boosted the morale of troops.

- Vera Lynn was a singer who was given her own BBC radio show. She sang patriotic songs like *We'll Meet Again* and *White Cliffs of Dover*, and broadcast messages to soldiers abroad. She also toured military bases to entertain the troops and became known as the 'Forces' Sweetheart'.

How effective was the use of the media?

The government control of the media was very effective. One way to judge how effective is to study people's reaction to war. For example, we know that:

- although censorship was a severe curtailment of the normal liberties of the British people, there were few complaints during either conflict
- the great majority of people accepted it as a necessity of wartime that would end once the enemy was defeated.

Source A: A queue of volunteers outside a British recruiting office in 1914.

Source B: A British soldier writing in 1914.

> I adore war. It is like a big picnic. I have never been so well or so happy. Nobody grumbles at you for being dirty. I have only had my boots off once in the last ten days and only washed twice.

Source C: Siegfried Sassoon served in the First World War. This is what he wrote in 1917. He is also a famous poet, one of many who became disillusioned with the war.

> I believe that the war is prolonged by those who have the power to end it. I believe that this war upon which I entered as a war of liberation and defence has now become a war of conquest and aggression. I have seen and endured the sufferings of the troops and I can no longer be a party to prolonging those sufferings for ends [aims] which I believe to be evil and unjust.

Source D: From a broadcast by the popular playwright and broadcaster, J. B. Priestley, 5 June 1940, the day after the Dunkirk evacuation ended.

> Among those paddle steamers that will never return was one I knew well, for it was the pride of our ferry service to the Isle of Wight… She has paddled and churned away – for ever. But now… this little steamer… is immortal. She'll go sailing proudly down the years in the epic of Dunkirk.

Source E: A cartoon from the *Daily Express,* November 1940, during the Blitz.

"IS IT ALL RIGHT NOW, HENRY?"
"YES, NOT EVEN SCRATCHED."

Source F: From 'World War II today', a modern web site.

> In a week when over 300 civilians were killed and over 600 seriously injured in bombing raids, the Ministry of Information was able to report to the Cabinet that morale on the Home Front was excellent. The daily reports were compiled from a variety of sources, including formal one-to-one surveys, as well as reports of conversations 'overheard' in public places.

Activities

1   Using these pages and pages 108-113, describe how the media was used for:
    a) campaigning for change
    b) censorship
    c) propaganda
    d) entertainment.

2   Look at Sources A-F. Overall, how effective do they suggest that government use of the media was? Explain your answer.

8.3 The impact of changes in industry

We have seen on pages 120-121 how the government reorganised industry during the First and Second World Wars. These changes in industry had a major impact on the lives of civilians.

More women working in industry was one change. So many women were employed to work in munitions factories in the First World War that it is estimated that women produced about 80 per cent of all munitions by 1917. It was a change which was even more marked in the Second World War, when eight times as many women took on war work as in the First World War. Eventually, during the Second World War, women made up one third of the total workforce in the metal and chemical industries, shipbuilding and vehicle manufacture.

There are various views of the impact of all this. For example:

- Some historians think that the status of women in society changed dramatically as a result of wartime work. They point out, for example, that their work during the First World War did much to further the cause of female suffrage.
- However, others maintain that it was only a short-term change. They would say that, despite changes in working practices *during* wartime, most women left their jobs once the war ended.

Another important change was that workers lost control over where they would work. During the Second World War, for example, the government could force them to take a job where the war effort needed them. Some workers enjoyed the change. See Source A for example.

Source A: A land girl, interviewed in 1941.

> When you were on pigs, which had to be cleaned out and fed before breakfast, no one would sit near you because of the smell. Before they let us loose on the dairy cows we had to train on a rubber udder, which was a laugh. We didn't get a lot of free time.

In the coal shortage of 1940, some 30,000 miners were told they had to leave the army and return to their old jobs. Additional men were conscripted into the mines; these were known as the 'Bevin Boys'.

Men from wealthier backgrounds experienced, for the first time, the often unpleasant working conditions down the mines. Not surprisingly, many were unhappy about this (see Source B).

Source B: *East Grinstead Observer*, November 1944. Courtesy of egcourier.co.uk.

> Thomas Lower, aged 18, of Grantham Cottages, Copthorne, pleaded guilty at East Grinstead Magistrates Court on Monday for not reporting for training in the coal mines.
>
> When interviewed, Lower said: "I will go into any of the Forces but not the mines. I would rather go to gaol."
>
> Mr. A. J. Burt told Lower that coal mining was as valuable a service as entering the Forces and it was in the nation's interest that the defendant should obey the directives of the government.

Workers' freedom was also severely restricted. Wages and hours of work were strictly controlled. Working conditions also changed. Workers were expected to work long hours, night shifts and right through the holidays.

Source C: An ex-land girl, interviewed many years later, in 2005.

> [On one] farm in Lincolnshire we worked for twelve hours a day at very hard work and received no training. Wages were £1.40 a week, out of which we had to pay £1 for our lodgings. At a smaller farm in Huntingdonshire… the farmer gave us no training and refused to pay us any wages.

In weapons factories, in particular, the demand for war munitions meant that factories worked almost round the clock. Long hours led to accidents as safety was sometimes seen as secondary to producing more munitions.

The worst factory accident was at Silvertown in the East End of London. On January 19th 1917, the munitions factory exploded and 69 people were killed and over 400 injured. Extensive damage was done to the area around the factory.

Source D: The memories of George Grainger, a Bevin Boy, written in 1985.

> I worked on one of the worst shifts one could imagine, 6.30p.m. till 2.30a.m. We would be going to work when most people have finished, or going out for the evening. But someone had it to do and we were the unlucky ones. I had one nasty accident during my time at Chester-Moor. We were working at one of the gates. Unknown to us some miners had pushed a tub into our gate, forgetting to tell us it was there… when me and my mate backed our full tub out… I'm afraid I wasn't quick enough to get my full body in between the pit props, and one of my hands got caught in two of the tub handles.

Summary

The wars which occurred in the first half of the 20th century changed the lives of British people.

There were three factors which shaped these changes:

- the actions of government
- the use of the media
- changes in industry.

Source E: The front page of a *Boy's Own* comic, 1944.

Activities

1 Record two examples of each of the following ways in which changes in industry impacted on the lives of workers during wartime:

   a) workers losing control of where they worked

   b) workers suffering harsh working conditions

   c) women working in unfamiliar jobs.

2 Look at sources A to E. For each source, consider it as evidence of working conditions during wartime. Make a list of:

   a) reasons why you might trust the source

   b) reasons why you might not trust it.

164

Introduction to the exam

The examination for this unit of your course tests your understanding of the way that a historian uses sources.

The examination:

- lasts 1 hour and 15 minutes
- has 5 questions
- contains 6 sources which you will need in order to to answer the questions.

All the questions will focus on source skills.

To answer Questions 2, 3, 4 and 5 you are told to use:

a) the sources

and

b) your own knowledge of the impact of war.

You will not be able to gain the highest marks for Questions 2, 3, 4 and 5 unless you use your own knowledge as well as the sources to answer the questions.

You do not have any choice in the questions so make sure that you have covered all of the specification in your revision and you are prepared for the sorts of question that are likely to be asked.

Self-evaluation checklist

When preparing for the examination, make sure that you know and understand the following:

The civilian experience of total war

- The experience of air raids, bombing and the Blitz, and its impact on morale.
- Civilian attitudes and responses to the First and Second World Wars: the role of volunteers.
- The use and experience of propaganda and censorship.

The impact of government war organisation

- DORA, recruitment for the armed forces, the reorganisation of industry, rationing and evacuation.
- The role of women.
- The economic and social legacy of the Second World War after 1945.
- The effects on society and industry of government actions in war.

The impact of war on society

- The Boer War and the Liberal Party reforms which followed it.
- The First World War and its impact on society, including welfare, and medical and health provision.
- The Second World War and its impact on society, including the Beveridge Report and Labour Party reforms after 1945.
- Changes in attitudes: social mobility and the changing role of women.
- The role of war in reducing social divisions.

Factors influencing change

- The role of government.
- The role of the media, propaganda, censorship and entertainment.
- The impact on civilians of changes in industry.

1 Are the following statements true or false? If they are false, what is the correct statement?

	True	False
The Defence of the Realm Act was introduced during the First World War.		
Zeppelins bombed Britain during the Second World War.		
Women over the age of 30 were given the vote in 1918.		
Lloyd George was Minister of Munitions 1915–1916.		
The flappers were women who wanted greater freedom.		
Rationing was only used in the Second World War.		
Conscription was introduced for the first time in 1939.		
Censorship was only used in the First World War.		
The Blitz destroyed the morale of the British people.		
The majority of women remained in their wartime jobs once both wars ended.		
The Emergency Powers Act was introduced during the Second World War.		

2 The following paragraph is not an accurate account.

   a) Find the errors.

   b) Write out the paragraph and correct the errors, replacing them with the correct answer.

> Before the First World War the suffragettes campaigned for the vote peacefully. Their campaign was supported by most men and women. Once the war broke out they called off their campaign. In 1915 Winston Churchill, the Minister of Munitions, decided to employ women due to labour shortages. Women earned less than they had done before the war. The government was not impressed with the work done by women. As a result, women over the age of 25 were given the vote in 1921.

Support activities

Making inferences

Source A: Extract from a letter by Humphrey Jennings to his wife, during the Blitz of 1940–1941.

> What warmth – what courage! What determination! People singing in public shelters. WVS (Women's Voluntary Service) girls serving hot drinks to fire-fighters during raids. Everyone secretly delighted with the privilege of holding up Hitler. Certainly of beating him.

Read Source A.

   a) What can you learn from Source A about the effects of the Blitz?

   b) Which of the statements on the following page are simple comprehension, inferences and/or supported inferences from the source?

Support activities

	Comprehension	Inference	Supported inference
The Blitz did not destroy the morale of people because they were singing in the shelters.			
The Blitz did not destroy the morale of people.			
The Blitz made people even more determined as they were confident Hitler would be defeated.			
People were singing in public shelters.			
Everyone was delighted with holding up Hitler.			

Support activities

Making comparisons

Working in groups, make a copy of, and complete, the following table comparing the impact of the two world wars. Use all the knowledge you have gained in this book.

	Similarities	Differences
Propaganda		
Censorship		
Recruitment		
Impact on women		
Role of government		
Rationing		
Impact of bombing		

Patterns of change, 1903–1954 activity

Below is an empty graph of Britain in the years 1900–1960 for you to use to show how the role of women in society (in red) and the role of government in society (in green) became greater and lesser at different times over this period.

Make a copy of the graph and complete it. Ensure you make entries at regular intervals; include 1900, 1910, 1915, 1920, 1939, 1945, 1950 and 1954.

What conclusions can you make from your graph about changes in:

- the role of women
- the role of government?

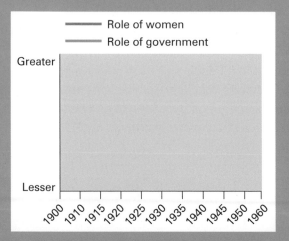

What can you learn from Source A about reactions to women working in the First World War? (6 marks)

Source A: A government report written after the war, describing reactions to women working in industry in 1915.

> In every industrial district there was continuous opposition from men to the introduction of women. There were cases of refusal to instruct women, or attempts to restrict the scope of their work to discredit their efforts. In some cases this opposition was overt to the point of striking.

Student answer	**Comments**	**Improved student answer**
Men in general did not like women working in industry at this time. Some would not work with women.	This is a valid inference about men's attitudes. To improve, the answer should: • provide support for the inference from the source • provide a second supported inference.	Source A shows that men in general did not like women working in industry. I can tell this because it says there was opposition in every industrial district to the introduction of women. Source A also infers that the opposition to women was deeply felt. I can tell this because the source says that the opposition was continuous and that some men even went to the extreme of striking to show their disapproval.

What was the purpose of this representation? (8 marks)
Explain your answer, using Source B and your own knowledge.

Source B: A poster produced by the government in 1916.

Student answer	**Comments**	**Improved student answer**
The purpose of the source is to get women to work. It shows a woman doing her bit by making munitions.	This is a valid statement of purpose, supported from the source. To improve the answer, the student needs to: • analyse the source more • explain his or her answer • use his/her own knowledge to provide support.	The purpose of the source is to encourage women to work to help the war effort. The source achieves this by showing that the soldier is grateful to the woman who is putting on her work clothes to make munitions. I know more munitions workers were needed in 1916, because of the munitions shortage in 1915. I also know that more women workers were needed in 1916, because conscription of men into the armed forces began in that year. Women were needed to fill jobs men had to leave.

examzone

Build better answers

Did women enjoy working in factories during the First World War? (10 marks)
Explain your answer, using Source C and your own knowledge.

Source C: One woman's experiences in the First World War, written in 1919.

> Over and over the foreman gave me the wrong or incomplete directions and altered them in such a way as to create hours more work. I had no tools that I needed. It was out of the question to borrow anything from the men. None of the men spoke to me for a long time, and would give me no help...

Student answer	Comments	Improved student answer
This woman didn't enjoy working much. The source says she got no support or company from the foreman or the male workers.	This is a supported statement. To improve, it needs to: • be developed into a wider answer • give support from other sources and from own knowledge.	[Student adds]... In fact it appears that her job was made harder by the male workers. Other women had a similar experience, e.g. Source A. But, from my own knowledge, I know that some women enjoyed the freedom and independence work gave them and, in a government survey of 1918, many wished to stay in their new jobs after the war. [Gives further examples.]

How reliable are Sources D and E as evidence of how successful women factory workers were in the First World War? (10 marks)
Explain your answer, using Sources D and E and your own knowledge.

Source D: Minister of Munitions, 1916.

> Women of every station have proved themselves able to undertake work that before the war was regarded solely the province of men. Where is a man now who would deny to women the civil rights which she has earned by her hard work?

Source E: The Reverend Clark, 1915.

> Mr Caldwell called. He had talked with a foreman, who said the women workers were doing splendidly. Lads were often selfishly thoughtless and larked about. The women worked thoughtfully and steadily.

Student answer	Comments	Improved student answer
Source D may not be reliable. Ministers were keen to get more women workers, so he may have ignored problems.	The answer makes a valid judgment based on *provenance* and uses some own knowledge to support the answer. To improve, the answer needs to: • consider *both* sources • make a judgement of reliability based on the *content* of the sources • use more knowledge of the *context* of the sources to judge their reliability.	[Student adds]... The Minister's view is also supported by Source E. This source is probably more reliable. I can see no reason for the reverend to be biased and the foreman's information is detailed, so it sounds informed. The content of Reverend Clark's opinion is also supported by a report in 1918, which showed that women's work was usually as good, if not better, than the men's. However, I also know that this report said that men remained better than women for some jobs, like shell making. So the sources are not reliable as evidence about every type of job.

Source F suggests that attitudes about women changed as a result of their work during the First World War. How far do you agree with this interpretation? (16 marks)

Explain your answer, using your own knowledge, Sources D, E and F and any other sources you find helpful.

Additional credit of up to 3 marks will be given for the quality of spelling, punctuation and grammar.

Source F: From a speech by Herbert Asquith, prime minister 1908-1916.

> How could we have carried on the war without women? Wherever we turn we see them doing work which three years ago we would have regarded as exclusively 'men's work'. But what I confess moves me still more in the matter is the problem of what to do when the war is over. The question will then arise about women's labour and women's functions in the new order of things. Things have changed. I would now find it impossible to withhold from them the power and the right of making their voices directly heard.

Student answer

Source F does show that Asquith's attitude to women changed.

The vicar in Source E has a good view of women workers too.

The minister in Source D has changed his views too. He says 'Where is a man now who would deny to women… civil rights…?'

Comments

The answer gives two valid examples (from Sources F and D) of men's views changing. The example from Source E, however, does not show *change*.

It also successfully finds an extract from Source D to support the answer.

To improve, the student should:

- consider both sides of the argument – that views may have changed and may not have changed
- move away from giving a series of statements and provide an argued case
- provide support for the answer based on his or her own knowledge
- come to a conclusion as to how far the student agrees or disagrees.

The student also needs to consider that the best answers need to show good spelling, punctuation and grammar, achieve a consistent level of accuracy and, when required, use specialist historical terms with precision.

Improved student answer

Source F does show that Asquith's attitude to women changed. He said that he now sees women doing work he used to think of as 'exclusively "men's work"'. I know from my own knowledge that, before the war, he opposed the suffragists and suffragettes. Now he says he would 'find it impossible'.

Source D also shows us men who had positive attitudes to women. For example, the Minister of Munitions states that women had proved themselves capable of undertaking work that before the war was 'regarded solely the province of men'.

The vicar in Source E has a good view of women workers too, though there is no evidence of <u>change</u> in this source.. But Sources F and D do not give us the whole picture. Sources A and C show that, amongst ordinary men on the shop floor, there was 'continuous opposition' to women at work. I know, from my own knowledge, that many men continued to oppose the idea of votes for women.

Overall, I think attitudes did change, but only a little and only amongst some men. Don't forget, they didn't allow women's lives to change that much. In 1911 only 10 per cent of married women worked. Although many more women went to work during the war, by 1931 still only 10 per cent were working and married women could still be barred from the workplace.

Welcome to exam zone

Revising for your exams can be a daunting prospect. In this part of the book we'll take you through the best way of revising for your exams, step by step, to help you perform as well as you can.

Zone In!

Have you ever become so absorbed in a task that suddenly it feels entirely natural and easy to perform? This is a feeling familiar to many athletes and performers. They work hard to recreate it in competition in order to do their very best. It's a feeling of being 'in the zone', and if you can achieve that same feeling in an examination, the chances are you'll perform brilliantly.

The good news is that you can get 'in the zone' by taking some simple steps in advance of the exam. Here are our top tips.

UNDERSTAND IT

Make sure you understand the exam process and what revision you need to do. This will give you confidence and also help you to get things into proportion. These pages are a good place to find some starting pointers for performing well in exams.

BUILD CONFIDENCE

Use your revision time not only to revise content, but also to build your confidence in readiness for tackling the examination. For example, try tackling a short sequence of easy tasks in record time.

DEAL WITH DISTRACTIONS

Think about the issues in your life that may interfere with revision. Write them all down. Then think about how you can deal with each so they don't affect your revision.

FRIENDS AND FAMILY

Make sure that your friends and family know when you want to revise. Even share your revision plan with them. Learn to control your times with them, so you don't get distracted. This means you can have better quality time with them when you aren't revising, because you aren't worrying about what you ought to be doing.

DIET AND EXERCISE

Make sure you eat sensibly and exercise as well! If your body is not in the right state, how can your mind be? A substantial breakfast will set you up for the day, and a light evening meal will keep your energy levels high. Also, make sure you drink plenty of water while revising, and during the exam. Even at rest, your brain uses up about 30% of your energy and fluid intake to work effectively!

COMPARTMENTALISE

You might not be able to deal with all the issues that can distract you. For example, you may be worried about a friend who is ill, or just be afraid of the exam. In this case, there is still a useful technique you can use. Put all of these worries into an imagined box in your mind at the start of your revision (or in the exam) and mentally lock it. Only open it again at the end of your revision session (or exam).

The key to success in exams and revision often lies in good planning. Knowing **what** you need to do and **when** you need to do it is your best path to a stress-free experience. Here are some top tips in creating a great personal revision plan.

First of all, **know your strengths and weaknesses**.

Go through each topic making a list of how well you think you know the topic. Use your mock examination results and/or any other test results that are available as a check on your self-assessment. This will help you to plan your personal revision effectively, putting extra time into your weaker areas.

Next, *create your plan!*
Remember to make time for considering how topics interrelate.

For example, in History you will be expected to know not just the date when an event happened, but why it happened, how important it was, and how one event relates to another.

The specification quite clearly states when you are expected to be able to link one topic to another so plan this into your revision sessions.

You will be tested on this in the exam and you can gain valuable marks by showing your ability to do this.

Finally, *follow the plan!*
You can use the revision sections in the following pages to kick-start your revision.

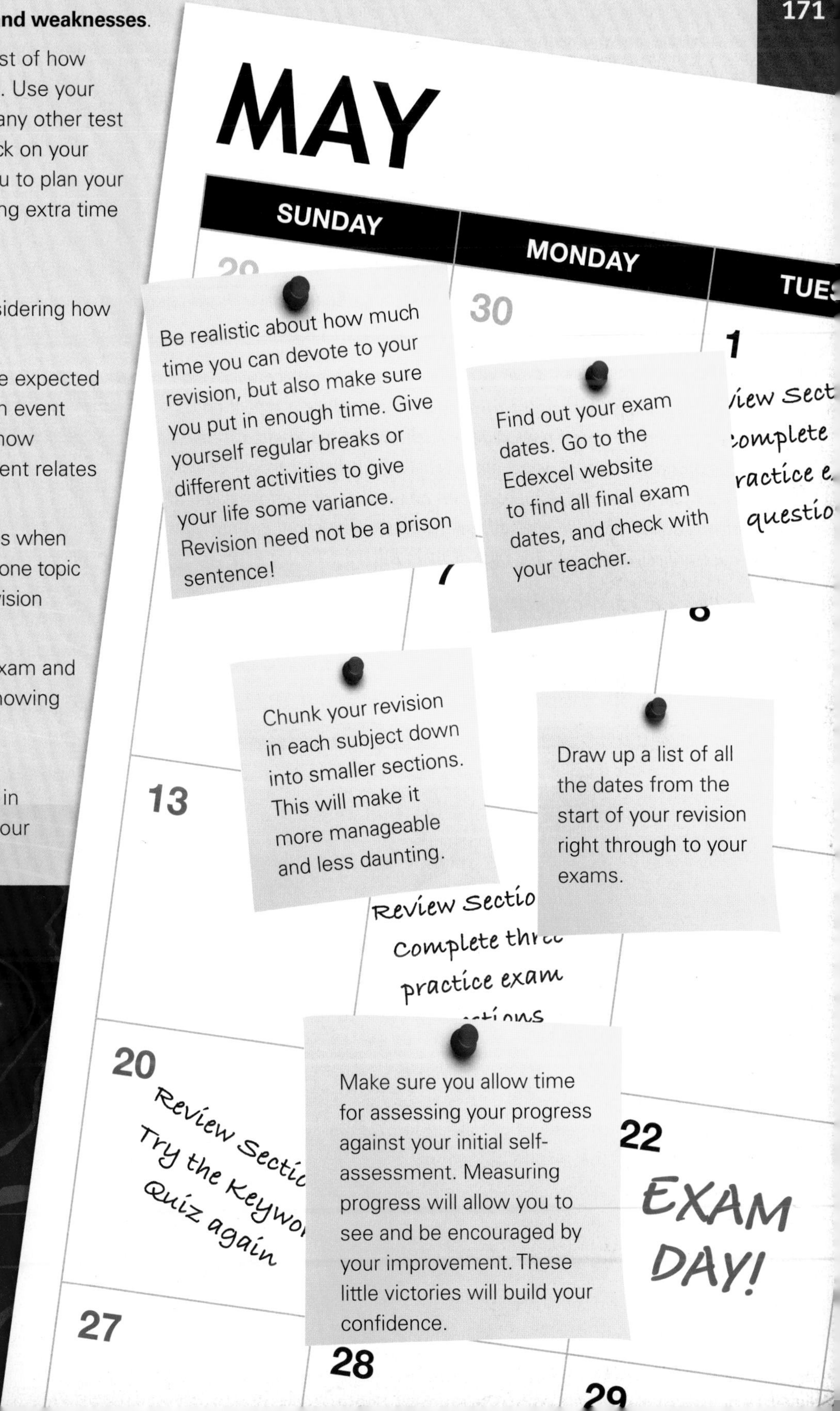

MAY

SUNDAY	MONDAY	TUES
29	30	1

Be realistic about how much time you can devote to your revision, but also make sure you put in enough time. Give yourself regular breaks or different activities to give your life some variance. Revision need not be a prison sentence!

Find out your exam dates. Go to the Edexcel website to find all final exam dates, and check with your teacher.

iew Sect
complete
ractice e.
questio

Chunk your revision in each subject down into smaller sections. This will make it more manageable and less daunting.

Draw up a list of all the dates from the start of your revision right through to your exams.

13

Review Sectio
Complete three
practice exam
...ions

20

Review Secti
Try the Keywo
Quiz again

Make sure you allow time for assessing your progress against your initial self-assessment. Measuring progress will allow you to see and be encouraged by your improvement. These little victories will build your confidence.

22

EXAM DAY!

27

28

29

As you get close to completing your revision, the Big Day will be getting nearer and nearer. Many students find this the most stressful time and tend to go into panic mode, either working long hours without really giving their brains a chance to absorb information or giving up and staring blankly at the wall.

Panicking simply makes your brain seize up and you find that information and thoughts simply cannot flow naturally. You become distracted and anxious, and things seem worse than they are. Many students build the exams up into more than they are. Remember: the exams are not trying to catch you out! If you have studied the course, there will be no surprises on the exam paper!

Student tip

I know how silly it is to panic, especially if you've done the work and know your stuff. I was asked by a teacher to produce a report on a project I'd done, and I panicked so much I spent the whole afternoon crying and worrying. I asked other people for help, but they were panicking too. In the end, I calmed down and looked at the task again. It turned out to be quite straightforward and, in the end, I got my report finished first and it was the best of them all!

In the exam you don't have much time, so you can't waste it by panicking. The best way to control panic is simply to do what you have to do. Think carefully for a few minutes, then start writing and as you do, the panic will drain away.

Don't panic

Make sure you know in which order you are sitting your exams and prepare for each accordingly – check with your teacher if you're not sure. They are likely to be about a week apart, so make sure you allow plenty of revision time for each before your first exam.

For the **Changing nature of warfare** paper, you will have an hour and a quarter for the exam, and in that time you have to answer five questions. You need to answer Questions 1, 2 and 3. Then you must choose to answer either Question 4 or Question 5, and then choose to answer one question from Questions 6 and 7.

For the **Impact of war on Britain c1903-c1954** paper, you will have an hour and a quarter and in that time you have to answer five questions. There are no choices for this exam.

Each question on each paper is worth a different number of marks and it is important that you use your time effectively. Don't waste precious time on a 6-mark question that might then leave you with too little time to spend on a question which is worth 16 marks – plus an extra 3 for SPaG!

Meet the exam paper

This diagram shows the front cover of the exam paper. These instructions, information and advice will always appear on the front of the paper. It is worth reading it carefully now. Check you understand it. Now is a good opportunity to ask your teacher about anything you are not sure of here.

Print your surname here, and your other names afterwards. This is an additional safeguard to ensure that the exam board awards the marks to the right candidate.

Here you fill in the school's exam number.

Ensure that you understand exactly how long the examination will last, and plan your time accordingly.

Note that in questions marked with an asterisk (*) the quality of your written communication will also be marked. Take particular care to present your thoughts and work at the highest standard you can.

Here you fill in your personal exam number. Take care when writing it down because the number is important to the exam board when writing your score.

In this box, the examiner will write the total marks you have achieved in the exam paper.

Make sure that you understand exactly which questions from which sections you should attempt.

Don't feel that you have to fill the answer space provided. Everybody's handwriting varies, so a long answer from you may take up as much space a short answer from someone else.

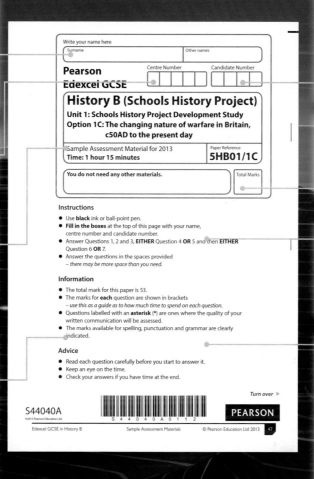

Understanding the language of the exam paper

Describe	The examiner is looking for a concise and organised account.
Explain how/why	The examiner is trying to discover whether you understand the key ideas about how and why developments happened in the history of warfare. The more detail you can give, the more marks you will receive.
How useful...? How reliable...?	These questions involve source evaluation skills – look for clues that tell you about origins, intention, nature, selection…
How far	Questions that ask 'How far do you agree…' with an interpretation are looking for you to consider different sides and come up with a balanced judgment.

ZoneOut

This section provides answers to the most common questions students have about what happens after they complete their exams. For more information, visit www.examzone.co.uk

About your grades

Whether you've done better than, worse than, or just as you expected, your grades are the final measure of your performance on your course and in the exams. On this page we explain some of the information that appears on your results slip and tell you what to do if you think something is wrong. We answer the most common questions about grades and look at some of the options facing you.

When will my results be published?

Results for GCSE History examinations are issued on the third Thursday in August.

Can I get my results online?

Visit www.resultsplusdirect.co.uk, where you will find detailed student results information including the 'Edexcel Gradeometer' which demonstrates how close you were to the nearest grade boundary.

I haven't done as well as I expected. What can I do now?

First of all, talk to your subject teacher. After all the teaching that you have had, and the tests and internal examinations you have done, he/she is the person who best knows what grade you are capable of achieving. Take your results slip to your subject teacher, and go through the information on it in detail. If you both think there is something wrong with the result, the school or college can apply to see your completed examination paper and then, if necessary, ask for a re-mark immediately.

Can I have a re-mark of my examination paper?

Yes, this is possible, but remember that only your school or college can apply for a re-mark, not you or your parents/carers. First of all, you should consider carefully whether or not to ask your school or college to make a request for a re-mark. It is worth knowing that very few re-marks result in a change to a grade, simply because a re-mark request has shown that the original marking was accurate. Check the closing date for re-marking requests with your Examinations Officer. Bear in mind that there is no guarantee that your grades will go up if your papers are re-marked. The original mark can be confirmed or lowered, as well as raised, as a result of a re-mark.

Glossary

This Glossary contains all the key word definitions, plus some other terms used in the book that may be unfamiliar to you. When appropriate the definitions are particularly directed to the period being studied.

Anaesthetic – A substance that affects your nervous system so that you are less aware of sensation and don't feel pain.

Anderson shelter – A small shelter made from corrugated iron sheets that was half buried in the ground and covered with earth for protection from bomb blasts.

Aqueduct – A bridge that allows water to flow over or past obstacles.

Arquebus – An early type of gun supported on a forked rest or tripod.

Artillery – Large guns used in warfare on land; light artillery could be pulled around quickly by horses, while heavy artillery were much larger, stationary cannon for attacking castle walls, etc.

Atomic bomb – An explosive device that gets its incredibly destructive force from a nuclear fission reaction.

Attrition – A process of steadily wearing down an enemy bit by bit over a period of time.

Auxiliary – Providing additional help or support.

Bastion – A projecting part of a fort's wall to increase the angle of fire.

Battering ram – A large wooden ram, the size of a tree trunk, often tipped with metal, which was swung from a harness against the gates of castles or fortified towns.

Bayonet – A long knife that could be attached to the end of the barrel of a musket or rifle, enabling soldiers to stab at the enemy in close combat.

Billet – Temporary accommodation for soldiers; before barracks, soldiers were often billeted in local homes or inns.

Blackout – A period of darkness imposed on citizens as protection against air raids; windows were blacked out with curtains or paint and all lights were turn off.

Blitzkrieg – Literally 'lightning war', consisting of rapid attacks, coordinating **artillery**, bombing, tanks, troops and dive bombers, such as the Blitz in 1940–1941.

Booty – The goods that soldiers took, during warfare, from prisoners, the bodies of the enemy or from captured villages or towns.

Boss – A raised mound or cone in the centre of a shield which helps to deflect blows from an opponent's weapon.

Bureaucratic – Dominated by rules, restrictions and paperwork.

Caltrop – An iron ball with protruding spikes, thrown on to the floor in the path of cavalry to injure the horses and disrupt their charge.

Camaraderie – A spirit of trust and friendship among a group of people.

Campaigning season – The months in the year, usually late spring until late autumn, when fighting was possible before modern times.

Catholic Church – That part of the Christian Church owing loyalty to the Pope in Rome.

Cavalry – Soldiers mounted on horseback and fighting in groups.

Censorship – The control by a government of the spread of all information that might be useful to the enemy or that might upset the **morale** of the public.

Centenaur – The leader of a group of one hundred archers.

Centurion – A Roman soldier who was in charge of a unit of soldiers – confusingly not 100 but usually about 80.

Chain mail – Protective clothing made up of many small interlinked pieces of chain that could be worn alone or with plate armour for extra protection.

Chaperone – An older woman who accompanied a younger one on social occasions, to keep her safe and make sure she behaved properly.

Chevauchée – A destructive raid into enemy territory, featuring mounted soldiers.

Chivalry – A code of conduct, for example among medieval knights, which emphasised social graces, such as courtesy and courage, and Christian virtues, such as mercy and forgiveness.

Civil Defence – The organisation of civilians to deal with enemy attacks.

Commission – Officers' posts, to be bought and sold for promotion in the 18th century especially

Conscientious objector – Someone who refuses to fight because of their moral or religious beliefs.

Conscription – The requirement that all men (and sometimes women) of a certain age group must join the armed forces.

Continuity – A period of continuity is when there is little change; things carry on much as they were before.

Depleted uranium – A very dense metal that can be used as armour to protect military vehicles, such as tanks, or for very hard points of **artillery** shells, which can pierce the armour on enemy vehicles.

Desertion – When a soldier leaves his post or leaves the army completely, without permission.

Dragoon – Lightly armed soldier who can fight on foot or on horseback; evolved in the 17th century to include those fighting with pistols.

Drill – Repeated training of soldiers in military exercises, so that they become second nature and to instil discipline.

Ducat – Gold coin accepted in most European countries from the 12th to 19th centuries.

Emetic – A substance given to people who were unwell, to make them vomit, which was believed to rid the body of bad substances.

Entrepreneur – A person who takes financial risks to set up a business.

Evacuation – The process of moving people from towns and cities to the countryside for safety, to protect them from German bombing.

Feigned retreat – When an attacking force pretends to be forced back, hoping that the enemy will abandon their disciplined, defensive position and chase the attackers out into the open, where they can be confronted on better ground.

Firearm – A **gunpowder** weapon small enough to be carried by a soldier, for example a pistol or a rifle.

Flappers – Young women who challenged traditional ideas about women's fashion and social habits.

Foraging – Searching the countryside for food to purchase or, more usually, to take.

Freeman – Someone in medieval times who was given their own land in exchange for services – including military duties – for the king.

Friendly fire – The term recently used to describe incidents when troops are accidentally killed by other troops on their side; such accidents have probably always happened, but the term was only coined after the deaths of UK soldiers caused by US troops in the Gulf War of 1991.

Front line – In general terms, the front line is the area of fighting in which opposing troops are in direct conflict with each other; in trench warfare, the front line was the trench closest to enemy troops.

Fyrd – The main body of the Saxon army; they were infantry, called up from the Saxons with small landholdings. Originally poorly armed and organised, by the time of King Harold, in 1066, many were experienced, well-armed soldiers.

Gaiter – Protective covering for the lower leg.

Galling – Harassing the enemy, for example with arrows, **firearms** or **artillery** fire.

Gambeson – A protective jacket worn by infantrymen, usually made of quilted linen or wool and stuffed to provide extra protection, it could be worn alone or under **chain mail** or plate armour.

Gladiator – Literally a 'swordsman', but in ancient Rome a slave or skilled professional fighter who fought other gladiators, criminals or animals for the entertainment of spectators.

Guerrilla warfare – From the French 'guerre' (war), this refers to small independent groups using irregular means to attack larger, regular forces.

Gunpowder – An explosive mixture of sulphur, charcoal and saltpetre that burns rapidly and can be used to propel bullets, cannonballs or shells from guns.

Halberd – A pike with a sharpened axe-head added to the spike on the end, producing a weapon that could not just stab, but also slash, hook and pull.

Hauberk – A tunic or shirt for protection, quilted or made of leather or **chain mail**, worn by a soldier on the upper body.

Herald – A person who carried official messages.

Home front – The support given and work performed by the civilian population during wartime.

Housecarls – The king's personal guard and most powerful troops of the Saxon army.

Howitzer – A cannon that fired at a very slow speed and steep angle to lob projectiles on to the enemy. Early versions used cannonballs; later versions used explosive shells.

Indenture – A contract under which a ruler would employ troops.

Inference – Identifying the underlying message or messages of a source rather than relying on what it says explicitly.

Intelligence – Useful information, usually about your enemy.

Jingoism – Extreme patriotism, especially involving an aggressive attitude towards other countries.

Legion – The heavy infantry that was the main military unit of the Roman army; legions usually consisted of about 4,000 legionaries, or heavily armed soldiers, and several hundred other supporting troops.

Limited warfare – A term used to describe warfare before modern times, when it was conducted with restricted resources and for limited aims.

Mangonel – A wooden **siege** engine that used twisted rope to catapult objects at the enemy.

Manoeuvre – To carefully move one's army into a position of advantage; manoeuvres are also large-scale military exercises.

Media – Methods of communicating information, including the press and radio.

Mercenary – A soldier who sells his services to any commander willing to pay him.

Militia – Part-time, volunteer soldiers, who act as a reserve or emergency military force.

Mobilisation – Preparing and organising people or resources for a particular task, especially war.

Morale – The confidence, enthusiasm and sense of purpose of a group of people at a particular time.

Mortar – A cannon that fired at a very slow speed, at an angle even steeper than **howitzers**, to lob projectiles on to the enemy. Early versions used cannonballs; later versions used explosive shells.

Munitions – Weapons, ammunition and shells.

New Model Army – A new army, set up by Parliament in 1645, during the English Civil War. It was an efficient, permanent, paid army recruited mostly from **Protestant** volunteers. See also **Ironsides**.

Nuclear weapons – Very powerful weapons that produce massive explosions caused by reactions in the nucleus of an atom.

Overpressure – This is caused when an explosion taking place overhead changes normal air pressure on the ground, causing terrible injuries.

Pillage (or **plunder**) – Stealing from the enemy or civilians.

Propaganda – One-sided information used to persuade people to support certain ideas or beliefs.

Protestant Church – That part of the Christian Church that became distinct from the **Catholic** and other churches, when their members 'protested' the centrality of the Bible and other beliefs.

Purging – Deliberately giving diarrhoea to people who were unwell, believed to rid the body of harmful substances and return a natural balance.

Quadrant – An instrument for measuring angles; gunners used one to calculate the angle of the cannon barrel needed to fire a given distance.

Radar – A name formed from radio detection and ranging to describe a system that sends out microwaves or radio waves and then picks up waves that are reflected back.

Ransom – Money demanded for the release of a captive.

Rationing – The setting of a fixed allowance of food and provisions to prevent shortages.

Recruitment – The way in which armies were raised; methods included feudal duty, paying **mercenaries**, volunteering, forced enlistment or **conscription**.

Regiment – A part of an army used as an organisational unit; because of their long history, regiments can vary in size from a few hundred to 5,000 soldiers.

Reserved occupations – Jobs considered so important to the war effort that people doing them were excluded from conscription into military service. They included miners, farmers and doctors.

Salvo – A volley of fire from a group of cannon or other **artillery** all firing together.

Scout – To send out small groups or individuals to gather information, usually about the enemy's position.

Scutage – A system, under the feudal system, in which rulers would accept payment from their subjects as a substitute for military service. They could then use the money to pay for troops.

Shield wall – A traditional form of defence, in which infantry interlock their shields to create a barrier against attack, through which the defenders can stab attackers with swords, spears, etc.

Siege – A blockade of a fortress or town, with the intent of starving it into surrender or using force to destroy its defences.

Siege tower – A large wooden tower, often on wheels, which was capable of carrying concealed soldiers and could be pushed up against a castle wall in a **siege**, to allow the soldiers to gain access to the top of the wall.

Skirmish – A brief fight between small groups of soldiers.

Standing army – A permanent army, employed during peacetime as well as during war; it is highly skilled and can form the core of fighting forces if the army is expanded in wartime.

Suffrage – The right to vote in political elections; Suffragettes were women who campaigned for the vote using more militant or illegal methods, while Suffragists used peaceful, law-abiding methods.

Telegraph – A system for sending messages from a distance by electrical means along a wire.

Tenants-in-chief – The most wealthy and senior supporters of a king or lord; they held their land in exchange for military service in their lord's army.

Total warfare – Unlimited warfare, fought with all possible or available resources, intended to destroy entirely all enemy resistance and affecting civilians as well as soldiers.

Trade union – An association of employees set up to improve their working conditions.

Trebuchet – A wooden **siege** machine, which used counterweights to sling objects at the enemy.

Tribunal – A type of court set up to judge certain types of cases, especially in the military.

Trunnions – The two projections on each side of the barrel of a cannon on which the barrel rests when it sits on the cannon carriage; they allowed the barrel to be raised or lowered to change the angle of the shot.

United Nations – An international body, made up of most nations of the world, which tries to promote international security, peace and human rights.

USSR – Union of Soviet Socialist Republics, sometimes called the Soviet Union, this was a collection of states in eastern Europe and northern Asia, dominated by Russia, which, between 1922 and 1991, acted as one, very powerful country.

Volley (of fire) – Pistol, musket or rifle fire in which, rather than firing separately, all the soldiers fire at the same time, to increase their impact.

A note on currency

In 1971, Britain adopted decimal currency. British money used before and after 1971 is shown below.

Before 1971:
- £1 = 20 shillings (s)
- 1s = 12 'old' pence (d)

Since 1971:
- £1 = 100 'new' pence (p)

So, for comparison:

Before 1971	After 1971
£1 =	£1
1s or 12d =	5p
2.4d =	1p

A note on abbreviations

The following abbreviations are not explained within the text:

RNR – Royal Navy Reserves

RAFVR – Royal Air Force Volunteer Reserve

Index

Definitions of terms that are in **bold** type can be found in the Glossary on pages 166–9.

Index